Tolkien Warriors
The House of the Wolfings

Interesting Tolkien Books

For the enjoyment of Tolkien fans everywhere, Inkling Books is releasing a series of new books. These titles are (or will be) available in both print and digital formats.

TOLKIEN TIMELINE. Tolkien spent many long hours getting the chronology of his tale just right and yet in the story itself he rarely gives us actual dates. In one edition he takes 328 pages and 22 chapters to cover a mere nine days and yet he never mentions a single date. That's because he's using a little-known but powerful literary technique called *interlacing* to lend realism. This detailed, day-by-day chronology of events allows readers to penetrate that literary veil and discover the hidden story. It also describes events from other sources that take place before or after the narrative of *The Lord of the Rings* and includes some 800 references to Tolkien's writings, including material published by Tolkien's son Christopher.

TOLKIEN ROMANCES—THE WELL AT THE WORLD'S END. Facing a dull future, Ralph, the youngest son of a minor king, sets off on an adventure that becomes a quest for the Well at the World's End, which bestows health and good fortune to all who drink from it. Along the way, he meets with far more romance.

TOLKIEN ROMANCES—THE WOOD BEYOND THE WORLD. Betrayed by his wife, Golden leaves home, discovers a magical land, rescues an enslaved maiden, and reaches as strange land. Look for romance and adventure in mysterious woods.

TOLKIEN WARRIORS—THE HOUSE OF THE WOLFINGS. Tales of brave warriors who, like the riders of Rohan, must defend their homes and freedom from the might of imperial Rome. There's even a magical coat of mail whose temptations are similar to the One Ring in Tolkien.

TOLKIEN WARRIORS—THE ROOTS OF THE MOUNTAINS. Has two peoples—the Sons of the Wolf, who are descendants of the Wolfings of the earlier volume, and the men of the Dale. Like the Dunedain, who quietly protected the Shire from barbarian attacks, the Sons of the Wolf have been secretly guarding the people of the Dale from the Dusky Men. Now they want an alliance along with a much expanded war.

CELEBRATING MIDDLE-EARTH. Six chapters about Tolkien from leading scholars, including Peter Kreeft, Joseph Pearce, and John West. Great for understanding its literary background.

TOLKIEN WARRIORS

THE HOUSE OF THE WOLFINGS

A STORY THAT INSPIRED

THE LORD OF THE RINGS

William Morris

Michael W. Perry

INKLING BOOKS   SEATTLE   2013

Description
In letter written at the end of 1960, J. R. R. Tolkien wrote that, while parts of *The Lord of the Rings*, "owe something to Northern France after the Battle of the Somme. They owe more to William Morris and his Huns and Romans, as in *The House of the Wolfings* or *The Roots of the Mountains*." For the enjoyment of Tolkien fans everywhere, those two books have been republished in Inkling's *Tolkien Warriors* series. *The Roots of the Mountains* describes a Germanic tribe called the Wolfings who bravely defend their homes, families and freedoms against imperialistic Rome, much as the warriors of Rohan fought against Saruman and Sauron. Careful proofing, professional formatting, chapters summaries and definitions of obscure words make the reading more enjoyable. This edition includes William Morris's never-completed third volume, "The Story of Desiderius."

Copyright Notice

Dedication
This book is dedicated to to the many Tolkien fans who, like myself, have longed for more books like J. R. R. Tolkien's marvelous *The Lord of the Rings*.

Publisher's Note
The House of the Wolfings was first published in December 1888 by Reeves and Turner. A 1904 edition by Longmans, Green and Co. was used to prepare this text, which was then carefully checked against the 1912 edition of *The Collected Works of William Morris* (Volume 14) by that same publisher. As William Morris' daughter, May Morris, noted in the 1912 edition, there was inconsistency in how her father handled "proper names and place-names" in his books. The tales were written with a "slight hurry and inattention to unessential things, and a sure touch and deliberation in the graver moments." She corrected some inconsistencies and left others intact.

While leaving the text unaltered, this book makes more improvements. It adds, [in square brackets] the meaning for obscure words. It alters quirky paragraph breaks to fit a modern reader's expectations. It includes a short summary at the start of every chapter, adds subheadings at major breaks in the plot, and bolds critical passages. The result should be more enjoyable reading.

Library Cataloging Data
Title: *Tolkien Warriors—The House of the Wolfings: A Story that Inspired The Lord of the Rings*
Authors: William Morris (1834–1896) and Michael W. Perry (1948–).
Description: 186 pages.
Size: 6 x 9 x 0.43 inches, 229 x 152 x 11 mm. Weight: 0.62 pounds, 282 grams.
Library of Congress Control Number: 2013931905 (paper edition).

BISAC Subject Headings
FIC009020 FICTION/FANTASY/EPIC
LIT004260 LITERARY CRITICISM/SCIENCE FICTION & FANTASY
FIC032000 FICTION/WAR & MILITARY

ISBN
ISBN for paperback: 978-1-58742-078-8
ISBN for iBookstore: 978-1-58742-079-5 (Apple)
ISBN for Kindle: 978-1-58742-080-1 (Amazon)
ISBN for Smashwords: 978-1-58742-081 (Others)

Publisher Information
Print edition published in the United States of America on acid-free paper.
First edition. First printing, February 2013
Publisher: Inkling Books, Seattle, Washington, USA
Internet: http://www.InklingBooks.com/

Contents

Literary Links Between William Morris and J. R. R. Tolkien

The Lord of the Rings was actually begun, as a separate thing, about 1937, and had reached the inn at Bree, before the shadow of the second war. Personally, I do not think that either the war (and of course not the atomic bomb) had any influence upon either the plot or the manner of its unfolding. Perhaps in landscape. The Dead Marshes and the approaches to the Morannon owe something to Northern France after the Battle of the Somme. They owe more to William Morris and his Huns and Romans, as in *The House of the Wolfings* or *The Roots of the Mountains*.— J. R. R. Tolkien to Professor L. W. Forster, December 31, 1960

In her introduction to the fourteenth volume of *The Collected Works of William Morris* (1912), Morris' daughter May said that, "In *The House of the Wolfings* and in *The Roots of the Mountains* my father seems to have got back to the atmosphere of the [ancient Northern European] Sagas. In that it is part metrical, part prose, the Wolfings may be held experimental, but in this tale of imaginary tribal life on the verge of Roman conquest—a period which had a great fascination for the writer, who read with critical enjoyment the more important modern studies of it as they came out."

The impact of those "modern studies" was great, for May Morris went on to note with amusement, a "German professor who, after the *Wolfings* came out, wrote and asked learned questions about the Mark, expecting, I fear, equally learned answers from our Poet who sometimes dreamed realities without having documentary evidence of them." Morris' own response to that professor was amusing. "Doesn't the fool realize," he shouted, "that it's a romance, a work of fiction—that it's all lies!"

As Morris well knew, we know almost nothing about the day-to-day life of these brave and intelligent, but typically illiterate European tribes. In the Middle East, a dry climate, the widespread use of stone and clay, and the early spread of a written language preserved much. In a region that J. R. R. Tolkien would also make such a prominent part of his Middle-earth, a wet climate, the limited use of writing, and the common use of wood and leather left little for future generations to study. What little we do know has as its source the far from objective remarks of their foes, such as the Romans, and the fragments that have come down to us across the centuries, preserved in poetic sagas about great heroes and their achievements.

Drinking from Ancient Wells

Both Morris and Tolkien drank deeply from those ancient literary wells of "Northerness." Morris did so as part of a wide artistic genius that included the translation of ancient tales—as in his 1870 *Volsunga Saga: The Story of the Volsungs and Niblungs*. Tolkien did so as part of a long professional life as an Oxford professor and a leading expert on the ancient languages and literature of Northern Europe.

These two men knew either much (Morris) or most (Tolkien) of all that was known about these people and their lives. They used that wealth of knowledge to create "dreamed realities" (Morris) or an "imaginary history" (Tolkien) about what it might have been like to live in those days. While what they wrote wasn't necessarily true in a strict sense, both knew enough about the past and were talented enough as writers that what they wrote creates a strong sense that what they describe might have been.

Their readers certainly sense this. One wrote Morris that his tales, "convey the impression of your having lived in the time to describe what you have seen." The effect of Tolkien is even more startling. Friends of his fans often complain that those who drink deeply of Middle-earth act as if Tolkien's created world were more real than the one in which they live. In his *Rehabilitations*, Tolkien's close friend C. S. Lewis said much the same when he noted of Morris, "All we need demand is that this invented world should have some intellectual or emotional relevance to the world we live in. And it has."

Without a doubt, both Morris and Tolkien achieved that most difficult of all tasks for an author. They imagined a world with such skill that those who inhabit it seem as real as our next-door neighbor. Morris made clear that was his intent in a July 1889 paper in which he discussed romantic literature and said that, "As for romance, what does romance mean? I have heard people miscalled for being romantic, but what romance means is the capacity for a true conception of history, a power of making the past part of the present." Both Morris and Tolkien were geniuses at doing just that.

Differences Between the Two

Of course there were also differences in how the two men wrote. Morris was relatively indifferent to the broader picture. In *The House of the Wolfings* it is enough for him that his tale roughly resembles the battles that Germanic tribes once fought with encroaching Roman armies. He has no desire to link his tale to actual battles fought on certain dates with specific Roman generals.

The same is true of geography in his later *The Roots of the Mountains*. His description of the local geography and its forests is as marvelous as anything in Tolkien and it plays a major role in his story. But we are left uncertain about what would seem to be an important fact, which particular mountain range provides a backdrop for the story. May Morris believed the story was set in "the wonderful land at the foot of the Italian Alps" that her father loved so dearly. Others, with perhaps more an eye on history, place it in the German Alps or even in the Carpathian Mountains of Eastern Europe.

Even more surprising, although we are left with the impression that some of the people in *Roots* are descendants of those in *Wolfings*, the actual ties between the two were left unclear. For Morris those things simply did not matter. It was enough for him that his tales can be fitted, however loosely, into European history.

In contrast, as his readers know, Tolkien did not even place his tale within the recorded history of Europe. The events he described are assumed to have taken place in a past so distant that no independent history or artifacts from the age remain. Only the faintest echoes of what happened then have been preserved in extinct languages and ancient tales about dwarves, elves and dragons. In fact, so much imaginary time has passed that even the geography of Middle-earth only loosely resembles that of the Western Europe on which it's modeled.

Tolkien saw this historical vacuum as an opportunity. Into that vast gap, he thrust his own history for a world that, by his account, was just over seven thousand years old when the main events of *The Lord of the Rings* took place. He gave his Middle-earth a history and geography so complex that numerous books have been written to describe it. In fact, I was able to write and publish a detailed chronology of *The Lord of the Rings* in which I describe, typically to the year, the complex and quite plausible chain of events that led to Frodo acquiring the Ring, as well as a precise and detailed, day-by-day account of Frodo's quest to rid Middle-earth of the Ring, aided by his friends. Morris, although almost as talented as a story teller, did nothing on that grand a scale. He lacked Tolkien's obsession with detail.

What the Two Men Shared

That said, what the two had in common was far more important than their differences. May Morris expressed it when she said that her father's writings were "experimental." In biblical language, he wanted to see if the 'old wine' in the ancient Northern tales that he loved so well—tales that were typically told in poetic forms that were no longer popular—could survive in the 'new wineskins' of a modern prose novel, with only an occasional burst of poetry. In that he proved quite successful, although much of his success would come through others, such as Tolkien, and through a new form of literature called fantasy that both men helped to create from ancient folk and fairy tales.

The fact that Morris was building on those tales, does not mean he slavishly followed them. C. S. Lewis readily admitted that, "Morris invented for his poems and perfected in his prose-romances a language which has never at any period been spoken in England." But Lewis went on to point out that, "The question about Morris's style is not whether it is an artificial language—all endurable language in longer works must be that—but whether it is a good one."

Lewis, creator of the Narnia series of children's stories and a great writer in his own right, believed that Morris had succeeded marvelously. Morris' style, he wrote, "is incomparably easier and clearer than any 'natural' style could possibly be, and the 'dull finish,' the careful avoidance of rhetoric, gloss and decoration, is of its very essence."

In words that also apply to Tolkien, Lewis said it was the very "matter-of-factness" of the tales, that make them seem true. "Other stories have only scenery: his have geography. He is not concerned with 'painting' landscapes; he tells you the lie of the land, and then you paint the landscape for yourself. To a reader long fed on the almost botanical and entomological niceties of much modern fiction—where, indeed, we mostly skip if the characters go through a jungle—the effect is at first very pale and cold, but also very fresh and spacious. We begin to relish what my friend called the 'Northerness.' No mountains in literature are as far away as distant mountains in Morris."

There is also, Lewis said, a remarkable vividness in Morris' descriptions of human society. Unlike many other romantic writers, Morris did not glorify the individual, making him almost God-like in his independence. Morris, Lewis wrote, "immerses the individual completely in the society. 'If thou diest today, where then shall our love be?' asks the leading woman in *The House of the Wolfings*. 'It shall abide with the soul of the Wolfings,' comes the answer."

Lewis points out that many writers who have tried to describe an ideal society are "dull" because they fail to define the value of "x" that describes the Good. But he goes on, "The tribal communities which Morris paints in *The House of the Wolfings* or *The Roots of the Mountains* are such attempts, perhaps the most successful attempts ever made, to give x a value…. A modern poet of the Left, praising that same solidarity with the group which Morris praises, invites a man to be 'one cog in the singing golden hive.' Morris, on the other hand, paints the actual goings on of the communal life, the sowing, planting, begetting, building, ditching, eating and conversation… Morris… brings back a sentiment that a man could really live by."

Lewis could have said the same of the imaginary communities that Tolkien created. The Shire, Rivendell and Rohan have ways of life many find appealing, however different they are from each other and from modern life. Each sets before us what seems to be a reasonable standard for our lives. All are places we can imagine as home. Rivendale, we should never forget, was called the "last Homely House east of the sea"—using homely in the British sense of a place "simple, but cozy and comfortable."

Bridging a Gap

Lewis also believed that Morris might bridge a gap he saw developing in 1939 society. "The old indeterminate, half-Christian, half-Pantheistic, piety of the last century is gone," he wrote. "The modern literary world is increasingly divided into two camps, that of the positive, militant Christians and that of the convinced materialists." Both camps, Lewis noted, can "find in him something that they need."

As a Pagan poet, Morris was "content to merely state the [ultimate human] question… uncontaminated by theorizing." Within his tales we sense the great Pagan "thirst for immortality, tingling alive," but also totally devoid of the answers that Christianity would later bring to a Pagan Europe. As a "prophet as unconscious, and therefore as far beyond suspicion as Balaam's ass," he testifies to the importance of that thirst in itself and not merely as a prelude to a presentation of the Christian gospel.

Because Morris considered himself a socialist, many on the Left consider him one of them. But Lewis saw a critical difference between Morris and his political allies. He believed that Morris might force an increasingly secular and politicized Left to face a question it would rather ignore. "The Left agrees with Morris that it is an absolute duty to labour for human happiness in this world," he wrote. "But the Left is deceiving itself if it thinks that any zeal for this object can permanently silence the reflection that every moment of this happiness must be lost as soon as gained, that all who enjoy it will die, that the race and the planet themselves must one day follow the individual into a state of being which has no significance—a universe of inorganic homogeneous matter moving at uniform speed in a low temperature. Hitherto the Left has been content, as far as I know, to pretend that this does not matter." Morris makes clear that such things do matter.

Morris can do this because of a peculiarity in his writings. Like Tolkien, the fact that he wrote of a long-ago world has led some to accuse him of being escapist. Not so, says Lewis. Morris (and by implication Tolkien) has "faced the facts" of modern life. "This is the paradox of him. He seems to retire far from the real world and to build a world out of his wishes; but when he has finished the result stands out as a picture of experience ineluctably true." Morris presents, "in one vision the ravishing sweetness and the heart-breaking melancholy of our experience." He shows, "how the one continually passes over into the other." Most important of all, he combines everything into "a stirring practical creed," that "all our adventures, worldly and other-worldly alike, must take into account."

The same can be said of Tolkien. By setting his tale in the past and avoiding both the trappings of modern religion and the controversies of contemporary politics, he created a world in which people of varied religious and political views find a home and he has described a way of life they find appealing.

Tolkien's Literary Debts

Early on, Tolkien recognized the literary debt he owned to those ancient tales and to Morris himself in a letter he wrote to his future wife in the fall of 1914 (now the first letter in *The Letters of J. R. R. Tolkien*). There he spoke of introducing a fellow student to the delights of "Kalevala the Finnish ballads." Tolkien went on to say that he was trying to turn one of those ballads, "which is really a great story and most tragic—into a short story somewhat on the lines of Morris' romances with chunks of poetry in between."

That remark by Tolkien is what inspired me to republished the two William Morris romantic quests that most influenced Frodo's own brave quest to destroy the One Ring. You can find them in *Tolkien Romances—The Well at the World's End* and *Tolkien Romances—The Wood Beyond the World*.

Forty-six years later, in a letter written at the very end of 1960, Tolkien continued to honor his literary debt to Morris when he wrote that the landscape of "The Dead Marshes and the approaches to the Morannon owe something to Northern France after the Battle of the Somme [where Tolkien fought in World War I]. They owe more to William Morris and his Huns and Romans, as in *The House of the Wolfings* or *The Roots of the Mountains*."

That remark was the inspiration for me to publish two other books, *Tolkien's Warriors—The House of the Wolfings* and *Tolkien Warriors—The Roots of the Mountains*. If you love what Tolkien had to say about the brave riders of Rohan, you'll love the warriors in those two tales.

The Hopes of Tolkien Fans

After Tolkien died in 1973, many of his admirers hoped stories similar to *The Lord of the Rings* existed in manuscript form among the author's large collection of papers. I know I felt that way. I even attempted to read Thomas Mann's 1922 novel, *The Magic Mountain*, in the hope of finding something similar. What could be more like Tolkien,

I naively thought, than a tale set on a magical mountain? After all, Tolkien centered both his major works—*The Hobbit* and *The Lord of the Rings*—on Hobbit quests to reach distant mountains, either to get dragon gold, or to be rid of the One Ring.

I was most disappointed, abandoning Mann's novel halfway through. Although it's considered by some to be one of the most influential works in twentieth-century German literature, I found it a bore. Set in a tuberculous sanatorium on a mountain in Switzerland before the First World War, it's cluttered with the idle chatter of a wealthy, cosmopolitan clientele. Those who're delighted by the adventures of Tolkien's characters aren't likely to find much pleasure in a story where the most dramatic event of a typical day was the dining hall arrival of a Russian noblewoman that commentators describe as symbolic of "passivity, irrationality, slackness, and submissiveness." In Morris and Tolkien we find characters who show us the joys, struggles and sorrows that give life meaning. In Mann's *The Magic Mountain* we are forced to endure to the petty quibbles of Europe's idle, chattering classes in the early years of the twentieth century.

Unfortunately, the passing of the years—some forty years as I write this— has demonstrated that our hope for great tales rescued from Tolkien's attic are only partly feasible. Fragments of tales and plots that might have become great stories do exist and have been published in books such as *The Silmarillion* and *Unfinished Tales*. Also, many possible plots and variations in the plot that lie behind *The Lord of Rings* have been described, thanks to the long labors of Tolkien's son Christopher and his helpful "History of Middle-earth" series. That gives us the 'backstory' for the novel itself, a fact I take advantage of in my Tolkien chronology, *Tolkien Timeline*. But almost all that material lacks the appeal of Tolkien's two great masterpieces. Sadly, what Tolkien left behind is simply too fragmentary—with incomplete plots and only partially developed characters—to create a great work of literature. For tales like those of Tolkien, we must go to one of his richest literary sources—William Morris.

C. S. Lewis would have agreed. Morris' stories, he wrote, provide readers with "a pleasure so inexhaustible that after twenty or fifty years of reading they find it worked so deeply into all their emotions as to defy analysis." Morris's stories were almost certainly among those Lewis meant when he told Tolkien, "if they won't write the kind of books we want to read, we shall have to write them ourselves."

Readers, however, should keep one thing in mind. In the warrior and romantic tales by Morris that I'm publishing, you will not find an epic as quite as broad or as extraordinarily complex as Tolkien's account of the One Ring. But you will find something almost as important. You will find stories having the same literary flavor, with heroes and heroines from long ago fighting to keep their freedom and their personal integrity in a hostile and dangerous world. You'll also find descriptions of forests and nature every bit as marvelous as anything in Tolkien, along with stories that stresses the importance of personal choice and the need to remain loyal to those close to us, whatever the cost. That you also find in Tolkien.

The plot of these tales is as complex as anything in Tolkien, although Morris isn't quite careful as Tolkien to highlight the critical points in his narrative. At times, for instance, he will introduce a character whose name isn't given for several pages. That's why I've written short introductions to each chapter. If you don't want plot details revealed in advance, skip over them.

Finally, you'll find in Morris something that Tolkien is often accused of neglecting, warm romances between men and women. My own suspicion is that Tolkien felt that the heroes in Morris were often so besotted with romance for some lovely maiden, that they were distracted from more serious tasks. You'll have to judge that for yourself as you read these tales.

In short, if you like what Tolkien wrote about Aragorn and his Rangers, if you admire the bravery of the Riders of Rohan, if you long for more tales of travel in an unspoiled wilderness and mysterious, magical woods, and if you wish that Tolkien had more to say about the courage of women or romances between men and women, then you'll be delighted by these two marvelous tales from the pen of William Morris, along with a fragment of a third, "The Story of Desiderius." You may also want to read the companion tales in a pair of books called *Tolkien Romances—The Well at the World's End* and *Tolkien Romances—The Wood Beyond the World.*

We should never forget that William Morris, the writer who delighted and inspired both Tolkien and his friend C. S. Lewis, can still delight and inspire those who love the wonderful stories that Tolkien and Lewis wrote.

Last of all, this bit of poetry, addressed to Morris's readers and not particularly relevant to the tale itself, was published with the original, so I include it here.

WHILES IN THE EARLY WINTER EVE
We pass amid the gathering night
Some homestead that we had to leave
Years past; and see its candles bright
Shine in the room beside the door
Where we were merry years agone
But now must never enter more,
As still the dark road drives us on.
E'en so the world of men may turn
At even of some hurried day
And see the ancient glimmer burn
Across the waste that hath no way;
Then with that faint light in its eyes
A while I bid it linger near
And nurse in wavering memories
The bitter-sweet of days that were.

Introducing The House of the Wolfings

In J. R. R. Tolkien's great epic, *The Lord of the Rings*, the climax of the Council of Elrond comes when a consensus is reached that "the Ruling Ring must be destroyed." When the noon-bell then rings, a silence falls on the group as they ponder who will take up the seemingly impossible task. At that moment the heart of Frodo, the central character in the tale, is filled with dread, "A overwhelming longing to rest and remain at peace by Bilbo's side in Rivendell filled all his heart." With much effort, he makes his choice, "I will take the Ring," he said, "though I do not know the way."

In this earlier tale by Morris, the central actor, Thiodolf, faces a similar choice, one linked to a magical Hauberk (a dwarf-made coat of chain mail so important that it's capitalized in this tale) rather than the One Ring. Like Frodo as he set out, Thiodolf can live and remain close to someone he loves (Wood-Sun) or he can face the near certainty of dying for his people. Morris himself said as much in a 1888 letter when he wrote that *The House of the Wolfings* "is a story of the life of the Gothic tribes on their way through Middle Europe, and their first meeting with the Romans in war. It is meant to illustrate the melting of the individual into the society of the tribes: I mean apart from the artistic side of things that is its moral—if it has one."

It is probably no more than a coincidence that both Frodo and Thiodolf see in its starkness the decision they must make in the fourteenth chapter of their respective tales. For Frodo the choice is clear beyond doubt. He must carry the Ring to Mordor. But for Thiodolf, the choice is built on a dark suspicion, "that a curse goeth with the Hauberk, then either for the sake of the folk I will not wear the gift and the curse, and I shall die in great glory, and because of me the House shall live; or else for thy sake I shall bear it and live, and the House shall live or die as may be, but I not helping, nay I no longer of the House nor in it."

Roman History

Although there is no exact parallel between Morris' tale and any particular historical event, the great struggle between Rome's drive to civilize and enslave their way into central Europe and the willingness of Germanic tribes to fight for their freedom is the fact of history on which *The Roots of the Mountains* is built. Perhaps the most important battle in that struggle between Romans and Germans was one that came in A.D. 9 between the Roman general Varus and Gothic soldiers led by Arminius, a German whose talent had been recognized the Romans, who had attempted to buy his allegiance by giving him Roman citizenship and military training. He would use that training against them.

Knowing that troop strength and military skill gave the advantage to Rome, in September Arminius lured Varus out of his Westphalian fortress to put down what he thought was a minor revolt. The Romans were tricked into entering a wooded and hilly region where heavy rains made movement difficult. Arminius then launched a series of lightning attacks on the Roman army, using every advantage he possessed. (As in Morris's tale, one key battle took place on a forested ridge.) In the end, Varus committed suicide to avoid capture and most of his army was either killed in battle or sacrificed to blood-thirsty pagan gods. Rome, angry and bitter, was forced to come to an uneasy truce with the Germanic tribes, with the Rhine River serving as a boundary line. Later, barbarian tribes coming out of central Europe (much like the Dusky Men will in *The Roots of the Mountains*) will first weaken and then destroy Rome's great empire.

Why would an Englishman such as Morris take pride in a long-ago victory by a distant tribe when his own homeland, England, was successfully occupied and colonized by Rome? The reason is simple. In his day, many educated Englishmen believed that their racial or 'blood' roots lay in the Germanic tribes of this era. In his oft-reprinted *Fifteen Decisive Battles of the World* (1851), Edward S. Creasy made the bold claim that, "an Englishman is entitled to claim a closer degree of relationship with Arminius than can be claimed by any German of modern Germany." That's why the Englishmen of Morris' day would have no problem imagining themselves as brave and fierce Wolfing warriors, even as they ruled a Rome-like empire that bore little resemblance to an ancient Gothic village.

Finally, those who have read Tolkien's *The Lord of the Rings* will notice some intriguing similarities. There is a forest named Mirkwood in Morris, although it is not as dark and mysterious as in Tolkien. In Chapter 2, a messenger brings to the Wolfings (as to Rohan in Tolkien) a "war-arrow ragged and burnt and bloody." And, much like Bilbo and Frodo's One Ring, Thiodolf acquires a protective coat of mail (Hauberk) made by dwarves and having powers that are dangerous to use. But, while the Ring bestows unimaginable power on its possessor, the Hauberk has a different effect, it weakens the bearer even as it protects him.

Most important of all, in both tales the plot hinges on the hero making the right choice about the powerful weapon he has been given. Will he act just for himself or will he act for the sake of others, including generations yet unborn? We see just that in Tolkien's tale where Gandalf warns that even casting the One Ring into the sea is not an answer because: "There are many things in the deep waters; and seas and lands may change. And it is not our part here to take thought only for a season, or for a few lives of Men, or for a passing age of the world. We should seek a final end of this menace, even if we do not hope to make one."

With that, I leave you to enjoy the first of William Morris' two great warrior tales. For the other, see *Tolkien's Warriors—The Roots of the Moutains*. For adventurous romantic quests into mysterious forests, try *Tolkien Romances—The Well at the World's End* and *Tolkien Romances—The Wood Beyond the World*. You'll be glad you did.

A Tale of the House of the Wolfings

And All the Kindreds of the Mark
Written in Prose and In Verse

William Morris

1. The Dwellings of Mid-mark

The history of the Wolfings and their House is given. Kine is an ancient word for cattle and a thrall is a servant or slave (some coming from captives taken in war). Their folk-mote is a meeting of the folk (people) similar to the Entmoot in *The Lord of the Rings* is for Ents. (Additional definitions are given in square brackets.) Notice the mention of Mirkwood. It's a mysterious wood, but in a different sense than in Tolkien.

The tale tells that in times long past there was a dwelling of men beside a great wood. Before it lay a plain, not very great, but which was, as it were, an isle in the sea of woodland, since even when you stood on the flat ground, you could see trees everywhere in the offing, though as for hills, you could scarce say that there were any; only swellings-up of the earth here and there, like the upheavings of the water that one sees at whiles going on amidst the eddies of a swift but deep stream.

On either side, to right and left the tree-girdle reached out toward the blue distance, thick close and unsundered, save where it and the plain which it begirdled was cleft amidmost by a river about as wide as the Thames at Sheene when the flood-tide is at its highest, but so swift and full of eddies, that it gave token of mountains not so far distant, though they were hidden. On each side moreover of the stream of this river was a wide space of stones, great and little, and in most places above this stony waste were banks of a few feet high, showing where the yearly winter flood was most commonly stayed.

You must know that this great clearing in the woodland was not a matter of haphazard; though the river had driven a road whereby men might fare on each side of its hurrying stream. It was men who had made that Isle in the woodland.

For many generations the folk that now dwelt there had learned the craft of iron-founding, so that they had no lack of wares of iron and steel, whether they were tools of handicraft or weapons for hunting and for war. It was the men of the Folk, who coming adown by the river-side had made that clearing. The tale tells not whence they came, but belike from the dales of the distant mountains, and from dales and mountains and plains further aloof and yet further.

Anyhow they came adown the river; on its waters on rafts, by its shores in wains or bestriding their horses or their kine, or afoot, till they had a mind to abide; and there as it fell they stayed their travel, and spread from each side of the river, and fought with the wood and its wild things, that they might make to themselves a dwelling-place on the face of the earth.

So they cut down the trees, and burned their stumps that the grass might grow sweet for their kine and sheep and horses; and they diked the river where need was all through the plain, and far up into the wild-wood to bridle the winter floods: and they made them boats to ferry them over, and to float down stream and track up-stream: they fished the river's eddies also with net and with line; and drew drift from out of it of far-travelled wood and other matters; and the gravel of its shallows they washed for gold; and it became their friend, and they loved it, and gave it a name, and called it the Dusky, and the Glassy, and the Mirkwood-water; for the names of it changed with the generations of man.

There then in the clearing of the wood that for many years grew greater yearly they drave their beasts to pasture in the new-made meadows, where year by year the grass grew sweeter as the sun shone on it and the standing waters went from it; and now in the year whereof the tale telleth it was a fair and smiling plain, and no folk might have a better meadow.

But long before that had they learned the craft of tillage and taken heed to the acres and begun to grow wheat and rye thereon round about their roofs; the spade came into their hands, and they bethought them of the plough-share, and the tillage spread and grew, and there was no lack of bread.

In such wise that Folk had made an island amidst of the Mirkwood, and established a home there, and upheld it with manifold toil too long to tell of. And from the beginning this clearing in the wood they called the Mid-mark: for you shall know that men might journey up and down the Mirkwood-water, and half a day's ride up or down they would come on another clearing or island in the woods, and these were the Upper-mark and the Nether-mark: and all these three were inhabited by men of one folk and one kindred, which was called the Markmen, though of many branches was that stem of folk, who bore divers signs in battle and at the council whereby they might be known.

Now in the Mid-mark itself were many Houses of men; for by that word had they called for generations those who dwelt together under one token of kinship. The river ran from South to North, and both on the East side and on the West were there Houses of the Folk, and their habitations were shouldered up nigh unto the wood, so that ever betwixt them and the river was there a space of tillage and pasture.

Tells the tale of one such House, whose habitations were on the west side of the water, on a gentle slope of land, so that no flood higher than common might reach them. It was straight down to the river mostly that the land fell off, and on its downward-reaching slopes was the tillage, "the Acres," as the men of that time always called tilled land; and beyond that was the meadow going fair and smooth, though with here and there a rising in it, down to the lips of the stony waste of the winter river.

The House of the Wolfings

Now the name of this House was the Wolfings, and they bore a Wolf on their banners, and their warriors were marked on the breast with the image of the Wolf, that they might be known for what they were if they fell in battle, and were stripped.

The house, that is to say the Roof, of the Wolfings of the Mid-mark stood on the topmost of the slope aforesaid with its back to the wild-wood and its face to the acres and the water. But you must know that in those days the men of one branch of kindred dwelt under one roof together, and had therein their place and dignity; nor were there many degrees amongst them as hath befallen afterwards, but all they of one blood were brethren and of equal dignity. Howbeit they had servants or thralls, men taken in battle, men of alien blood, though true it is that from time to time were some of such men taken into the House, and hailed as brethren of the blood.

Also (to make an end at once of these matters of kinship and affinity) the men of one House might not wed the women of their own House: to the Wolfing men all Wolfing women were as sisters: they must needs wed with the Hartings or the Elkings or the Bearings, or other such Houses of the Mark as were not so close akin to the blood of the Wolf; and this was a law that none dreamed of breaking. Thus then dwelt this Folk and such was their Custom.

As to the Roof of the Wolfings, it was a great hall and goodly, after the fashion of their folk and their day; not built of stone and lime, but framed of the goodliest trees of the wild-wood squared with the adze, and betwixt the framing filled with clay wattled with reeds. Long was that house, and at one end anigh the gable was the Man's-door, not so high that a man might stand on the threshold and his helmcrest clear the lintel; for such was the custom, that a tall man must bow himself as he came into the hall; which custom maybe was a memory of the days of onslaught when the foemen were mostly wont to beset the hall; whereas in the days whereof the tale tells they drew out into the fields and fought unfenced; unless at whiles when the odds were over great, and then they drew their wains about them and were fenced by the Wain-burg.

At least it was from no niggardry [stinginess] that the door was made thus low, as might be seen by the fair and manifold carving of knots and dragons that was wrought above the lintel of the door for some three foot's space. But a like door was there anigh the other gable-end, whereby the women entered, and it was called the Woman's-door.

Near to the house on all sides except toward the wood were there many bowers and cots round about the penfolds and the byres: and these were booths for the stowage of wares, and for crafts and smithying that were unhandy to do in the house; and withal they were the dwelling-places of the thralls. And the lads and young men often abode there many days and were cherished there of the thralls that loved them, since at whiles they shunned the Great Roof that they might be the freer to come and go at their pleasure, and deal as they would. Thus was there a clustering on the slopes and bents betwixt the acres of the Wolfings and the wild-wood wherein dwelt the wolves.

The House's Interior

As to the house within, two rows of pillars went down it endlong, fashioned of the mightiest trees that might be found, and each one fairly wrought with base and chapiter, and wreaths and knots, and fighting men and dragons; so that it was like a church of later days that has a nave and aisles: windows there were above the aisles, and a passage underneath the said windows in their roofs. In the aisles were the sleeping-places of the Folk, and down the nave under the crown of the roof were three hearths for the fires, and above each hearth a luffer or smoke-bearer to draw the smoke up when the fires were lighted.

Forsooth on a bright winter afternoon it was strange to see the three columns of smoke going wavering up to the dimness of the mighty roof, and one maybe smitten athwart by the sunbeams. As for the timber of the roof itself and its framing, so exceeding great and high it was, that the tale tells how that none might see the fashion of it from the hall-floor unless he were to raise aloft a blazing faggot on a long pole: since no lack of timber was there among the men of the Mark.

At the end of the hall anigh the Man's-door was the dais, and a table thereon set thwartwise of the hall; and in front of the dais was the noblest and greatest of the hearths; (but of the others one was in the very midmost, and another in the Woman's Chamber) and round about the dais, along the gable-wall, and hung from pillar to pillar were woven cloths pictured with images of ancient tales and the deeds of the Wolfings, and the deeds of the Gods from whence they came. And this was the fairest place of all the house and the best-beloved of the Folk, and especially of the older and the mightier men: and there were tales told, and songs sung, especially if they were new: and thereto also were messengers brought if any tidings were abroad: there also would the elders talk together about matters concerning the House or the Mid-mark or the whole Folk of the Markmen.

Yet you must not think that their solemn councils were held there, the folk-motes whereat it must be determined what to do and what to forbear doing; for according as such councils, (which they called Things) were of the House or of the Mid-mark or of the whole Folk, were they held each at the due Thing-steads in the Wood aloof from either acre or meadow, (as was the custom of our forefathers for long after) and at such Things would all the men of the House or the Mid-mark or the Folk be present man by man. And in each of these steads was there a Doomring wherein Doom was given by the neighbours chosen, (whom now we call the Jury) in matters between man and man; and no such doom of neighbours was given, and no such voice of the Folk proclaimed in any house or under any roof, nor even as aforesaid on the tilled acres or the depastured meadows. This was the custom of our forefathers, in memory, belike, of the days when as yet there was neither house nor tillage, nor flocks and herds, but the Earth's face only and what freely grew thereon.

But over the dais there hung by chains and pulleys fastened to a tie-beam of the roof high aloft a wondrous lamp fashioned of glass; yet of no such glass as the folk made then and there, but of a fair and clear green like an emerald, and all done with figures and knots in gold, and strange beasts, and a warrior slaying a dragon, and the sun rising on the earth: nor did any tale tell whence this lamp came, but it was held as an ancient and holy thing by all the Markmen, and the kindred of the Wolf had it in charge to keep a light burning in it night and day for ever; and they appointed a maiden of their own kindred to that office; which damsel must needs be unwedded, since no wedded woman dwelling under that roof could be a Wolfing woman, but would needs be of the houses wherein the Wolfings wedded.

This lamp which burned ever was called the Hall-Sun, and the woman who had charge of it, and who was the fairest that might be found was called after it the Hall-Sun also. At the other end of the hall was the Woman's Chamber, and therein were the looms and other gear for the carding and spinning of wool and the weaving of cloth.

Such was the Roof under which dwelt the kindred of the Wolfings; and the other kindreds of the Mid-mark had roofs like to it; and of these the chiefest were the El-kings, the Vallings, the Alftings, the Beamings, the Galtings, and the Bearings; who bore on their banners the Elk, the Falcon, the Swan, the Tree, the Boar, and the Bear. But other lesser and newer kindreds there were than these: as for the Hartings above named, they were a kindred of the Upper-mark.

2. THE FLITTING OF THE WAR-ARROW

A lovely summer's day and evening in the Mark are described. Thiodolf is introduced as the Wolfing's chief and Hall-Sun as his twenty-year-old, mysteriously acquired "foster-daughter." (Recall in Tolkien that the king of Rohan has a similar name, Théoden and an adopted daughter named Éowyn.) A neat-herd is a herd of cattle, milch-kine are dairy cattle, and a byre is a barn. The children's singing is compared to that of a young throstle or song thrush. Dight refers to making ready, as for war. Notice the arrival of a war-arrow, dipped in blood, which is a call to war against the Roman invaders, much as Gondor used an arrow to call for Rohan's aid in their war. If you are confused by the passage saying "Welsh is their tongue" for these Latin-speaking Romans, May Morris adds a clarifying note to some editions: "Welsh with these men means Foreign, and is used for all people of Europe who are not of Gothic or Teutonic blood."

Tells the tale that it was an evening of summer, when the wheat was in the ear, but yet green; and the neat-herds were done driving the milch-kine to the byre, and the horseherds and the shepherds had made the night-shift, and the out-goers were riding two by two and one by one through the lanes between the wheat and the rye towards the meadow. Round the cots of the thralls were gathered knots of men and women both thralls and freemen, some talking together, some hearkening a song or a tale, some singing and some dancing together; and the children gambolling [running and jumping] about from group to group with their shrill and tuneless voices, like young throstles who have not yet learned the song of their race. With these were mingled dogs, dun of colour, long of limb, sharp-nosed, gaunt and great; they took little heed of the children as they pulled them about in their play, but lay down, or loitered about, as though they had forgotten the chase and the wild-wood.

Merry was the folk with that fair tide, and the promise of the harvest, and the joy of life, and there was no weapon among them so close to the houses, save here and there the boar-spear of some herdman or herd-woman late come from the meadow.

Tall and for the most part comely were both men and women; the most of them light-haired and grey-eyed, with cheek-bones somewhat high; white of skin but for the sun's burning, and the wind's parching, and whereas they were tanned of a very ruddy and cheerful hue. But the thralls were some of them of a shorter and darker breed, black-haired also and dark-eyed, lighter of limb; sometimes better knit, but sometimes crookeder of leg and knottier of arm. But some also were of build and hue not much unlike to the freemen; and these doubtless came of some other Folk of the Goths which had given way in battle before the Men of the Mark, either they or their fathers.

Moreover some of the freemen were unlike their fellows and kindred, being slenderer and closer-knit, and black-haired, but grey-eyed withal; and amongst these were one or two who exceeded in beauty all others of the House.

Evening Comes

Now the sun was set and the glooming was at point to begin and the shadowless twilight lay upon the earth. The nightingales on the borders of the wood sang ceaselessly from the scattered hazel-trees above the greensward where the grass was cropped down close by the nibbling of the rabbits; but in spite of their song and the divers voices of the men-folk about the houses, it was an evening on which sounds from aloof can be well heard, since noises carry far at such tides.

Suddenly they who were on the edges of those throngs and were the less noisy, held themselves as if to listen; and a group that had gathered about a minstrel to hear his story fell hearkening also round about the silenced and hearkening tale-teller: some of the dancers and singers noted them and in their turn stayed the dance and kept silence to hearken; and so from group to group spread the change, till all were straining their ears to hearken the tidings. Already the men of the night-shift had heard it, and the shepherds of them had turned about, and were trotting smartly back through the lanes of the tall wheat: but the horse-herds were now scarce seen on the darkening meadow, as they galloped on fast toward their herds to drive home the stallions. For what they had heard was the tidings of war.

News of War

There was a sound in the air as of a humble-bee close to the ear of one lying on a grassy bank; or whiles as of a cow afar in the meadow lowing in the afternoon when milking-time draws nigh: but it was ever shriller than the one, and fuller than the other; for it changed at whiles, though after the first sound of it, it did not rise or fall, because the eve was windless. You might hear at once that for all it was afar, it was a great and mighty sound; nor did any that hearkened doubt what it was, but all knew it for the blast of the great war-horn of the Elkings, whose Roof lay up Mirkwood-water next to the Roof of the Wolfings.

So those little throngs broke up at once; and all the freemen, and of the thralls a good many, flocked, both men and women, to the Man's-door of the hall, and streamed in quietly and with little talk, as men knowing that they should hear all in due season.

Within under the Hall-Sun, amidst the woven stories of time past, sat the elders and chief warriors on the dais, and amidst of all a big strong man of forty winters, his dark beard a little grizzled, his eyes big and grey. Before him on the board lay the great War-horn of the Wolfings carved out of the tusk of a sea-whale of the North and with many devices on it and the Wolf amidst them all; its golden mouth-piece and rim wrought finely with flowers. There it abode the blowing, until the spoken word of some messenger should set forth the tidings borne on the air by the horn of the Elkings.

But the name of the dark-haired chief was Thiodolf (to wit Folk-wolf) and he was deemed the wisest man of the Wolfings, and the best man of his hands, and of heart most dauntless. Beside him sat the fair woman called the Hall-Sun; for she was his foster-daughter before men's eyes; and she was black-haired and grey-eyed like to her fosterer, and never was woman fashioned fairer: she was young of years, scarce twenty winters old.

There sat the chiefs and elders on the dais, and round about stood the kindred intermingled with the thralls, and no man spake, for they were awaiting sure and certain tidings: and when all were come in who had a mind to, there was so great a silence in the hall, that the song of the nightingales on the wood-edge sounded clear and loud therein, and even the chink of the bats about the upper windows could be heard.

A Messenger Arrives with a War-Arrow

Then amidst the hush of men-folk, and the sounds of the life of the earth came another sound that made all turn their eyes toward the door; and this was the pad-pad of one running on the trodden and summer-dried ground anigh the hall: it stopped for a moment at the Man's-door, and the door opened, and the throng parted, making way for the man that entered and came hastily up to the midst of the table that stood on the dais athwart the hall, and stood there panting, holding forth in his outstretched hand something which not all could see in the dimness of the hall-twilight, but which all knew nevertheless.

The man was young, lithe and slender, and had no raiment but linen breeches round his middle, and skin shoes on his feet. As he stood there gathering his breath for speech, Thiodolf stood up, and poured mead into a drinking horn and held it out towards the new-comer, and spake, but in rhyme and measure:

WELCOME, THOU EVENING-FARER, AND HOLY BE THINE HEAD,
Since thou hast sought unto us in the heart of the Wolfings' stead;
Drink now of the horn of the mighty, and call a health if thou wilt
O'er the eddies of the mead-horn to the washing out of guilt.

For thou com'st to the peace of the Wolfings, and our very guest thou art,
And meseems as I behold thee, that I look on a child of the Hart.

But the man put the horn from him with a hasty hand, and none said another word to him until he had gotten his breath again; and then he said:

ALL HAIL YE WOOD-WOLFS' CHILDREN! NOUGHT MAY I DRINK THE WINE,
For the mouth and the maw that I carry this eve are nought of mine;
And my feet are the feet of the people, since the word went forth that tide,
'O Elf here of the Hartings, no longer shalt thou bide
In any house of the Markmen than to speak the word and wend,
Till all men know the tidings and thine errand hath an end.'
Behold, O Wolves, the token and say if it be true!
I bear the shaft of battle that is four-wise cloven through,
And its each end dipped in the blood-stream, both the iron and the horn,
And its midmost scathed with the fire; and the word that I have borne
Along with this war-token is, Wolfings of the Mark
Whenso ye see the war-shaft, by the daylight or the dark,
Busk ye to battle faring, and leave all work undone
Save the gathering for the handplay at the rising of the sun.
Three days hence is the hosting, and thither bear along
Your wains and your kine for the slaughter lest the journey should be long.
For great is the Folk, saith the tidings, that against the Markmen come;
In a far off land is their dwelling, whenso they sit at home,
And Welsh is their tongue, and we wot not of the word that is in their mouth,
As they march a many together from the cities of the South.'

Therewith he held up yet for a minute the token of the war-arrow ragged and burnt and bloody; and turning about with it in his hand went his ways through the open door, none hindering; and when he was gone, it was as if the token were still in the air there against the heads of the living men, and the heads of the woven warriors, so intently had all gazed at it; and none doubted the tidings or the token. Then said Thiodolf:

FORTH WILL WE WOLFING CHILDREN, AND CAST A SOUND ABROAD:
The mouth of the sea-beast's weapon shall speak the battle-word;
And ye warriors hearken and hasten, and dight the weed of war,
And then to acre and meadow wend ye adown no more,
For this work shall be for the women to drive our neat from the mead,
And to yoke the wains, and to load them as the men of war have need.

Preparing for War

Out then they streamed from the hall, and no man was left therein save the fair Hall-Sun sitting under the lamp whose name she bore. But to the highest of the slope they went, where was a mound made higher by man's handiwork; thereon stood

Thiodolf and handled the horn, turning his face toward the downward course of Mirk-wood-water; and he set the horn to his lips, and blew a long blast, and then again, and yet again the third time; and all the sounds of the gathering night were hushed under the sound of the roaring of the war-horn of the Wolfings; and the Kin of the Beamings heard it as they sat in their hall, and they gat them ready to hearken to the bearer of the tidings who should follow on the sound of the war-blast.

BUT WHEN THE LAST SOUND OF THE HORN HAD DIED AWAY, THEN SAID THIODOLF:
Now Wolfing children hearken, what the splintered War-shaft saith,
The fire scathed blood-stained aspen! we shall ride for life or death,
We warriors, a long journey with the herd and with the wain;
But unto this our homestead shall we wend us back again,
All the gleanings of the battle; and here for them that live
Shall stand the Roof of the Wolfings, and for them shall the meadow thrive,
And the acres give their increase in the harvest of the year;
Now is no long departing since the Hall-Sun bideth here
'Neath the holy Roof of the Fathers, and the place of the Wolfing kin,
And the feast of our glad returning shall yet be held therein
Hear the bidding of the War-shaft! All men, both thralls and free,
'Twixt twenty winters and sixty, beneath the shield shall be,
And the hosting is at the Thing-stead, the Upper-mark anigh;
And we wend away to-morrow ere the Sun is noon-tide high.

Therewith he stepped down from the mound, and went his way back to the hall; and manifold talk arose among the folk; and of the warriors some were already dight for the journey, but most not, and a many went their ways to see to their weapons and horses, and the rest back again into the hall.

By this time night had fallen, and between then and the dawning would be no darker hour, for the moon was just rising; a many of the horse-herds had done their business, and were now making their way back again through the lanes of the wheat, driving the stallions before them, who played together kicking, biting and squealing, paying but little heed to the standing corn on either side. Lights began to glitter now in the cots of the thralls, and brighter still in the stithies [forges] where already you might hear the hammers clinking on the anvils, as men fell to looking to their battle gear.

But the chief men and the women sat under their Roof on the eve of departure: and the tuns [casks] of mead were broached, and the horns filled and borne round by young maidens, and men ate and drank and were merry; and from time to time as some one of the warriors had done with giving heed to his weapons, he entered into the hall and fell into the company of those whom he loved most and by whom he was best beloved; and whiles they talked, and whiles they sang to the harp up and down that long house; and the moon risen high shone in at the windows, and there was much laughter and merriment, and talk of deeds of arms of the old days on the eve of that departure: till little by little weariness fell on them, and they went their ways to slumber, and the hall was fallen silent.

3. Thiodolf Talketh with the Wood-Sun

In the night, Thiodolf enters the wood and embraces Wood-Sun, daughter of the gods and Chooser of the Slain in battle. She's been his lover since he was a young man, and Hall-Sun is their daughter. (Wood-Sun lives in the *woods*, while Hall-Sun lives in the *hall* with Thiodolf.) They talk of their life and how she has guarded him in forty battles. Fearing his death in the battle to come, Wood-Sun offers a magical Hauberk (coat of mail) for protection. Recognizing it as dwarf-made, he fears its unknown effects. (Think of Bilbo and Frodo wearing the One Ring, unaware of its real power.) She pleads with him to wear it, and in the morning when he returns to the Wolfings he is.

But yet sat Thiodolf under the Hall-Sun for a while as one in deep thought; till at last as he stirred, his sword clattered on him; and then he lifted up his eyes and looked down the hall and saw no man stirring, so he stood up and settled his raiment on him, and went forth, and so took his ways through the hall-door, as one who hath an errand.

The moonlight lay in a great flood on the grass without, and the dew was falling in the coldest hour of the night, and the earth smelled sweetly: the whole habitation was asleep now, and there was no sound to be known as the sound of any creature, save that from the distant meadow came the lowing of a cow that had lost her calf, and that a white owl was flitting about near the eaves of the Roof with her wild cry that sounded like the mocking of merriment now silent.

Thiodolf turned toward the wood, and walked steadily through the scattered hazel-trees, and thereby into the thick of the beech-trees, whose boles grew smooth and silver-grey, high and close-set: and so on and on he went as one going by a well-known path, though there was no path, till all the moonlight was quenched under the close roof of the beech-leaves, though yet for all the darkness, no man could go there and not feel that the roof was green above him.

Still he went on in despite of the darkness, till at last there was a glimmer before him, that grew greater till he came unto a small wood-lawn whereon the turf grew again, though the grass was but thin, because little sunlight got to it, so close and thick were the tall trees round about it. In the heavens above it by now there was a light that was not all of the moon, though it might scarce be told whether that light were the memory of yesterday or the promise of to-morrow, since little of the heavens could be seen thence, save the crown of them, because of the tall tree-tops.

Thiodlf Meets with Wood-Sun

Nought looked Thiodolf either at the heavens above, or the trees, as he strode from off the husk-strewn floor of the beech wood on to the scanty grass of the lawn, but his eyes looked straight before him at that which was amidmost of the lawn: and little wonder was that; for there on a stone chair sat a woman exceeding fair, clad in glittering raiment, her hair lying as pale in the moonlight on the grey stone as the barley acres in the August night before the reaping-hook goes in amongst them.

She sat there as though she were awaiting someone, and he made no stop nor stay, but went straight up to her, and took her in his arms, and kissed her mouth and her eyes, and she him again; and then he sat himself down beside her. But her eyes looked kindly on him as she said: "O Thiodolf, hardy art thou, that thou hast no fear to take me in thine arms and to kiss me, as though thou hadst met in the meadow with a maiden of the Elkings: and I, who am a daughter of the Gods of thy kindred, and a Chooser of the Slain! Yea, and that upon the eve of battle and the dawn of thy departure to the stricken field!"

"O Wood-Sun," he said "thou art the treasure of life that I found when I was young, and the love of life that I hold, now that my beard is grizzling. Since when did I fear thee, Wood-Sun? Did I fear thee when first I saw thee, and we stood amidst the hazelled field, we twain living amongst the slain? But my sword was red with the blood of the foe, and my raiment with mine own blood; and I was a-weary with the day's work, and sick with many strokes, and methought I was fainting into death. And there thou wert before me, full of life and ruddy and smiling both lips and eyes; thy raiment clean and clear, thine hands unstained with blood: then didst thou take me by my bloody and weary hand, and didst kiss my lips grown ashen pale, and thou saidst 'Come with me.' And I strove to go, and might not; so many and sore were my hurts. Then amidst my sickness and my weariness was I merry; for I said to myself, This is the death of the warrior, and it is exceeding sweet. What meaneth it? Folk said of me; he is over young to meet the foeman; yet am I not over young to die?"

Therewith he laughed out amid the wild-wood, and his speech became song, and he said:

WE WROUGHT IN THE RING OF THE HAZELS, AND THE WINE OF WAR WE DRANK:
From the tide when the sun stood highest to the hour wherein she sank:
And three kings came against me, the mightiest of the Huns,
The evil-eyed in battle, the swift-foot wily ones;
And they gnashed their teeth against me, and they gnawed on the shield-rims there,
On that afternoon of summer, in the high-tide of the year.
Keen-eyed I gazed about me, and I saw the clouds draw up
Till the heavens were dark as the hollow of a wine-stained iron cup,
And the wild-deer lay unfeeding on the grass of the forest glades,
And all earth was scared with the thunder above our clashing blades.

THEN SANK A King before me, and on fell the other twain,
And I tossed up the reddened sword-blade in the gathered rush of the rain
And the blood and the water blended, and fragrant grew the earth.

THERE LONG I turned and twisted within the battle-girth

Before those bears of onset: while out from the grey world streamed
The broad red lash of the lightening and in our byrnies gleamed.
And long I leapt and laboured in that garland of the fight
'Mid the blue blades and the lightening; but ere the sky grew light
The second of the Hun-kings on the rain-drenched daisies lay;
And we twain with the battle blinded a little while made stay,
And leaning on our sword-hilts each on the other gazed.

THEN THE RAIN grew less, and one corner of the veil of clouds was raised,
And as from the broidered covering gleams out the shoulder white
Of the bed-mate of the warrior when on his wedding night
He layeth his hand to the linen; so, down there in the west
Gleamed out the naked heaven: but the wrath rose up in my breast,
And the sword in my hand rose with it, and I leaped and hewed at the Hun;
And from him too flared the war-flame, and the blades danced bright in the sun
Come back to the earth for a little before the ending of day.

THERE THEN WITH all that was in him did the Hun play out the play,
Till he fell, and left me tottering, and I turned my feet to wend
To the place of the mound of the mighty, the gate of the way without end.
And there thou wert. How was it, thou Chooser of the Slain,
Did I die in thine arms, and thereafter did thy mouth-kiss wake me again?

Ere the last sound of his voice was done she turned and kissed him; and then she said; "Never hadst thou a fear and thine heart is full of hardihood."
Then he said:

'TIS THE HARDY HEART, BELOVED, THAT KEEPETH ME ALIVE,
As the king-leek in the garden by the rain and the sun doth thrive,
So I thrive by the praise of the people; it is blent with my drink and my meat;
As I slumber in the night-tide it laps me soft and sweet;
And through the chamber window when I waken in the morn
With the wind of the sun's arising from the meadow is it borne
And biddeth me remember that yet I live on earth:
Then I rise and my might is with me, and fills my heart with mirth,
As I think of the praise of the people; and all this joy I win
By the deeds that my heart commandeth and the hope that lieth therein.

"Yea," she said, "but day runneth ever on the heels of day, and there are many and many days; and betwixt them do they carry eld."

"Yet art thou no older than in days bygone," said he. "Is it so, O Daughter of the Gods, that thou wert never born, but wert from before the framing of the mountains, from the beginning of all things?"

But she said:

Nay, nay; I began, I was born; although it may be indeed
That not on the hills of the earth I sprang from the godhead's seed.
And e'en as my birth and my waxing shall be my waning and end.
But thou on many an errand, to many a field dost wend
Where the bow at adventure bended, or the fleeing dastard's spear
Oft lulleth the mirth of the mighty. Now me thou dost not fear,
Yet fear with me, beloved, for the mighty Maid I fear;
And Doom is her name, and full often she maketh me afraid
And even now meseemeth on my life her hand is laid.

But he laughed and said:

In what land is she abiding? Is she near or far away?
Will she draw up close beside me in the press of the battle play?
And if then I may not smite her 'midst the warriors of the field
With the pale blade of my fathers, will she bide the shove of my shield?

But sadly she sang in answer:

In many a stead Doom dwelleth, nor sleepeth day nor night:
The rim of the bowl she kisseth, and beareth the chambering light
When the kings of men wend happy to the bride-bed from the board.
It is little to say that she wendeth the edge of the grinded sword,
When about the house half builded she hangeth many a day;
The ship from the strand she shoveth, and on his wonted way
By the mountain-hunter fareth where his foot ne'er failed before:
She is where the high bank crumbles at last on the river's shore:
The mower's scythe she whetteth; and lulleth the shepherd to sleep
Where the deadly ling-worm wakeneth in the desert of the sheep.
Now we that come of the God-kin of her redes for ourselves we wot,
But her will with the lives of men-folk and their ending know we not.
So therefore I bid thee not fear for thyself of Doom and her deed,
But for me: and I bid thee hearken to the helping of my need.
Or else—Art thou happy in life, or lusteth thou to die
In the flower of thy days, when thy glory and thy longing bloom on high?

But Thiodolf answered her:

I have deemed, and long have I deemed that this is my second life,
That my first one waned with my wounding when thou cam'st to the ring of strife.
For when in thine arms I wakened on the hazelled field of yore,
Meseemed I had newly arisen to a world I knew no more,
So much had all things brightened on that dewy dawn of day.
It was dark dull death that I looked for when my thought had died away.

It was lovely life that I woke to; and from that day henceforth
My joy of the life of man-folk was manifolded of worth.
Far fairer the fields of the morning than I had known them erst,
And the acres where I wended, and the corn with its half-slaked thirst;
And the noble Roof of the Wolfings, and the hawks that sat thereon;
And the bodies of my kindred whose deliverance I had won;
And the glimmering of the Hall-Sun in the dusky house of old;
And my name in the mouth of the maidens, and the praises of the bold,
As I sat in my battle-raiment, and the ruddy spear well steeled
Leaned 'gainst my side war-battered, and the wounds thine hand had healed.
Yea, from that morn thenceforward has my life been good indeed,
The gain of to-day was goodly, and good to-morrow's need,
And good the whirl of the battle, and the broil I wielded there,
Till I fashioned the ordered onset, and the unhoped victory fair.
And good were the days thereafter of utter deedless rest
And the prattle of thy daughter, and her hands on my unmailed breast.
Ah good is the life thou hast given, the life that mine hands have won.
And where shall be the ending till the world is all undone?
Here sit we twain together, and both we in Godhead clad,
We twain of the Wolfing kindred, and each of the other glad.

But she answered, and her face grew darker withal:

O MIGHTY MAN AND JOYOUS, ART THOU OF THE WOLFING KIN?
'Twas no evil deed when we mingled, nor lieth doom therein.
Thou lovely man, thou black-haired, thou shalt die and have done no ill.
Fame-crowned are the deeds of thy doing, and the mouths of men they fill.
Thou betterer of the Godfolk, enduring is thy fame:
Yet as a painted image of a dream is thy dreaded name.
Of an alien folk thou comest, that we twain might be one indeed.
Thou shalt die one day. So hearken, to help me at my need.

His face grew troubled and he said: "What is this word that I am no chief of the Wolfings?"

"Nay," she said, "but better than they. Look thou on the face of our daughter the Hall-Sun, thy daughter and mine: favoureth she at all of me?"

He laughed: "Yea, whereas she is fair, but not otherwise. This is a hard saying, that I dwell among an alien kindred, and it wotteth not thereof. Why hast thou not told me hereof before?"

She said: "It needed not to tell thee because thy day was waxing, as now it waneth. Once more I bid thee hearken and do my bidding though it be hard to thee."

He answered: "Even so will I as much as I may; and thus wise must thou look upon it, that I love life, and fear not death."

Then she spake, and again her words fell into rhyme:

IN FORTY FIGHTS HAST THOU FOUGHTEN, AND BEEN WORSTED BUT IN FOUR;
And I looked on and was merry; and ever more and more
Wert thou dear to the heart of the Wood-Sun, and the Chooser of the Slain.
But now whereas ye are wending with slaughter-herd and wain
To meet a folk that ye know not, a wonder, a peerless foe,
I fear for thy glory's waning, and I see thee lying alow.

Then he brake in: "Herein is little shame to be worsted by the might of the mightiest: if this so mighty folk sheareth a limb off the tree of my fame, yet shall it wax again."

But she sang:

IN FORTY FIGHTS HAST THOU FOUGHTEN, AND BESIDE THEE WHO BUT I
Beheld the wind-tossed banners, and saw the aspen fly?
But to-day to thy war I wend not, for Weird withholdeth me
And sore my heart forebodeth for the battle that shall be.
To-day with thee I wend not; so I feared, and lo my feet,
That are wont to the woodland girdle of the acres of the wheat,
For thee among strange people and the foeman's throng have trod,
And I tell thee their banner of battle is a wise and a mighty God.
For these are the folk of the cities, and in wondrous wise they dwell
'Mid confusion of heaped houses, dim and black as the face of hell;
Though therefrom rise roofs most goodly, where their captains and their kings
Dwell amidst the walls of marble in abundance of fair things;
And 'mid these, nor worser nor better, but builded otherwise
Stand the Houses of the Fathers, and the hidden mysteries.
And as close as are the tree-trunks that within the beech-wood thrive
E'en so many are their pillars; and therein like men alive
Stand the images of god-folk in such raiment as they wore
In the years before the cities and the hidden days of yore.
Ah for the gold that I gazed on! and their store of battle gear,
And strange engines that I knew not, or the end for which they were.
Ah for the ordered wisdom of the war-array of these,
And the folks that are sitting about them in dumb down-trodden peace!
So I thought now fareth war-ward my well-beloved friend,
And the weird of the Gods hath doomed it that no more with him may I wend!
Woe's me for the war of the Wolfings wherefrom I am sundered apart,
And the fruitless death of the war-wise, and the doom of the hardy heart!"

Then he answered, and his eyes grew kind as he looked on her:

For thy fair love I thank thee, and thy faithful word, O friend!
But how might it otherwise happen but we twain must meet in the end,
The God of this mighty people and the Markmen and their kin?
Lo, this is the weird of the world, and what may we do herein?

Then mirth came into her face again as she said: "Who wotteth of Weird [fate], and what she is till the weird is accomplished? Long hath it been my weird to love thee and to fashion deeds for thee as I may; nor will I depart from it now." And she sang:

Keen-edged is the sword of the city, and bitter is its spear,
But thy breast in the battle, beloved, hath a wall of the stithy's gear.
What now is thy wont in the handplay with the helm and the hauberk of rings?
Farest thou as the thrall and the cot-carle, or clad in the raiment of kings?

He started, and his face reddened as he answered:

O Wood-Sun thou wottest our battle and the way wherein we fare:
That oft at the battle's beginning the helm and the hauberk we bear;
Lest the shaft of the fleeing coward or the bow at adventure bent
Should slay us ere the need be, ere our might be given and spent.
Yet oft ere the fight is over, and Doom hath scattered the foe,
No leader of the people by his war-gear shall ye know,
But by his hurts the rather, from the cot-carle and the thrall:
For when all is done that a man may, 'tis the hour for a man to fall.

She yet smiled as she said in answer:

O Folk-wolf, heed and hearken; for when shall thy life be spent
And the Folk wherein thou dwellest with thy death be well content?
Whenso folk need the fire, do they hew the apple-tree,
And burn the Mother of Blossom and the fruit that is to be?
Or me wilt thou bid to thy grave-mound because thy battle-wrath
May nothing more be bridled than the whirl wind on his path?
So hearken and do my bidding, for the Hauberk shalt thou bear
E'en when the other warriors cast off their battle-gear.
So come thou, come unwounded from the war-field of the south,
And sit with me in the beech-wood, and kiss me, eyes and mouth.

And she kissed him in very deed, and made much of him, and fawned on him, and laid her hand on his breast, and he was soft and blithe with her, but at last he laughed and said:

God's Daughter, long hast thou lived, and many a matter seen,
And men full often grieving for the deed that might have been;
But here my heart thou wheedlest as a maid of tender years
When first in the arms of her darling the horn of war she hears.

Thou knowest the axe to be heavy, and the sword, how keen it is;
But that Doom of which thou hast spoken, wilt thou not tell of this,
God's Daughter, how it sheareth, and how it breaketh through
Each wall that the warrior buildeth, yea all deeds that he may do?
What might in the hammer's leavings, in the fire's thrall shall abide
To turn that Folks' o'erwhelmer from the fated warrior's side?

Then she laughed in her turn, and loudly; but so sweetly that the sound of her voice mingled with the first song of a newly awakened wood-thrush sitting on a rowan twig on the edge of the Wood-lawn. But she said:

YEA, I THAT AM GOD'S DAUGHTER MAY TELL THEE NEVER A WHIT
From what land cometh the Hauberk nor what smith smithied it,
That thou shalt wear in the handplay from the first stroke to the last;
But this thereof I tell thee, that it holdeth firm and fast
The life of the body it lappeth, if the gift of the Godfolk it be.
Lo this is the yoke-mate of doom, and the gift of me unto thee.

The Hauberk Given

Then she leaned down from the stone whereon they sat, and her hand was in the dewy grass for a little, and then it lifted up a dark grey rippling coat of rings; and she straightened herself in the seat again, and laid that Hauberk on the knees of Thiodolf, and he put his hand to it, and turned it about, while he pondered long: then at last he said:

WHAT EVIL THING ABIDETH WITH THIS WARDER OF THE STRIFE,
This burg and treasure chamber for the hoarding of my life?
For this is the work of the dwarfs, and no kindly kin of the earth;
And all we fear the dwarf-kin and their anger and sorrow and mirth.

She cast her arms about him and fondled him, and her voice grew sweeter than the voice of any mortal thing as she answered:

NO ILL FOR THEE, BELOVED, OR FOR ME IN THE HAUBERK LIES;
No sundering grief is in it, no lonely miseries.
But we shall abide together, and that new life I gave,
For a long while yet henceforward we twain its joy shall have.
Yea, if thou dost my bidding to wear my gift in the fight
No hunter of the wild-wood at the changing of the night
Shall see my shape on thy grave-mound or my tears in the morning find
With the dew of the morning mingled; nor with the evening wind
Shall my body pass the shepherd as he wandereth in the mead
And fill him with forebodings on the eve of the Wolfings' need.
Nor the horse-herd wake in the midnight and hear my fateful cry;

Nor yet shall the Wolfing women hear words on the wind go by
As they weave and spin the night down when the House is gone to the war,
And weep for the swains they wedded and the children that they bore.
Yea do my bidding, O Folk-wolf, lest a grief of the Gods should weigh
On the ancient House of the Wolfings and my death o'ercloud its day.

And still she clung about him, while he spake no word of yea or nay: but at the last he let himself glide wholly into her arms, and the dwarf-wrought Hauberk fell from his knees and lay on the grass.

So they abode together in that wood-lawn till the twilight was long gone, and the sun arisen for some while. **And when Thiodolf stepped out of the beech-wood into the broad sunshine dappled with the shadow of the leaves of the hazels moving gently in the fresh morning air, he was covered from the neck to the knee by a Hauberk of rings dark and grey and gleaming, fashioned by the dwarfs of ancient days.**

4. THE HOUSE FARETH TO THE WAR

The Wolfings prepare for war. Their wains are large wagons that can create a defensive garth (enclosure) they call a Wain-burg (wagon-city). Carles are rude and rustic men (common laborers), and a trencher-licker seems to be man mostly interested in eating from wooden platters (trenchers). Both are contrasted with well-equipped and trained warriors. Notice that at this point Thiodolf chooses to go to war clad in the dwarf-made Hauberk that Wood-Sun gave him rather than the one he usually wears. In Morris, as in the "weird sisters" of Shakespeare's *Macbeth*, the term weird refers to fate or destiny. As they march to war, they meet the Beamings, a sister tribe whose sign is a green tree.

Now when Thiodolf came back to the habitations of the kindred the whole House was astir, both thrall-men and women, and free women hurrying from cot to stithy [forge], and from stithy to hall bearing the last of the war-gear or raiment for the fighting-men. But they for their part were some standing about anigh the Man's-door, some sitting gravely within the hall, some watching the hurry of the thralls and women from the midmost of the open space amidst of the habitations, whereon there stood yet certain wains which were belated: for the most of the wains were now standing with the oxen already yoked to them down in the meadow past the acres, encircled by a confused throng of kine and horses and thrall-folk, for thither had all the beasts for the slaughter, and the horses for the warriors been brought; and there were the horses tethered or held by the thralls; some indeed were already saddled and bridled, and on others were the thralls doing the harness.

But as for the wains of the Markmen, they were stoutly framed of ash-tree with panels of aspen, and they were broad-wheeled so that they might go over rough and smooth. They had high tilts over them well framed of willow-poles covered over with squares of black felt over-lapping like shingles; which felt they made of the rough of their fleeces, for they had many sheep. And these wains were to them for houses upon the way if need were, and therein as now were stored their meal and their war-store and after fight they would flit their wounded men in them, such as were too sorely hurt to back a horse: nor must it be hidden that whiles they looked to bring back with them the treasure of the south.

Moreover the folk if they were worsted in any battle, instead of fleeing without more done, would often draw back fighting into a garth [enclosed area] made by these wains, and guarded by some of their thralls; and there would abide the onset of those who had thrust them back in the field. And this garth they called the Wain-burg.

So now stood three of these wains aforesaid belated amidst of the habitations of the House, their yoke-beasts standing or lying down unharnessed as yet to them: but in the very midst of that place was a wain unlike to them; smaller than they but higher; square of shape as to the floor of it; built lighter than they, yet far stronger; as the warrior is stronger than the big carle and trencher-licker that loiters about the hall; and from the midst of this wain arose a mast made of a tall straight fir-tree, and thereon hung the banner of the Wolfings, wherein was wrought the image of the Wolf, but red of hue as a token of war, and with his mouth open and gaping upon the foemen.

Also whereas the other wains were drawn by mere oxen, and those of divers colours, as chance would have it, the wain of the banner was drawn by ten black bulls of the mightiest of the herd, deep-dewlapped, high-crested and curly-browed; and their harness was decked with gold, and so was the wain itself, and the woodwork of it painted red with vermilion. There then stood the Banner of the House of the Wolfings awaiting the departure of the warriors to the hosting.

So Thiodolf stood on the top of the bent beside that same mound wherefrom he had blown the War-horn yester-eve, and which was called the Hill of Speech, and he shaded his eyes with his hand and looked around him; and even therewith the carles fell to yoking the beasts to the belated wains, and the warriors gathered together from out of the mixed throngs, and came from the Roof and the Man's-door and all set their faces toward the Hill of Speech.

So Thiodolf knew that all was ready for departure, and it wanted but an hour of high-noon; so he turned about and went into the Hall, and there found his shield and his spear hanging in his sleeping place beside the hauberk he was wont to wear; then he looked, as one striving with thought, at his empty hauberk and his own body covered with the dwarf-wrought rings; nor did his face change as he took his shield and his spear and turned away.

Meeting with Hall-Sun

Then he went to the dais and there sat his foster-daughter (as men deemed her) sitting amidst of it as yester-eve, and now arrayed in a garment of fine white wool, on the breast whereof were wrought in gold two beasts ramping up against a fire-altar whereon a flame flickered; and on the skirts and the hems were other devices, of wolves chasing deer, and men shooting with the bow; and that garment was an ancient treasure; but she had a broad girdle of gold and gems about her middle, and on her arms and neck she wore great gold rings wrought delicately.

By then there were few save the Hall-Sun under the Roof, and they but the oldest of the women, or a few very old men, and some who were ailing and might not go abroad. But before her on the thwart table lay the Great War-horn awaiting the coming of Thiodolf to give signal of departure.

Then went Thiodolf to the Hall-Sun and kissed and embraced her fondly, and she gave the horn into his hands, and he went forth and up on to the Hill of Speech, and blew thence a short blast on the horn, and then came all the Warriors flocking to the Hill of Speech, each man stark in his harness, alert and joyous.

Then presently through the Man's-door came the Hall-Sun in that ancient garment, which fell straight and stiff down to her ankles as she stepped lightly and slowly along, her head crowned with a garland of eglantine. In her right hand also she held a great torch of wax lighted, whose flame amidst the bright sunlight looked like a wavering leaf of vermilion.

The warriors saw her, and made a lane for her, and she made her way through it up to the Hill of Speech, and she went up to the top of it and stood there holding the lighted candle in her hand, so that all might see it. Then suddenly was there as great a silence as there may be on a forenoon of summer; for even the thralls down in the meadow had noted what was toward, and ceased their talking and shouting, for as far off as they were, since they could see that the Hall-Sun stood on the Hill of Speech, for the wood was dark behind her; so they knew the Farewell Flame was lighted, and that the maiden would speak; and to all men her speech was a boding of good or of ill.

Hall-Sun's Speech

So she began in a sweet voice yet clear and far-reaching:

O WARRIORS OF THE WOLFINGS by the token of the flame
That here in my right hand flickers, come aback to the House of the Name!
For there yet burneth the Hall-Sun beneath the Wolfing roof,
And this flame is litten from it, nor as now shall it fare aloof
Till again it seeth the mighty and the men to be gleaned from the fight.
So wend ye as weird willeth and let your hearts be light;
For through your days of battle all the deeds of our days shall be fair.
To-morrow beginneth the haysel, as if every carle were here;
And who knoweth ere your returning but the hook shall smite the corn?
But the kine shall go down to the meadow as their wont is every morn,
And each eve shall come back to the byre; and the mares and foals afield
Shall ever be heeded duly; and all things shall their increase yield.
And if it shall befal us that hither cometh a foe
Here have we swains of the shepherds good players with the bow,
And old men battle-crafty whose might is nowise spent,

And women fell and fearless well wont to tread the bent
Amid the sheep and the oxen; and their hands are hard with the spear
And their arms are strong and stalwart the battle shield to bear;
And store of weapons have we and the mighty walls of the stead;
And the Roof shall abide you steadfast with the Hall-Sun overhead.
Lo here I quench this candle that is lit from the Hall-Sun's flame
Which unto the Wild-wood clearing with the kin of the Wolfings came
And shall wend with their departure to the limits of the earth;
Nor again shall the torch be lighted till in sorrow or in mirth,
Overthrown or overthrowing, ye come aback once more,
And bid me bear the candle before the Wolf of War.

As she spake the word she turned the candle downward, and thrust it against the grass and quenched it indeed; but the whole throng of warriors turned about, for the bulls of the banner-wain lowered their heads in the yokes and began to draw, lowing mightily; and the wain creaked and moved on, and all the men-at-arms followed after, and down they went through the lanes of the corn, and a many women and children and old men went down into the mead with them.

In their hearts they all wondered what the Hall-Sun's words might signify; for she had told them nought about the battles to be, saving that some should come back to the Mid-mark; whereas aforetime somewhat would she foretell to them concerning the fortune of the fight, and now had she said to them nothing but what their own hearts told them.

Marching to War

Nevertheless they bore their crests high as they followed the Wolf down into the meadow, where all was now ready for departure. There they arrayed themselves and went down to the lip of Mirkwood-water; and such was their array that the banner went first, save that a band of fully armed men went before it; and behind it and about were the others as well arrayed as they. Then went the wains that bore their munition, with armed carles of the thrall-folk about them, who were ever the guard of the wains, and should never leave them night or day; and lastly went the great band of the warriors and the rest of the thralls with them.

As to their war-gear, all the freemen had helms of some kind, but not all of iron or steel; for some bore helms fashioned of horse-hide and bull-hide covered over with the similitude of a Wolf's muzzle; nor were these ill-defence against a sword-stroke. Shields they all had, and all these had the image of the Wolf marked on them, but for many their thralls bore them on the journey. As to their body-armour some carried long byrnies of ring-mail, some coats of leather covered with splinters of horn laid like the shingles of a roof, and some skin-coats only: whereof indeed there were some of which tales went that they were better than the smith's hammer-work, because they had had spells sung over them to keep out steel or iron.

But for their weapons, they bore spears with shafts not very long, some eight feet of our measure; and axes heavy and long-shafted; and bills with great and broad heads; and some few, but not many of the kindred were bowmen, and every freeman was girt with a sword; but of the swords some were long and two-edged, some short and heavy, cutting on one edge, and these were of the kind which they and our forefathers long after called 'sax.' Thus were the freemen arrayed.

But for the thralls, there were many bows among them, especially among those who were of blood alien from the Goths; the others bore short spears, and feathered broad arrows, and clubs bound with iron, and knives and axes, but not every man of them had a sword. Few iron helms they had and no ringed byrnies, but most had a buckler at their backs with no sign or symbol on it.

Thus then set forth the fighting men of the House of the Wolf toward the Thing-stead of the Upper-mark where the hosting was to be, and by then they were moving up along the side of Mirkwood-water it was somewhat past high-noon.

But the stay-at-home people who had come down with them to the meadow lingered long in that place; and much foreboding there was among them of evil to come; and of the old folk, some remembered tales of the past days of the Markmen, and how they had come from the ends of the earth, and the mountains where none dwell now but the Gods of their kindreds; and many of these tales told of their woes and their wars as they went from river to river and from wild-wood to wild-wood before they had established their Houses in the Mark, and fallen to dwelling there season by season and year by year whether the days were good or ill. And it fell into their hearts that now at last mayhappen was their abiding wearing out to an end, and that the day should soon be when they should have to bear the Hall-Sun through the wild-wood, and seek a new dwelling-place afar from the troubling of these newly arisen Welsh foemen.

And so those of them who could not rid themselves of this foreboding were somewhat heavier of heart than their wont was when the House went to the War. For long had they abided there in the Mark, and the life was sweet to them which they knew, and the life which they knew not was bitter to them: and Mirkwood-water was become as a God to them no less than to their fathers of old time; nor lesser was the mead where fed the horses that they loved and the kine that they had reared, and the sheep that they guarded from the Wolf of the Wild-wood: and they worshipped the kind acres which they themselves and their fathers had made fruitful, wedding them to the seasons of seed-time and harvest, that the birth that came from them might become a part of the kindred of the Wolf, and the joy and might of past springs and summers might run in the blood of the Wolfing children.

And a dear God indeed to them was the Roof of the Kindred, that their fathers had built and that they yet warded against the fire and the lightening and the wind and the snow, and the passing of the days that devour and the years that heap the dust over the work of men. They thought of how it had stood, and seen so many generations of men come and go; how often it had welcomed the new-born babe, and given farewell to the old man: how many secrets of the past it knew; how many tales which men of the present had forgotten, but which yet mayhap men of times to come should learn of it; for to them yet living it had spoken time and again, and had told them what their fathers had not told them, and it held the memories of the generations and the very life of the Wolfings and their hopes for the days to be.

Thus these poor people thought of the Gods whom they worshiped, and the friends whom they loved, and could not choose but be heavy-hearted when they thought that the wild-wood was awaiting them to swallow all up, and take away from them their Gods and their friends and the mirth of their life, and burden them with hunger and thirst and weariness, that their children might begin once more to build the House and establish the dwelling, and call new places by old names, and worship new Gods with the ancient worship.

Such imaginations of trouble then were in the hearts of the stay-at-homes of the Wolfings; the tale tells not indeed that all had such forebodings, but chiefly the old folk who were nursing the end of their life-days amidst the cherishing Kindred of the House.

But now they were beginning to turn them back again to the habitations, and a thin stream was flowing through the acres, when they heard a confused sound drawing near blended of horns and the lowing of beasts and the shouting of men; and they looked and saw a throng of brightly clad men coming up stream alongside of Mirkwood-water; and they were not afraid, for they knew that it must be some other company of the Markmen journeying to the hosting of the Folk: and presently they saw that it was the House of the Beamings following their banner on the way to the Thing-stead.

But when the new-comers saw the throng out in the meads, some of their young men pricked on their horses and galloped on past the women and old men, to whom they threw a greeting, as they ran past to catch up with the bands of the Wolfings; for between the two houses was there affinity, and much good liking lay between them; and the stay-at-homes, many of them, lingered yet till the main body of the Beamings came with their banner: and their array was much like to that of the Wolfings, but gayer; for whereas it pleased the latter to darken all their wargear to the colour of the grey Wolf, the Beamings polished all their gear as bright as might be, and their raiment also was mostly bright green of hue and much beflowered; and the sign on their banner was a green leafy tree, and the wain was drawn by great white bulls.

So when their company drew anear to the throng of the stay-at-homes they went to meet and greet each other, and tell tidings to each other; but their banner held steadily onward amidst their converse, and in a little while they followed it, for the way was long to the Thing-stead of the Upper-mark.

So passed away the fighting men by the side of Mirkwood-water, and the throng of the stay-at-homes melted slowly from the meadow and trickled along through the acres to the habitations of the Wolfings, and there they fell to doing whatso of work or play came to their hands.

5. Concerning the Hall-Sun

On the Hill of Speech we learn more of Wall-Sun's mysterious origins and the visions she has seen. The old woman is Wall-Sun's mother, Wood-Sun, who has the power to change her appearance, as Hall-Sun realizes.

When the warriors and the others had gone down to the mead, the Hall-Sun was left standing on the Hill of Speech, and she stood there till she saw the host in due array going on its ways dark and bright and beautiful; then she made as if to turn aback to the Great Roof; but all at once it seemed to her as if something held her back, as if her will to move had departed from her, and that she could not put one foot before the other. So she lingered on the Hill, and the quenched candle fell from her hand, and presently she sank adown on the grass and sat there with the face of one thinking intently.

Yet was it with her that a thousand thoughts were in her mind at once and no one of them uppermost, and images of what had been and what then was flickered about in her brain, and betwixt them were engendered images of things to be, but unstable and not to be trowed in. So sat the Hall-Sun on the Hill of Speech lost in a dream of the day, whose stories were as little clear as those of a night-dream.

Hall-Sun speaks with Her Mother Disguised

But as she sat musing thus, came to her a woman exceeding old to look on, whom she knew not as one of the kindred or a thrall; and this carline [old woman] greeted her by the name of Hall-Sun and said:

Hail, Hall-Sun of the Markmen! how fares it now with thee
When the whelps of the Woodbeast wander with the Leafage of the Tree
All up the Mirkwood-water to seek what they shall find,
The oak-boles of the battle and the war-wood stark and blind?

Then answered the maiden:

It fares with me, O mother, that my soul would fain go forth
To behold the ways of the battle, and the praise of the warriors' worth.
But yet is it held entangled in a maze of many a thing,
As the low-grown bramble holdeth the brake-shoots of the Spring.
I think of the thing that hath been, but no shape is in my thought;
I think of the day that passeth, and its story comes to nought.
I think of the days that shall be, nor shape I any tale.
I will hearken thee, O mother, if hearkening may avail.

The carline gazed at her with dark eyes that shone brightly from amidst her brown wrinkled face: then she sat herself down beside her and spake:

From a far folk have I wandered and I come of an alien blood,
But I know all tales of the Wolfings and their evil and their good;

And when I heard of thy fairness, thereof I heard it said,
That for thee should be never a bridal nor a place in the warrior's bed.

The maiden neither reddened nor paled, but looking with calm steady eyes into the carline's face she answered:

YEA TRUE IT IS, I AM WEDDED TO THE MIGHTY ONES OF OLD,
And the fathers of the Wolfings ere the days of field and fold.

Then a smile came into the eyes of the old woman and she said.

HOW GLAD SHALL BE THY MOTHER OF THY WORSHIP AND THY WORTH,
And the father that begat thee if yet they dwell on earth!

But the Hall-Sun answered in the same steady manner as before:

NONE KNOWETH WHO IS MY MOTHER, NOR MY VERY FATHER'S NAME;
But when to the House of the Wolfings a wild-wood waif I came,
They gave me a foster-mother an ancient dame and good,
And a glorious foster-father the best of all the blood.

Spake the carline.

YEA, I HAVE HEARD THE STORY, BUT SCARCE THEREIN MIGHT I TROW
That thou with all thy beauty wert born 'neath the oaken bough,
And hast crawled a naked baby o'er the rain-drenched autumn-grass;
Wilt thou tell the wandering woman what wise it cometh to pass
That thou art the Mid-mark's Hall-Sun, and the sign of the Wolfings' gain?
Thou shalt pleasure me much by the telling, and there of shalt thou be fain.

Then answered the Hall-Sun.

YEA; THUS MUCH I REMEMBER FOR THE FIRST OF MY MEMORIES;
That I lay on the grass in the morning and above were the boughs of the trees.
But nought naked was I as the wood-whelp, but clad in linen white,
And adown the glades of the oakwood the morning sun lay bright.
Then a hind came out of the thicket and stood on the sunlit glade,
And turned her head toward the oak tree and a step on toward me made.
Then stopped, and bounded aback, and away as if in fear,
That I saw her no more; then I wondered, though sitting close anear
Was a she-wolf great and grisly. But with her was I wont to play,
And pull her ears, and belabour her rugged sides and grey,
And hold her jaws together, while she whimpered, slobbering
For the love of my love; and nowise I deemed her a fearsome thing.
There she sat as though she were watching, and o'er head a blue-winged jay
Shrieked out from the topmost oak-twigs, and a squirrel ran his way
Two tree-trunks off. But the she-wolf arose up suddenly

And growled with her neck-fell bristling, as if danger drew anigh;
And therewith I heard a footstep, for nice was my ear to catch
All the noises of the wild-wood; so there did we sit at watch
While the sound of feet grew nigher: then I clapped hand on hand
And crowed for joy and gladness, for there out in the sun did stand
A man, a glorious creature with a gleaming helm on his head,
And gold rings on his arms, in raiment gold-broidered crimson-red.
Straightway he strode up toward us nor heeded the wolf of the wood
But sang as he went in the oak-glade, as a man whose thought is good,
And nought she heeded the warrior, but tame as a sheep was grown,
And trotted away through the wild-wood with her crest all laid adown.
Then came the man and sat down by the oak-bole close unto me
And took me up nought fearful and set me on his knee.
And his face was kind and lovely, so my cheek to his cheek I laid
And touched his cold bright war-helm and with his gold rings played,
And hearkened his words, though I knew not what tale they had to tell,
Yet fain was my heart of their music, and meseemed I loved him well.
So we fared for a while and were fain, till he set down my feet on the grass,
And kissed me and stood up himself, and away through the wood did he pass.
And then came back the she-wolf and with her I played and was fain.
Lo the first thing I remember: wilt thou have me babble again?

Spake the carline and her face was soft and kind:

NAY DAMSEL, LONG WOULD I HEARKEN TO THY VOICE THIS SUMMER DAY.
But how didst thou leave the wild-wood, what people brought thee away?

Then said the Hall-Sun:

I AWOKE ON A TIME IN THE EVEN, AND VOICES I HEARD AS I WOKE;
And there was I in the wild-wood by the bole of the ancient oak,
And a ring of men was around me, and glad was I indeed
As I looked upon their faces and the fashion of their weed.
For I gazed on the red and the scarlet and the beaten silver and gold,
And blithe were their noble faces and kindly to behold,
And nought had I seen of such-like since that hour of the other day
When that warrior came to the oak glade with the little child to play.
And forth now he came, with the face that my hands had fondled before,
And a battle shield wrought fairly upon his arm he bore,
And thereon the wood-wolf's image in ruddy gold was done.
Then I stretched out my little arms towards the glorious shining one
And he took me up and set me on his shoulder for a while
And turned about to his fellows with a blithe and joyous smile;

And they shouted aloud about me and drew forth gleaming swords
And clashed them on their bucklers; but nought I knew of the words
Of their shouting and rejoicing. So thereafter was I laid
And borne forth on the warrior's warshield, and our way through the wood we
 made
'Midst the mirth and great contentment of those fair-clad shielded men.

But no tale of the wolf and the wild-wood abides with me since then,
And the next thing I remember is a huge and dusky hall,
A world for my little body from ancient wall to wall;
A world of many doings, and nought for me to do,
A world of many noises, and known to me were few.

Time wore, and I spoke with the Wolfings and knew the speech of the kin,
And was strange 'neath the roof no longer, as a lonely waif therein;
And I wrought as a child with my playmates and every hour looked on,
Unto the next hour's joyance till the happy day was done.
And going and coming amidst us was a woman tall and thin
With hair like the hoary barley and silver streaks therein.
And kind and sad of visage, as now I remember me,
And she sat and told us stories when we were aweary with glee,
And many of us she fondled, but me the most of all.

And once from my sleep she waked me and bore me down the hall,
In the hush of the very midnight, and I was feared thereat.
But she brought me unto the dais, and there the warrior sat,
Who took me up and kissed me, as erst within the wood;
And meseems in his arms I slumbered: but I wakened again and stood
Alone with the kindly woman, and gone was the goodly man,
And athwart the hush of the Folk-hall the moon shone bright and wan,
And the woman dealt with a lamp hung up by a chain aloft,
And she trimmed it and fed it with oil, while she chanted sweet and soft
A song whose words I knew not: then she ran it up again,
And up in the darkness above us died the length of its wavering chain.

"Yea," said the carline, "this woman will have been the Hall-Sun that came before
thee. What next dost thou remember?"
Said the maiden:

Next I mind me of the hazels behind the People's Roof,
And the children running thither and the magpie flitting aloof,
And my hand in the hand of the Hall-Sun, as after the others we went,
And she soberly hearkening my prattle and the words of my intent.
And now would I call her 'Mother,' and indeed I loved her well.

So I WAXED; and now of my memories the tale were long to tell;
But as the days passed over, and I fared to field and wood,
Alone or with my playmates, still the days were fair and good.
But the sad and kindly Hall-Sun for my fosterer now I knew,
And the great and glorious warrior that my heart clung sorely to
Was but my foster-father; and I knew that I had no kin
In the ancient House of the Wolfings, though love was warm therein.

Then smiled the carline and said: "Yea, he is thy foster-father, and yet a fond one."

"Sooth is that," said the Hall-Sun. "But wise art thou by seeming. Hast thou come to tell me of what kindred I am, and who is my father and who is my mother?"

Said the carline: "Art thou not also wise? Is it not so that the Hall-Sun of the Wolfings seeth things that are to come?"

"Yea," she said, "yet have I seen waking or sleeping no other father save my foster-father; yet my very mother I have seen, as one who should meet her in the flesh one day."

"And good is that," said the carline; and as she spoke her face waxed kinder, and she said: "Tell us more of thy days in the House of the Wolfings and how thou faredst there."

Said the Hall-Sun:

I WAXED 'NEATH THE ROOF OF THE WOLFINGS, TILL NOW TO LOOK UPON
I was of sixteen winters, and the love of the Folk I won,
And in lovely weed they clad me like the image of a God:
And lonely now full often the wild-wood ways I trod,
And I feared no wild-wood creature, and my presence scared them nought;
And I fell to know of wisdom, and within me stirred my thought,
So that oft anights would I wander through the mead and far away,
And swim the Mirkwood-water, and amidst his eddies play
When earth was dark in the dawn-tide; and over all the folk
I knew of the beasts' desires, as though in words they spoke.

So I SAW of things that should be, were they mighty things or small,
And upon a day as it happened came the war-word to the hall,
And the House must wend to the warfield, and as they sang, and played
With the strings of the harp that even, and the mirth of the war-eve made,
Came the sight of the field to my eyes, and the words waxed hot in me,
And I needs must show the picture of the end of the fight to be.
Then I showed them the Red Wolf bristling o'er the broken fleeing foe;
And the war-gear of the fleers, and their banner did I show,
To wit the Ling-worm's image with the maiden in his mouth;
There I saw my foster-father 'mid the pale blades of the South,
Till aloof swept all the handplay and the hurry of the chase,

And he lay along by an ash-tree, no helm about his face,
No byrny on his body; and an arrow in his thigh,
And a broken spear in his shoulder. Then I saw myself draw nigh
To sing the song blood-staying. Then saw I how we twain
Went 'midst of the host triumphant in the Wolfings' banner-wain,
The black bulls lowing before us athwart the warriors' song,
As up from Mirkwood-water we went our ways along
To the Great Roof of the Wolfings, whence streamed the women out
And the sound of their rejoicing blent with the warriors' shout.

THEY HEARD ME and saw the picture, and they wotted how wise I was grown,
And they loved me, and glad were their hearts at the tale my lips had shown;
And my body clad as an image of a God to the field they bore,
And I held by the mast of the banner as I looked upon their war,
And endured to see unblenching on the wind-swept sunny plain
All the picture of my vision by the menfolk done again.
And over my Foster-father I sang the staunching-song,
Till the life-blood that was ebbing flowed back to his heart the strong,
And we wended back in the war-wain 'midst the gleanings of the fight
Unto the ancient dwelling and the Hall-Sun's glimmering light.

SO FROM THAT day henceforward folk hung upon my words,
For the battle of the autumn, and the harvest of the swords;
And e'en more was I loved than aforetime.
So wore a year away, And heavy was the burden of the lore that on me lay.

BUT MY FOSTERER the Hall-Sun took sick at the birth of the year,
And changed her life as the year changed, as summer drew anear.
But she knew that her life was waning, and lying in her bed
She taught me the lore of the Hall-Sun, and every word to be said
At the trimming in the midnight and the feeding in the morn,
And she laid her hands upon me ere unto the howe she was borne
With the kindred gathered about us; and they wotted her weird and her will,
And hailed me for the Hall-Sun when at last she lay there still.
And they did on me the garment, the holy cloth of old,
And the neck-chain wrought for the goddess, and the rings of the hallowed gold.
So here am I abiding, and of things to be I tell,
Yet know not what shall befall me nor why with the Wolfings I dwell.

Then said the carline:

WHAT SEEST THOU, O DAUGHTER, of the journey of to-day?
And why wendest thou not with the war-host on the battle-echoing way?

Said the Hall-Sun.

O MOTHER, HERE DWELLETH THE HALL-SUN WHILE THE KIN HATH A DWELLING-
    PLACE,
Nor ever again shall I look on the onset or the chase,
Till the day when the Roof of the Wolfings looketh down on the girdle of foes,
And the arrow singeth over the grass of the kindred's close;
Till the pillars shake with the shouting and quivers the roof-tree dear,
When the Hall of the Wolfings garners the harvest of the spear.

Therewith she stood on her feet and turned her face to the Great Roof, and gazed long at it, not heeding the crone by her side; and she muttered words of whose signification the other knew not, though she listened intently, and gazed ever at her as closely as might be.

Then fell the Hall-Sun utterly silent, and the lids closed over her eyes, and her hands were clenched, and her feet pressed hard on the daisies: her bosom heaved with sore sighs, and great tear-drops oozed from under her eyelids and fell on to her raiment and her feet and on to the flowery summer grass; and at the last her mouth opened and she spake, but in a voice that was marvelously changed from that she spake in before:

WHY WENT YE FORTH, O WOLFINGS, FROM THE GARTH YOUR FATHERS BUILT,
And the House where sorrow dieth, and all unloosed is guilt?
Turn back, turn back, and behold it! lest your feet be over slow
When your shields are heavy-burdened with the arrows of the foe;
How ye totter, how ye stumble on the rough and corpse-strewn way!
And lo, how the eve is eating the afternoon of day!
O why are ye abiding till the sun is sunk in night
And the forest trees are ruddy with the battle-kindled light?
O rest not yet, ye Wolfings, lest void be your resting-place,
And into lands that ye know not the Wolf must turn his face,
And ye wander and ye wander till the land in the ocean cease,
And your battle bring no safety and your labour no increase.

Then was she silent for a while, and her tears ceased to flow; but presently her eyes opened once more, and she lifted up her voice and cried aloud -

I SEE, I SEE! O GODFOLK BEHOLD IT FROM ALOOF,
How the little flames steal flickering along the ridge of the Roof!
They are small and red 'gainst the heavens in the summer afternoon;
But when the day is dusking, white, high shall they wave to the moon.
Lo, the fire plays now on the windows like strips of scarlet cloth
Wind-waved! but look in the night-tide on the onset of its wrath,
How it wraps round the ancient timbers and hides the mighty roof
But lighteth little crannies, so lost and far aloof,

That no man yet of the kindred hath seen them ere to-night,
Since first the builder builded in loving and delight!

Then again she stayed her speech with weeping and sobbing, but after a while was still again, and then she spoke pointing toward the roof with her right hand.

I SEE THE FIRE-RAISERS AND IRON-HELMED THEY ARE,
Brown-faced about the banners that their hands have borne afar.
And who in the garth of the kindred shall bear adown their shield
Since the onrush of the Wolfings they caught in the open field,
As the might of the mountain lion falls dead in the hempen net?
O Wolfings, long have ye tarried, but the hour abideth yet.
What life for the life of the people shall be given once for all,
What sorrow shall stay sorrow in the half-burnt Wolfing Hall?
There is nought shall quench the fire save the tears of the Godfolk's kin,
And the heart of the life-delighter, and the life-blood cast therein.

Then once again she fell silent, and her eyes closed again, and the slow tears gushed out from them, and she sank down sobbing on the grass, and little by little the storm of grief sank and her head fell back, and she was as one quietly asleep. Then the carline hung over her and kissed her and embraced her; and then through her closed eyes and her slumber did the Hall-Sun see a marvel; for she who was kissing her was young in semblance and unwrinkled, and lovely to look on, with plenteous long hair of the hue of ripe barley, and clad in glistening raiment such as has been woven in no loom on earth.

And indeed it was the Wood-Sun in the semblance of a crone, who had come to gather wisdom of the coming time from the foreseeing of the Hall-Sun; since now at last she herself foresaw nothing of it, though she was of the kindred of the Gods and the Fathers of the Goths. So when she had heard the Hall-Sun she deemed that she knew but too well what her words meant, and what for love, what for sorrow, she grew sick at heart as she heard them.

So at last she arose and turned to look at the Great Roof; and strong and straight, and cool and dark grey showed its ridge against the pale sky of the summer afternoon all quivering with the heat of many hours' sun: dark showed its windows as she gazed on it, and stark and stiff she knew were its pillars within.

Then she said aloud, but to herself: "What then if a merry and mighty life be given for it, and the sorrow of the people be redeemed; yet will not I give the life which is his; nay rather let him give the bliss which is mine. But oh! How may it be that he shall die joyous and I shall live unhappy!" Then she went slowly down from the Hill of Speech, and whoso saw her deemed her but a gangrel carline. So she went her ways and let the wood cover her.

But in a little while the Hall-Sun awoke alone, and sat up with a sigh, and she re-membered nothing concerning her sight of the flickering flame along the hall-roof, and the fire-tongues like strips of scarlet cloth blown by the wind, nor had she any memory of her words concerning the coming day.

But the rest of her talk with the carline she remembered, and also the vision of the beautiful woman who had kissed and embraced her; and she knew that it was her very mother. Also she perceived that she had been weeping, therefore she knew that she had uttered words of wisdom. For so it fared with her at whiles, that she knew not her own words of foretelling, but spoke them out as if in a dream.

So now she went down from the Hill of Speech soberly, and turned toward the Woman's-door of the hall, and on her way she met the women and old men and youths coming back from the meadow with little mirth: and there were many of them who looked shyly at her as though they would gladly have asked her somewhat, and yet durst not. But for her, her sadness passed away when she came among them, and she looked kindly on this and that one of them, and entered with them into the Woman's Chamber, and did what came to her hand to do.

6. THEY TALK ON THE WAY TO THE FOLK-THING

Various tribes of Markmen meet and talk as they travel north along both sides of the Mirkwood-water to a Folk-Thing (meeting) in the Upper-mark. They talk about the visions some have had of the coming battle. An escaped Roman slave, Hiarandi, tells of the many cities of their foe. As in Chapter 2, "Welshman" here refers to any foreigner.

All day long one standing on the Speech-hill of the Wolfings might have seen men in their war-array streaming along the side of Mirkwood-water, on both sides thereof; and the last comers from the Nether-mark came hastening all they might; for they would not be late at the trysting-place. But these were of a kindred called the Laxings, who bore a salmon on their banner; and they were somewhat few in number, for they had but of late years become a House of the Markmen. Their banner-wain was drawn by white horses, fleet and strong, and they were no great band, for they had but few thralls with them, and all, free men and thralls, were a-horseback; so they rode by hastily with their banner-wain, their few munition-wains following as they might.

Now tells the tale of the men-at-arms of the Wolfings and the Beamings, that soon they fell in with the Elking host, which was journeying but leisurely, so that the Wolfings might catch up with them: they were a very great kindred, the most numerous of all Mid-mark, and at this time they had affinity with the Wolfings. But old men of the House remembered how they had heard their grandsires and very old men tell that there had been a time when the Elking House had been established by men from out of the Wolfing kindred, and how they had wandered away from the Mark in the days when it had been first settled, and had abided aloof for many generations of men; and so at last had come back again to the Mark, and had taken up their habitation at a place in Mid-mark where was dwelling but a remnant of a House called the Thyrings, who had once been exceeding mighty, but had by that time almost utterly perished in a great sickness which befell in those days. So then these two Houses, the wanderers come back and the remnant left by the sickness of the Gods, made one House together, and increased and throve after their coming together, and wedded with the Wolfings, and became a very great House.

Gallant and glorious was their array now, as they marched along with their banner of the Elk, which was drawn by the very beasts themselves tamed to draught to that end through many generations; they were fatter and sleeker than their wild-wood brethren, but not so mighty.

So were the men of the three kindreds somewhat mingled together on the way. The Wolfings were the tallest and the biggest made; but of those dark-haired men aforesaid, were there fewest amongst the Beamings, and most among the Elkings, as though they had drawn to them more men of alien blood during their wanderings aforesaid. So they talked together and made each other good cheer, as is the wont of companions in arms on the eve of battle; and the talk ran, as may be deemed, on that journey and what was likely to come of it: and spake an Elking warrior to a Wolfing by whom he rode: "O Wolfkettle, hath the Hall-Sun had any foresight of the day of battle?"

"Nay," said the other, "when she lighted the farewell candle, she bade us come back again, and spoke of the day of our return; but that methinks, as thou and I would talk of it, thinking what would be likely to befal. Since we are a great host of valiant men, and these Welshmen most valiant, and as the rumour runneth bigger-bodied men than the Hun-folk, and so well ordered as never folk have been. So then if we overthrow them we shall come back again; and if they overthrow us, the remnant of us shall fall back before them till we come to our habitations; for it is not to be looked for that they will fall in upon our rear and prevent us, since we have the thicket of the wild-wood on our flanks."

"Sooth is that," said the Elking; "and as to the mightiness of this folk and their customs, ye may gather somewhat from the songs which our House yet singeth, and which ye have heard wide about in the Mark; for this is the same folk of which a many of them tell, making up that story-lay which is called the South-Welsh Lay; which telleth how we have met this folk in times past when we were in fellowship with a folk of the Welsh of like customs to ourselves: for we of the Elkings were then but a feeble folk.

So we marched with this folk of the Kymry and met the men of the cities, and whiles we overthrew and whiles were overthrown, but at last in a great battle were overthrown with so great a slaughter, that the red blood rose over the wheels of the wains, and the city-folk fainted with the work of the slaughter, as men who mow a match in the meadows when the swathes are dry and heavy and the afternoon of midsummer is hot; and there they stood and stared on the field of the slain, and knew not whether they were in Home or Hell, so fierce the fight had been."

Tales Recalled

Therewith a man of the Beamings, who was riding on the other side of the Elking, reached out over his horse's neck and said: "Yea friend, but is there not some telling of a tale concerning how ye and your fellowship took the great city of the Welshmen of the South, and dwelt there long."

"Yea," said the Elking, "Hearken how it is told in the South-Welsh Lay:

'Have ye not heard
Of the ways of Weird?
How the folk fared forth
Far away from the North?
And as light as one wendeth
Whereas the wood endeth,
When of nought is our need,
And none telleth our deed,

So Rodgeir unwearied and Reidfari wan
The town where none tarried the shield-shaking man.
All lonely the street there, and void was the way
And nought hindered our feet but the dead men that lay
Under shield in the lanes of the houses heavens-high,
All the ring-bearing swains that abode there to die.'

"Tells the Lay, that none abode the Goths and their fellowship, but such as were mighty enough to fall before them, and the rest, both man and woman, fled away before our folk and before the folk of the Kymry, and left their town for us to dwell in; as saith the Lay:

'Glistening of gold
Did men's eyen behold;
Shook the pale sword
O'er the unspoken word,
No man drew nigh us
With weapon to try us,
For the Welsh-wrought shield
Lay low on the field.

By man's hand unbuilded all seemed there to be,
The walls ruddy gilded, the pearls of the sea:
Yea all things were dead there save pillar and wall,
But they lived and they said us the song of the hall;
The dear hall left to perish by men of the land,
For the Goth-folk to cherish with gold gaining hand.'

"See ye how the Lay tells that the hall was bolder than the men, who fled from it, and left all for our fellowship to deal with in the days gone by?"

Said the Wolfing man: "And as it was once, so shall it be again. Maybe we shall go far on this journey, and see at least one of the garths of the Southlands, even those which they call cities. For I have heard it said that they have more cities than one only, and that so great are their kindreds, that each liveth in a garth full of mighty houses, with a wall of stone and lime around it; and that in every one of these garths lieth wealth untold heaped up. And wherefore should not all this fall to the Markmen and their valiancy [courage]?"

Said the Elking: "As to their many cities and the wealth of them, that is sooth; but as to each city being the habitation of each kindred, it is otherwise: for rather it may be said of them that they have forgotten kindred, and have none, nor do they heed whom they wed, and great is the confusion amongst them. And mighty men among them ordain where they shall dwell, and what shall be their meat, and how long they shall labour after they are weary, and in all wise what manner of life shall be amongst them; and though they be called free men who suffer this, yet may no house or kindred gainsay this rule and order. In sooth they are a people mighty, but unhappy."

Said Wolfkettle: "And hast thou learned all this from the ancient story lays, O Hiarandi? For some of them I know, though not all, and therein have I noted nothing of all this. Is there some new minstrel arisen in thine House of a memory excelling all those that have gone before? If that be so, I bid him to the Roof of the Wolfings as soon as may be; for we lack new tales."

News of the Roman Invaders

"Nay," said Hiarandi, "This that I tell thee is not a tale of past days, but a tale of to-day. For there came to us a man from out of the wild-wood, and prayed us peace, and we gave it him; and he told us that he was of a House of the Gael, and that his House had been in a great battle against these Welshmen, whom he calleth the Romans; and that he was taken in the battle, and sold as a thrall in one of their garths; and howbeit, it was not their master-garth, yet there he learned of their customs: and sore was the lesson! Hard was his life amongst them, for their thralls be not so well entreated as their draught-beasts, so many do they take in battle; for they are a mighty folk; and these thralls and those aforesaid unhappy freemen do all tilling and herding and all deeds of craftsmanship: and above these are men whom they call masters and lords who do nought, nay not so much as smithy their own edge-weapons, but linger out their days in their dwellings and out of their dwellings, lying about in the sun or the hall-cinders, like cur-dogs who have fallen away from kind.

"So this man made a shift to flee away from out of that garth, since it was not far from the great river; and being a valiant man, and young and mighty of body, he escaped all perils and came to us through the Mirkwood. But we saw that he was no liar, and had been very evilly handled, for upon his body was the mark of many a stripe, and of the shackles that had been soldered on to his limbs; also it was more than one of these accursed people whom he had slain when he fled. So he became our guest and we loved him, and he dwelt among us and yet dwelleth, for we have taken him into our House. But yesterday he was sick and might not ride with us; but may be he will follow on and catch up with us in a day or two. And if he come not, then will I bring him over to the Wolfings when the battle is done."

Then laughed the Beaming man, and spake: "How then if ye come not back, nor Wolfkettle, nor the Welsh Guest, nor I myself? Meseemeth no one of these Southland Cities shall we behold, and no more of the Southlanders than their war-array."

"These are evil words," said Wolfkettle, "though such an outcome must be thought on. But why deemest thou this?"

Said the Beaming: "There is no Hall-Sun sitting under our Roof at home to tell true tales concerning the Kindred every day. Yet forsooth from time to time is a word said in our Folk-hall for good or for evil; and who can choose but hearken thereto? And yestereve was a woeful word spoken, and that by a man-child of ten winters."

Said the Elking: "Now that thou hast told us thus much, thou must tell us more, yea, all the word which was spoken; else belike we shall deem of it as worse than it was."

A Child's Warning

Said the Beaming: "Thus it was; this little lad brake out weeping yestereve, when the Hall was full and feasting; and he wailed, and roared out, as children do, and would not be pacified, and when he was asked why he made that to do, he said: 'Well away! Raven hath promised to make me a clay horse and to bake it in the kiln with the pots next week; and now he goeth to the war, and he shall never come back, and never shall my horse be made.'

Thereat we all laughed as ye may well deem. But the lad made a sour countenance on us and said, 'why do ye laugh? look yonder, what see ye?'

'Nay,' said one, 'nought but the Feast-hall wall and the hangings of the High-tide thereon.'

Then said the lad sobbing: 'Ye see ill: further afield see I: I see a little plain, on a hill top, and fells beyond it far bigger than our speech-hill: and there on the plain lieth Raven as white as parchment; and none hath such hue save the dead.'

Then said Raven, (and he was a young man, and was standing thereby). 'And well is that, swain, to die in harness! Yet hold up thine heart; here is Gunbert who shall come back and bake thine horse for thee.'

'Nay never more,' quoth the child, 'For I see his pale head lying at Raven's feet; but his body with the green gold-broidered kirtle I see not.'

Then was the laughter stilled, and man after man drew near to the child, and questioned him, and asked, 'dost thou see me?' 'dost thou see me?' And he failed to see but few of those that asked him. Therefore now meseemeth that not many of us shall see the cities of the South, and those few belike shall look on their own shackles therewithal."

"Nay," said Hiarandi, "What is all this? heard ye ever of a company of fighting men that fared afield, and found the foe, and came back home leaving none behind them?"

Said the Beaming: "Yet seldom have I heard a child foretell the death of warriors. I tell thee that hadst thou been there, thou wouldst have thought of it as if the world were coming to an end."

"Well," said Wolfkettle, "let it be as it may! Yet at least I will not be led away from the field by the foemen. Oft may a man be hindered of victory, but never of death if he willeth it."

Therewith he handled a knife that hung about his neck, and went on to say: "But indeed, I do much marvel that no word came into the mouth of the Hall-Sun yestereven or this morning, but such as any woman of the kindred might say."

They Ride Further Upstream

Therewith fell their talk awhile, and as they rode they came to where the wood drew nigher to the river, and thus the Mid-mark had an end; for there was no House had a dwelling in the Mid-mark higher up the water than the Elkings, save one only, not right great, who mostly fared to war along with the Elkings: and this was the Os-elings, whose banner bore the image of the Wood-ousel, the black bird with the yellow neb; and they had just fallen into the company of the greater House.

So now Mid-mark was over and past, and the serried trees of the wood came down like a wall but a little way from the lip of the water; and scattered trees, mostly quicken-trees, grew here and there on the very water side. But Mirkwood-water ran deep, swift and narrow between high clean-cloven banks, so that none could dream of fording, and not so many of swimming its dark green dangerous waters.

And the day wore on towards evening and the glory of the western sky was unseen because of the wall of high trees. And still the host made on, and because of the narrowness of the space between river and wood it was strung out longer and looked a very great company of men. And moreover the men of the eastern-lying part of Mid-mark, were now marching thick and close on the other side of the river but a little way from the Wolfings and their fellows; for nothing but the narrow river sundered them.

So night fell, and the stars shone, and the moon rose, and yet the Wolfings and their fellows stayed not, since they wotted that behind them followed a many of the men of the Mark, both the Mid and the Nether, and they would by no means hinder their march.

So wended the Markmen between wood and stream on either side of Mirkwood-water, till now at last the night grew deep and the moon set, and it was hard on midnight, and they had kindled many torches to light them on either side of the water. So whereas they had come to a place where the trees gave back somewhat from the river, which was well-grassed for their horses and neat, and was called Baitmead, the companies on the western side made stay there till morning. And they drew the wains right up to the thick of the wood, and all men turned aside into the mead from the beaten road, so that those who were following after might hold on their way if so they would. There then they appointed watchers of the night, while the rest of them lay upon the sward by the side of the trees, and slept through the short summer night.

The tale tells not that any man dreamed of the fight to come in such wise that there was much to tell of his dream on the morrow; many dreamed of no fight or faring to war, but of matters little, and often laughable, mere mingled memories of bygone time that had no waking wits to marshal them.

But that man of the Beamings dreamed that he was at home watching a potter, a man of the thralls of the House working at his wheel, and fashioning bowls and ewers: and he had a mind to take of his clay and fashion a horse for the lad that had bemoaned the promise of his toy. And he tried long and failed to fashion anything; for the clay fell to pieces in his hands; till at last it held together and grew suddenly, not into an image of a horse, but of the Great Yule Boar, the similitude of the Holy Beast of Frey.

So he laughed in his sleep and was glad, and leaped up and drew his sword with his clay-stained hands that he might wave it over the Earth Boar, and swear a great oath of a doughty deed. And therewith he found himself standing on his feet indeed, just awakened in the cold dawn, and holding by his right hand to an ash-sapling that grew beside him. So he laughed again, and laid him down, and leaned back and slept his sleep out till the sun and the voices of his fellows stirring awakened him.

7. THE GATHER TO THE FOLK-MOTE

The Markmen cross a plain that had once been the scene of a fierce, three-day battle. They reach the Battleford, those on the east side of the river cross over to the west to meet at the Thing-stead, the "holiest place of the Markmen." Thiodolf is praised as a warrior, going where the fighting was the fiercest. Also there is Heriulf, a giant of a man. Note that in this chapter Thiodolf is still wearing the dwarf-made Hauberk, although strangely without a helmet or shield.

When it was the morning, all the host of the Markmen was astir on either side of the water, and when they had broken their fast, they got speedily into array, and were presently on the road again; and the host was now strung out longer yet, for the space between water and wood once more diminished till at last it was no wider than ten men might go abreast, and looking ahead it was as if the wild-wood swallowed up both river and road.

But the fighting-men hastened on merrily with their hearts raised high, since they knew that they would soon be falling in with more of their people, and the coming fight was growing a clearer picture to their eyes; so from side to side of the river they shouted out the cries of their Houses, or friend called to friend across the eddies of Mirkwood-water, and there was game and glee enough.

So they fared till the wood gave way before them, and lo, the beginning of another plain, somewhat like the Mid-mark. There also the water widened out before them, and there were eyots in it with stony shores crowned with willow or with alder, and aspens rising from the midst of them.

But as for the plain, it was thus much different from Mid-mark, that the wood which begirt it rose on the south into low hills, and away beyond them were other hills blue in the distance, for the most bare of wood, and not right high, the pastures of the wild-bull and the bison, whereas now dwelt a folk somewhat scattered and feeble; hunters and herdsmen, with little tillage about their abodes, a folk akin to the Mark-men and allied to them. They had come into those parts later than the Markmen, as the old tales told; which said moreover that in days gone by a folk dwelt among those hills who were alien from the Goths, and great foes to the Markmen; and how that on a time they came down from their hills with a great host, together with new-comers of their own blood, and made their way through the wild-wood, and fell upon the Up-per-mark; and how that there befel a fearful battle that endured for three days; and the first day the Aliens worsted the Markmen, who were but a few, since they were they of the Upper-mark only.

So the Aliens burned their houses and slew their old men, and drave off many of their women and children; and the remnant of the men of the Upper-mark with all that they had, which was now but little, took refuge in an island of Mirkwood-water, where they fenced themselves as well as they could for that night; for they expected the succour of their kindred of the Mid-mark and the Nether-mark, unto whom they had sped the war-arrow when they first had tidings of the onset of the Aliens.

So at the sun-rising they sacrificed to the Gods twenty chieftains of the Aliens whom they had taken, and therewithal a maiden of their own kindred, the daughter of their war-duke, that she might lead that mighty company to the House of the Gods; and thereto was she nothing loth, but went right willingly.

There then they awaited the onset. But the men of Mid-mark came up in the morn-ing, when the battle was but just joined, and fell on so fiercely that the aliens gave back, and then they of the Upper-mark stormed out of their eyot [small island], and fell on over the ford, and fought till the water ran red with their blood, and the blood of the foemen.

So the Aliens gave back before the onset of the Markmen all over the meads; but when they came to the hillocks and the tofts [homesteads] of the half-burned habita-tions, and the wood was on their flank, they made a stand again, and once more the battle waxed hot, for they were very many, and had many bow-men: there fell the War-duke of the Markmen, whose daughter had been offered up for victory, and his name was Agni, so that the tofts where he fell have since been called Agni's Tofts.

So that day they fought all over the plain, and a great many died, both of the Aliens and the Markmen, and though these last were victorious, yet when the sun went down there still were the Aliens abiding in the Upper-mark, fenced by their Wain-burg, beaten, and much diminished in number, but still a host of men: while of the Markmen many had fallen, and many more were hurt, because the Aliens were good bowmen.

But on the morrow again, as the old tale told, came up the men of the Nether-mark fresh and unwounded; and so the battle began again on the southern limit of the Upper-mark where the Aliens had made their Wain-burg. But not long did it endure; for the Markmen fell on so fiercely, that they stormed over the Wain-burg, and slew all before them, and there was a very great slaughter of the Aliens; so great, tells the old tale, that never again durst they meet the Markmen in war.

Traveling the Upper-mark

Thus went forth the host of the Markmen, faring along both sides of the water into the Upper-mark; and on the west side, where went the Wolfings, the ground now rose by a long slope into a low hill, and when they came unto the brow thereof, they beheld before them the whole plain of the Upper-mark, and the dwellings of the kindred therein all girdled about by the wild-wood; and beyond, the blue hills of the herdsmen, and beyond them still, a long way aloof, lying like a white cloud on the verge of the heavens, the snowy tops of the great mountains. And as they looked down on to the plain they saw it embroidered, as it were, round about the habitations which lay within ken by crowds of many people, and the banners of the kindreds and the arms of men; and many a place they saw named after the ancient battle and that great slaughter of the Aliens.

On their left hand lay the river, and as it now fairly entered with them into the Upper-mark, it spread out into wide rippling shallows beset with yet more sandy eyots, amongst which was one much greater, rising amidmost into a low hill, grassy and bare of tree or bush; and this was the island whereon the Markmen stood on the first day of the Great Battle, and it was now called the Island of the Gods.

Thereby was the ford, which was firm and good and changed little from year to year, so that all Markmen knew it well and it was called Battleford: thereover now crossed all the eastern companies, footmen and horsemen, freemen and thralls, wains and banners, with shouting and laughter, and the noise of horns and the lowing of neat, till all that plain's end was flooded with the host of the Markmen.

But when the eastern-abiders had crossed, they made no stay, but went duly ordered about their banners, winding on toward the first of the abodes on the western side of the water; because it was but a little way south-west of this that the Thing-stead of the Upper-mark lay; and the whole Folk was summoned thither when war threatened from the South, just as it was called to the Thing-stead of the Nether-mark, when the threat of war came from the North. But the western companies stayed on the brow of that low hilt till all the eastern men were over the river, and on their way to the Thing-stead, and then they moved on.

Reaching the Daylings

So came the Wolfings and their fellows up to the dwellings of the northernmost kindred, who were called the Daylings, and bore on their banner the image of the rising sun. Thereabout was the Mark somewhat more hilly and broken than in the Midmark, so that the Great Roof of the Daylings, which was a very big house, stood on a hillock whose sides had been cleft down sheer on all sides save one (which was left as a bridge) by the labour of men, and it was a very defensible place.

Thereon were now gathered round about the Roof all the stay-at-homes of the kindred, who greeted with joyous cries the men-at-arms as they passed. Albeit one very old man, who sat in a chair near to the edge of the sheer hill looking on the war array, when he saw the Wolfing banner draw near, stood up to gaze on it, and then shook his head sadly, and sank back again into his chair, and covered his face with his hands: and when the folk saw that, a silence bred of the coldness of fear fell on them, for that elder was deemed a foreseeing man.

But as those three fellows, of whose talk of yesterday the tale has told, drew near and beheld what the old carle did (for they were riding together this day also) the Beaming man laid his hand on Wolfkettle's rein and said: "Lo you, neighbour, if thy Vala hath seen nought, yet hath this old man seen somewhat, and that somewhat even as the little lad saw it. Many a mother's son shall fall before the Welshmen."

But Wolfkettle shook his rein free, and his face reddened as of one who is angry, yet he kept silence, while the Elking said: "Let be, Toti! for he that lives shall tell the tale to the foreseers, and shall make them wiser than they are to-day."

Then laughed Toti, as one who would not be thought to be too heedful of the morrow. But Wolfkettle brake out into speech and rhyme, and said:

O warriors, the Wolfing kindred shall live or it shall die;
And alive it shall be as the oak-tree when the summer storm goes by;
But dead it shall be as its bole, that they hew for the corner-post
Of some fair and mighty folk-hall, and the roof of a war-fain host.

So therewith they rode their ways past the abode of the Daylings. Straight to the wood went all the host, and so into it by a wide way cleft through the thicket, and in some thirty minutes they came thereby into a great wood-lawn cleared amidst of it by the work of men's hands. There already was much of the host gathered, sitting or standing in a great ring round about a space bare of men, where amidmost rose a great mound raised by men's hands and wrought into steps to be the sitting-places of the chosen elders and chief men of the kindred; and atop the mound was flat and smooth save for a turf bench or seat that went athwart it whereon ten men might sit.

The Sacred Thing-stead

All the wains save the banner-wains had been left behind at the Dayling abode, nor was any beast there save the holy beasts who drew the banner-wains and twenty white horses, that stood wreathed about with flowers within the ring of warriors, and these were for the burnt offering to be given to the Gods for a happy day of battle. Even the war-horses of the host they must leave in the wood without the wood-lawn, and all men were afoot who were there.

For this was the Thing-stead of the Upper-mark, and the holiest place of the Markmen, and no beast, either neat, sheep, or horse might pasture there, but was straightway slain and burned if he wandered there; nor might any man eat therein save at the holy feasts when offerings were made to the Gods.

Thiodolf as a Warrior

So the Wolfings took their place there in the ring of men with the Elkings on their right hand and the Beamings on their left. And in the midst of the Wolfing array stood Thiodolf clad in the dwarf-wrought Hauberk: but his head was bare; for he had sworn over the Cup of Renown that he would fight unhelmed throughout all that trouble, and would bear no shield in any battle thereof however fierce the onset might be.

Short, and curling close to his head was his black hair, a little grizzled, so that it looked like rings of hard dark iron: his forehead was high and smooth, his lips full and red, his eyes steady and wide-open, and all his face joyous with the thought of the fame of his deeds, and the coming battle with a foeman whom the Markmen knew not yet.

He was tall and wide-shouldered, but so exceeding well fashioned of all his limbs and body that he looked no huge man. He was a man well beloved of women, and children would mostly run to him gladly and play with him. A most fell warrior was he, whose deeds no man of the Mark could equal, but blithe of speech even when he was sorrowful of mood, a man that knew not bitterness of heart: and for all his exceeding might and valiancy, he was proud and high to no man; so that the very thralls loved him. He was not abounding in words in the field; nor did he use much the custom of those days in reviling and defying with words the foe that was to be smitten with swords.

There were those who had seen him in the field for the first time who deemed him slack at the work: for he would not always press on with the foremost, but would hold him a little aback, and while the battle was young he forbore to smite, and would do nothing but help a kinsman who was hard pressed, or succour the wounded. So that if men were dealing with no very hard matter, and their hearts were high and over-weening, he would come home at whiles with unbloodied blade. But no man blamed him save those who knew him not: for his intent was that the younger men should win themselves fame, and so raise their courage, and become high-hearted and stout.

But when the stour [struggle] was hard, and the battle was broken, and the hearts of men began to fail them, and doubt fell upon the Markmen, then was he another man to see: wise, but swift and dangerous, rushing on as if shot out by some mighty engine: heedful of all, on either side and in front; running hither and thither as the fight failed and the fire of battle faltered; his sword so swift and deadly that it was as if he wielded the very lightening of the heavens: for with the sword it was ever his wont to fight.

But it must be said that when the foemen turned their backs, and the chase began, then Thiodolf would nowise withhold his might as in the early battle, but ever led the chase, and smote on the right hand and on the left, sparing none, and crying out to the men of the kindred not to weary in their work, but to fulfil all the hours of their day.

FOR THUSWISE WOULD HE SAY AND THIS WAS A WORD OF HIS:
Let us rest to-morrow, fellows, since to-day we have fought amain!
Let not these men we have smitten come aback on our hands again,

And say 'Ye Wolfing warriors, ye have done your work but ill,
Fall to now and do it again, like the craftsman who learneth his skill.'

Such then was Thiodolf, and ever was he the chosen leader of the Wolfings and often the War-duke of the whole Folk.

Heriulf Described

By his side stood the other chosen leader, whose name was Heriulf; a man well stricken in years, but very mighty and valiant; wise in war and well renowned; of few words save in battle, and therein a singer of songs, a laugher, a joyous man, a merry companion. He was a much bigger man than Thiodolf; and indeed so huge was his stature, that he seemed to be of the kindred of the Mountain Giants; and his bodily might went with his stature, so that no one man might deal with him body to body. His face was big; his cheek-bones high; his nose like an eagle's neb, his mouth wide, his chin square and big; his eyes light-grey and fierce under shaggy eyebrows: his hair white and long.

Such were his raiment and weapons, that he wore a coat of fence of dark iron scales sewn on to horse-hide, and a dark iron helm fashioned above his brow into the similitude of the Wolf's head with gaping jaws; and this he had wrought for himself with his own hands, for he was a good smith. A round buckler he bore and a huge twibill, which no man of the kindred could well wield save himself; and it was done both blade and shaft with knots and runes in gold; and he loved that twibill well, and called it the Wolf's Sister.

There then stood Heriulf, looking no less than one of the forefathers of the kindred come back again to the battle of the Wolfings. He was well-beloved for his wondrous might, and he was no hard man, though so fell a warrior, and though of few words, as aforesaid, was a blithe companion to old and young. In numberless battles had he fought, and men deemed it a wonder that Odin had not taken to him a man so much after his own heart; and they said it was neighbourly done of the Father of the Slain to forbear his company so long, and showed how well he loved the Wolfing House.

For a good while yet came other bands of Markmen into the Thing-stead; but at last there was an end of their coming. Then the ring of men opened, and ten warriors of the Daylings made their way through it, and one of them, the oldest, bore in his hand the War-horn of the Daylings; for this kindred had charge of the Thing-stead, and of all appertaining to it. So while his nine fellows stood round about the Speech-Hill, the old warrior clomb up to the topmost of it, and blew a blast on the horn. Thereon they who were sitting rose up, and they who were talking each to each held their peace, and the whole ring drew nigher to the hill, so that there was a clear space behind them 'twixt them and the wood, and a space before them between them and the hill, wherein were those nine warriors, and the horses for the burnt-offering, and the altar of the Gods; and now were all well within ear-shot of a man speaking amidst the silence in a clear voice.

But there were gathered of the Markmen to that place some four thousand men, all chosen warriors and doughty men; and of the thralls and aliens dwelling with them they were leading two thousand. But not all of the freemen of the Upper-mark could be at the Thing; for needs must there be some guard to the passes of the wood toward the south and the hills of the herdsmen, whereas it was no wise impassable to a wisely led host: so five hundred men, what of freemen, what of thralls, abode there to guard the wild-wood; and these looked to have some helping from the hill-men.

Now came an ancient warrior into the space between the men and the wild-wood holding in his hand a kindled torch; and first he faced due south by the sun, then, turning, he slowly paced the whole circle going from east to west, and so on till he had reached the place he started from: then he dashed the torch to the ground and quenched the fire, and so went his ways to his own company again.

Then the old Dayling warrior on the mound-top drew his sword, and waved it flashing in the sun toward the four quarters of the heavens; and thereafter blew again a blast on the War-horn. Then fell utter silence on the whole assembly, and the wood was still around them, save here and there the stamping of a war-horse or the sound of his tugging at the woodland grass; for there was little resort of birds to the depths of the thicket, and the summer morning was windless.

8. THE FOLK-MOTE OF THE MARKMEN

The Roman historian, Tacitus (56–117 AD), described these events when he wrote in his *Agricola* in 92 AD: "To ravage, to slaughter, to usurp under false titles, they call empire; and where they make a desert, they call it peace." The Romans usually stayed west of the "Great River" (Rhine), but at times they grew more aggressive. At the Folk-thing, Bork of the Geirings reports that the Romans have crossed the Great River, attacking Goth villages, building a fortress, and showing an intent to stay. Geirmund from the Shieldings describes the killing of the men of the Hundings and the enslavement of their women and children. Fox the Red reports of spying on the Romans and discovering their plans to "win the Mark and waste it." The Markmen vote unanimously to go to war and choose Thiodolf as their war-duke and Otter of the Laxings as his second.

S o the Dayling warrior lifted up his voice and said:

O kindreds of the Markmen, hearken the words I say;
  For no chancehap assembly is gathered here to-day.
The fire hath gone around us in the hands of our very kin,
And twice the horn hath sounded, and the Thing is hallowed in.
Will ye hear or forbear to hearken the tale there is to tell?
There are many mouths to tell it, and a many know it well.

And the tale is this, that the foemen against our kindreds fare
Who eat the meadows desert, and burn the desert bare.

Then sat he down on the turf seat; but there arose a murmur in the assembly as of men eager to hearken; and without more ado came a man out of a company of the Upper-mark, and clomb up to the top of the Speech-Hill, and spoke in a loud voice:

Bork Tells of the Invasion

"I am Bork, a man of the Geirings of the Upper-mark: two days ago I and five others were in the wild-wood a-hunting, and we wended through the thicket, and came into the land of the hill-folk; and after we had gone a while we came to a long dale with a brook running through it, and yew-trees scattered about it and a hazel copse at one end; and by the copse was a band of men who had women and children with them, and a few neat, and fewer horses; but sheep were feeding up and down the dale; and they had made them booths of turf and boughs, and were making ready their cooking fires, for it was evening. So when they saw us, they ran to their arms, but we cried out to them in the tongue of the Goths and bade them peace. Then they came up the bent to us and spake to us in the Gothic tongue, albeit a little diversely from us; and when we had told them what and whence we were, they were glad of us, and bade us to them, and we went, and they entreated us kindly, and made us such cheer as they might, and gave us mutton to eat, and we gave them venison of the wild-wood which we had taken, and we abode with them there that night.

"But they told us that they were a house of the folk of the herdsmen, and that there was war in the land, and that the people thereof were fleeing before the cruelty of a host of warriors, men of a mighty folk, such as the earth hath not heard of, who dwell in great cities far to the south; and how that this host had crossed the mountains, and the Great Water that runneth from them, and had fallen upon their kindred, and overcome their fighting-men, and burned their dwellings, slain their elders, and driven their neat and their sheep, yea, and their women and children in no better wise than their neat and sheep.

"And they said that they had fled away thus far from their old habitations, which were a long way to the south, and were now at point to build them dwellings there in that Dale of the Hazels, and to trust to it that these Welshmen, whom they called Romans, would not follow so far, and that if they did, they might betake them to the wild-wood, and let the thicket cover them, they being so nigh to it.

"Thus they told us; wherefore we sent back one of our fellowship, Birsti of the Geirings, to tell the tale; and one of the herdsmen folk went with him, but we ourselves went onward to hear more of these Romans; for the folk when we asked them, said that they had been in battle against them, but had fled away for fear of their rumour only. Therefore we went on, and a young man of this kindred, who named themselves the Hrutings of the Fell-folk, went along with us. But the others were sore afeard, for all they had weapons.

"So as we went up the land we found they had told us the very sooth, and we met divers Houses, and bands, and broken men, who were fleeing from this trouble, and many of them poor and in misery, having lost their flocks and herds as well as their roofs; and this last be but little loss to them, as their dwellings are but poor, and for the most part they have no tillage.

"Now of these men, we met not a few who had been in battle with the Roman host, and much they told us of their might not to be dealt with, and their mishandling of those whom they took, both men and women; and at the last we heard true tidings how they had raised them a garth, and made a stronghold in the midst of the land, as men who meant abiding there, so that neither might the winter drive them aback, and that they might be succoured by their people on the other side of the Great River; to which end they have made other garths, though not so great, on the road to that water, and all these well and wisely warded by tried men.

"For as to the Folks on the other side of the Water, all these lie under their hand already, what by fraud what by force, and their warriors go with them to the battle and help them; of whom we met bands now and again, and fought with them, and took men of them, who told us all this and much more, over long to tell of here."

He paused and turned about to look on the mighty assembly, and his ears drank in the long murmur that followed his speaking, and when it had died out he spake again, but in rhyme:

Lo thus much of my tidings! But this too it behoveth to tell,
That these masterful men of the cities of the Markmen know full well:
And they wot of the well-grassed meadows, and the acres of the Mark,
And our life amidst of the wild-wood like a candle in the dark;
And they know of our young men's valour and our women's loveliness,
And our tree would they spoil with destruction if its fruit they may never possess.
For their lust is without a limit, and nought may satiate
Their ravening maw; and their hunger if ye check it turneth to hate,
And the blood-fever burns in their bosoms, and torment and anguish and woe
O'er the wide field ploughed by the sword-blade for the coming years they sow;
And ruth is a thing forgotten and all hopes they trample down;
And whatso thing is steadfast, whatso of good renown,
Whatso is fair and lovely, whatso is ancient sooth
In the bloody marl shall they mingle as they laugh for lack of ruth.
Lo the curse of the world cometh hither; for the men that we took in the land
Said thus, that their host is gathering with many an ordered band
To fall on the wild-wood passes and flood the lovely Mark,
As the river over the meadows upriseth in the dark.
Look to it, O ye kindred! availeth now no word
But the voice of the clashing of iron, and the sword-blade on the sword.

Therewith he made an end, and deeper and longer was the murmur of the host of freemen, amidst which Bork gat him down from the Speech-Hill, his weapons clattering about him, and mingled with the men of his kindred.

Geirmund the Minstrel Speaks

Then came forth a man of the kin of the Shieldings of the Upper-mark, and clomb the mound; and he spake in rhyme from beginning to end; for he was a minstrel of renown:

Lo I AM A MAN OF THE SHIELDINGS AND GEIRMUND IS MY NAME;
A half-moon back from the wild-wood out into the hills I came,
And I went alone in my war-gear; for we have affinity
With the Hundings of the Fell-folk, and with them I fain would be;
For I loved a maid of their kindred. Now their dwelling was not far
From the outermost bounds of the Fell-folk, and bold in the battle they are,
And have met a many people, and held their own abode.
Gay then was the heart within me, as over the hills I rode
And thought of the mirth of to-morrow and the sweet-mouthed Hunding maid
And their old men wise and merry and their young men unafraid,
And the hall-glee of the Hundings and the healths o'er the guesting cup.
But as I rode the valley, I saw a smoke go up
O'er the crest of the last of the grass-hills 'twixt me and the Hunding roof,
And that smoke was black and heavy: so a while I bided aloof,
And drew my girths the tighter, and looked to the arms I bore
And handled my spear for the casting; for my heart misgave me sore,
For nought was that pillar of smoke like the guest-fain cooking-fire.
I lingered in thought for a minute, then turned me to ride up higher,
And as a man most wary up over the bent I rode,
And nigh hid peered o'er the hill-crest adown on the Hunding abode;
And forsooth 'twas the fire wavering all o'er the roof of old,
And all in the garth and about it lay the bodies of the bold;
And bound to a rope amidmost were the women fair and young,
And youths and little children, like the fish on a withy strung
As they lie on the grass for the angler before the beginning of night.
Then the rush of the wrath within me for a while nigh blinded my sight;
Yet about the cowering war-thralls, short dark-faced men I saw,
Men clad in iron armour, this way and that way draw,
As warriors after the battle are ever wont to do.
Then I knew them for the foemen and their deeds to be I knew,
And I gathered the reins together to ride down the hill amain,
To die with a good stroke stricken and slay ere I was slain.

When lo, on the bent before me rose the head of a brown-faced man,
Well helmed and iron-shielded, who some Welsh speech began
And a short sword brandished against me; then my sight cleared and I saw
Five others armed in likewise up hill and toward me draw,
And I shook the spear and sped it and clattering on his shield
He fell and rolled o'er smitten toward the garth and the Fell-folk's field.

BUT MY HEART changed with his falling and the speeding of my stroke,
And I turned my horse; for within me the love of life awoke,
And I spurred, nor heeded the hill-side, but o'er rough and smooth I rode
Till I heard no chase behind me; then I drew rein and abode.
And down in a dell was I gotten with a thorn-brake in its throat,
And heard but the plover's whistle and the blackbird's broken note
'Mid the thorns; when lo! from a thorn-twig away the blackbird swept,
And out from the brake and towards me a naked man there crept,
And straight I rode up towards him, and knew his face for one
I had seen in the hall of the Hundings ere its happy days were done.
I asked him his tale, but he bade me forthright to bear him away;
So I took him up behind me, and we rode till late in the day,
Toward the cover of the wild-wood, and as swiftly as we might.
But when yet aloof was the thicket and it now was moonless night,
We stayed perforce for a little, and he told me all the tale:
How the aliens came against them, and they fought without avail
Till the Roof o'er their heads was burning and they burst forth on the foe,
And were hewn down there together; nor yet was the slaughter slow.
But some they saved for thralldom, yea, e'en of the fighting men,
Or to quell them with pains; so they stripped them; and this man espying just then
Some chance, I mind not whatwise, from the garth fled out and away.

Now MANY A thing noteworthy of these aliens did he say,
But this I bid you hearken, lest I wear the time for nought,
That still upon the Markmen and the Mark they set their thought;
For they questioned this man and others through a go-between in words
Of us, and our lands and our chattels, and the number of our swords;
Of the way and the wild-wood passes and the winter and his ways.
Now look to see them shortly; for worn are fifteen days
Since in the garth of the Hundings I saw them dight for war,
And a hardy folk and ready and a swift-foot host they are.

Therewith Geirmund went down clattering from the Hill and stood with his company.

But a man came forth from the other side of the ring, and clomb the Hill: he was a red-haired man, rather big, clad in a skin coat, and bearing a bow in his hand and a quiver of arrows at his back, and a little axe hung by his side. He said: "I dwell in the House of the Hrossings of the Mid-mark, and I am now made a man of the kindred: howbeit I was not born into it; for I am the son of a fair and mighty woman of a folk of the Kymry, who was taken in war while she went big with me; I am called Fox the Red.

"These Romans have I seen, and have not died: so hearken! for my tale shall be short for what there is in it. I am, as many know, a hunter of Mirkwood, and I know all its ways and the passes through the thicket somewhat better than most.

"A moon ago I fared afoot from Mid-mark through Upper-mark into the thicket of the south, and through it into the heath country; and I went over a neck and came in the early dawn into a little dale when somewhat of mist still hung over it. At the dale's end I saw a man lying asleep on the grass under a quicken tree, and his shield and sword hanging over his head to a bough thereof, and his horse feeding hoppled higher up the dale. I crept up softly to him with a shaft nocked on the string, but when I drew near I saw him to be of the sons of the Goths. So I doubted nothing, but laid down my bow, and stood upright, and went to him and roused him, and he leapt up, and was wroth.

"I said to him, 'Wilt thou be wroth with a brother of the kindred meeting him in unpeopled parts?' But he reached out for his weapons; but ere he could handle them I ran in on him so that he gat not his sword, and had scant time to smite at me with a knife which he drew from his waist. I gave way before him for he was a very big man, and he rushed past me, and I dealt him a blow on the side of the head with my little axe which is called the War-babe, and gave him a great wound: and he fell on the grass, and as it happened that was his bane.

"I was sorry that I had slain him, since he was a man of the Goths: albeit otherwise he had slain me, for he was very wroth and dazed with slumber. He died not for a while; and he bade me fetch him water; and there was a well hard by on the other side of the tree; so I fetched it him in a great shell that I carry, and he drank. I would have sung the blood-staunching song over him, for I know it well. But he said, 'It availeth nought: I have enough: what man art thou?' "I said, 'I am a fosterling of the Hrossings, and my mother was taken in war: my name is Fox.'

"Said he; 'O Fox, I have my due at thy hands, for I am a Markman of the Elkings, but a guest of the Burgundians beyond the Great River; and the Romans are their masters and they do their bidding: even so did I who was but their guest: and I a Markman to fight against the Markmen, and all for fear and for gold! And thou an alien-born hast slain their traitor and their dastard [sneaking coward]! This is my due. Give me to drink again.' "So did I; and he said; 'Wilt thou do an errand for me to thine own house?' 'Yea,' said I.

"Said he, 'I am a messenger to the garth of the Romans, that I may tell the road to the Mark, and lead them through the thicket; and other guides are coming after me: but not yet for three days or four. So till they come there will be no man in the Roman garth to know thee that thou art not even I myself. If thou art doughty, strip me when I am dead and do my raiment on thee, and take this ring from my neck, for that is my token, and when they ask thee for a word say, 'no limit;' for that is the token-word. Go south-east over the dales keeping Broadshield-fell square with thy right hand, and let thy wisdom, O Fox, lead thee to the Garth of the Romans, and so back to thy kindred with all tidings thou hast gathered—for indeed they come—a many of them. Give me to drink.' So he drank again, and said, 'The bearer of this token is called Hrosstyr of the River Goths. He hath that name among dastards. Thou shalt lay a turf upon my head. Let my death pay for my life.'

"Therewith he fell back and died. So I did as he bade me and took his gear, worth six kine, and did it on me; I laid turf upon him in that dale, and hid my bow and my gear in a blackthorn brake hard by, and then took his horse and rode away.

"Day and night I rode till I came to the garth of the Romans; there I gave myself up to their watchers, and they brought me to their Duke, a grim man and hard. He said in a terrible voice, 'Thy name?' I said, 'Hrosstyr of the River Goths.' He said, 'What limit?' I answered, 'No limit.' 'The token!' said he, and held out his hand. I gave him the ring. 'Thou art the man,' said he.

"I thought in my heart, 'thou liest, lord,' and my heart danced for joy. Then he fell to asking me questions a many, and I answered every one glibly enough, and told him what I would, but no word of truth save for his hurt, and my soul laughed within me at my lies; thought I, the others, the traitors, shall come, and they shall tell him the truth, and he will not trow it, or at the worst he will doubt them. But me he doubted nothing, else had he called in the tormentors to have the truth of me by pains; as I well saw afterwards, when they questioned with torments a man and a woman of the hill-folk whom they had brought in captive.

"I went from him and went all about that garth espying everything, fearing noth-ing; albeit there were divers woeful captives of the Goths, who cursed me for a dastard, when they saw by my attire that I was of their blood. I abode there three days, and learned all that I might of the garth and the host of them, and the fourth day in the morning I went out as if to hunt, and none hindered me, for they doubted me not. So I came my ways home to the Upper-mark, and was guested with the Geirings. Will ye that I tell you somewhat of the ways of these Romans of the garth? The time presses, and my tale runneth longer than I would. What will ye?"

Then there arose a murmur, "Tell all, tell all." "Nay," said the Fox, "All I may not tell; so much did I behold there during the three days' stay; but this much it behoveth you to know: that these men have no other thought save to win the Mark and waste it, and slay the fighting men and the old carles, and enthrall such as they will, that is, all that be fair and young, and they long sorely for our women either to have or to sell.

"As for their garth, it is strongly walled about with a dyke newly dug; on the top thereof are they building a wall made of clay, and burned like pots into ashlar stones hard and red, and these are laid in lime. It is now the toil of the thralls of our blood whom they have taken, both men and women, to dig that clay and to work it, and bear it to kilns, and to have for reward scant meat and many stripes. For it is a grim folk, that laugheth to see others weep.

"Their men-at-arms are well dight and for the most part in one way: they are helmed with iron, and have iron on their breasts and reins, and bear long shields that cover them to the knees. They are girt with a sax [short sword] and have a heavy casting-spear. They are dark-skinned and ugly of aspect, surly and of few words: they drink little, and eat not much.

"They have captains of tens and of hundreds over them, and that War-duke over all; he goeth to and fro with gold on his head and his breast, and commonly hath a cloak cast over him of the colour of the crane's-bill blossom.

"They have an altar in the midst of their burg, and thereon they sacrifice to their God, who is none other than their banner of war, which is an image of the ravening eagle with outspread wings; but yet another God they have, and look you! It is a wolf, as if they were of the kin of our brethren; a she-wolf and two man-children at her dugs [teats]; wonderful is this.

"I tell you that they are grim; and know it by this token: those captains of tens, and of hundreds, spare not to smite the warriors with staves even before all men, when all goeth not as they would; and yet, though they be free men, and mighty warriors, they endure it and smite not in turn. They are a most evil folk.

"As to their numbers, they of the burg are hard on three thousand footmen of the best; and of horsemen five hundred, nowise good; and of bowmen and slingers six hundred or more: their bows weak; their slingers cunning beyond measure. And the talk is that when they come upon us they shall have with them some five hundred warriors of the Over River Goths, and others of their own folk." Then he said:

O MEN OF THE MARK, WILL YE MEET THEM IN THE MEADOWS AND THE FIELD,
Or will ye flee before them and have the wood for a shield?
Or will ye wend to their war-burg with weapons cast away,
With your women and your children, a peace of them to pray?
So doing, not all shall perish; but most shall long to die
Ere in the garths of the Southland two moons have loitered by.

Then rose the rumour loud and angry mingled with the rattle of swords and the clash of spears on shields; but Fox said: "Needs must ye follow one of these three ways. Nay, what say I? there are but two ways and not three; for if ye flee they shall follow you to the confines of the earth. Either these Welsh shall take all, and our lives to boot, or we shall hold to all that is ours, and live merrily. The sword doometh; and in three days it may be the courts shall be hallowed: small is the space between us." Therewith he also got him down from the Hill, and joined his own house: and men said that he had spoken well and wisely.

Otter Gives Advice

But there arose a noise of men talking together on these tidings; and amidst it an old warrior of the Nether-mark strode forth and up to the Hill-top. Gaunt and stark he was to look on; and all men knew him and he was well-beloved, so all held their peace as he said:

"I am Otter of the Laxings: now needeth but few words till the War-duke is chosen, and we get ready to wend our ways in arms. Here have ye heard three good men and true tell of our foes, and this last, Fox the Red, hath seen them and hath more to tell when we are on the way; nor is the way hard to find. It were scarce well to fall upon these men in their garth and war-burg; for hard is a wall to slay. Better it were to meet them in the Wild-wood, which may well be a friend to us and a wall, but to them a net. O Agni of the Daylings, thou warder of the Thing-stead, bid men choose a War-duke if none gainsay it." And without more words he clattered down the Hill, and went and stood with the Laxing band.

Voting for War and Thiodolf as War-duke

But the old Dayling arose and blew the horn, and there was at once a great silence, amidst which he said: "Children of Slains-father, doth the Folk go to the war?"

There was no voice but shouted "yea," and the white swords sprang aloft, and the westering sun swept along a half of them as they tossed to and fro, and the others showed dead-white and fireless against the dark wood.

Then again spake Agni: "Will ye choose the War-duke now and once, or shall it be in a while, after others have spoken?"

And the voice of the Folk went up, "Choose! Choose!"

Said Agni: "Sayeth any aught against it?" But no voice of a gainsayer was heard, and Agni said: "Children of Tyr, what man will ye have for a leader and a duke of war?"

Then a great shout sprang up from amidst the swords: "We will have Thiodolf; Thiodolf the Wolfing!"

Said Agni: "I hear no other name; are ye of one mind? hath any aught to say against it? If that be so, let him speak now, and not forbear to follow in the wheatfield of the spears. Speak, ye that will not follow Thiodolf!"

No voice gainsaid him: then said the Dayling: "Come forth thou War-duke of the Markmen! take up the gold ring from the horns of the altar, set it on thine arm and come up hither!"

Then came forth Thiodolf into the sun, and took up the gold ring from where it lay, and did it on his arm. And this was the ring of the leader of the folk whenso one should be chosen: it was ancient and daintily wrought, but not very heavy: so ancient it was that men said it had been wrought by the dwarfs.

So Thiodolf went up on to the hill, and all men cried out on him for joy, for they knew his wisdom in war. Many wondered to see him unhelmed, but they had a deeming that he must have made oath to the Gods thereof and their hearts were glad of it. They took note of the dwarf-wrought Hauberk, and even from a good way off they could see what a treasure of smith's work it was, and they deemed it like enough that spells had been sung over it to make it sure against point and edge: for they knew that Thiodolf was well beloved of the Gods.

But when Thiodolf was on the Hill of Speech, he said: "Men of the kindreds, I am your War-duke to-day; but it is oftenest the custom when ye go to war to choose you two dukes, and I would it were so now. No child's play is the work that lies before us; and if one leader chance to fall let there be another to take his place without stop or stay. Thou Agni of the Daylings, bid the Folk choose them another duke if so they will."

Said Agni: "Good is this which our War-duke hath spoken; say then, men of the Mark, who shall stand with Thiodolf to lead you against the Aliens?"

Then was there a noise and a crying of names, and more than two names seemed to be cried out; but by far the greater part named either Otter of the Laxings, or Heriulf of the Wolfings. True it is that Otter was a very wise warrior, and well known to all the men of the Mark; yet so dear was Heriulf to them, that none would have named Otter had it not been mostly their custom not to choose both War-dukes from one House.

Now spake Agni: "Children of Tyr, I hear you name more than one name: now let each man cry out clearly the name he nameth.

So the Folk cried the names once more, but this time it was clear that none was named save Otter and Heriulf; so the Dayling was at point to speak again, but or ever a word left his lips, Heriulf the mighty, the ancient of days, stood forth: and when men saw that he would take up the word there was a great silence. So he spake: "Hearken, children! I am old and war-wise; but my wisdom is the wisdom of the sword of the mighty warrior, that knoweth which way it should wend, and hath no thought of turning back till it lieth broken in the field. Such wisdom is good against Folks that we have met heretofore; as when we have fought with the Huns, who would sweep us away from the face of the earth, or with the Franks or the Burgundians, who would quell us into being something worser than they be. But here is a new foe, and new wisdom, and that right shifty, do we need to meet them. One wise duke have ye gotten, Thiodolf to wit; and he is young beside me and beside Otter of the Laxings. And now if ye must needs have an older man to stand beside him, (and that is not ill) take ye Otter; for old though his body be, the thought within him is keen and supple like the best of Welsh-wrought blades, and it liveth in the days that now are: whereas for me, meseemeth, my thoughts are in the days bygone. Yet look to it, that I shall not fail to lead as the sword of the valiant leadeth, or the shaft shot by the cunning archer. Choose ye Otter; I have spoken over long."

Then spoke Agni the Dayling, and laughed withal: "One man of the Folk hath spoken for Otter and against Heriulf—now let others speak if they will!"

So the cry came forth, "Otter let it be, we will have Otter!"

"Speaketh any against Otter?" said Agni. But there was no voice raised against him.

Then Agni said: "Come forth, Otter of the Laxings, and hold the ring with Thiodolf."

Then Otter went up on to the hill and stood by Thiodolf, and they held the ring together; and then each thrust his hand and arm through the ring and clasped hands together, and stood thus awhile, and all the Folk shouted together.

Then spake Agni: "Now shall we hew the horses and give the gifts to the Gods."

Therewith he and the two War-dukes came down from the hill; and stood before the altar; and the nine warriors of the Daylings stood forth with axes to hew the horses and with copper bowls wherein to catch the blood of them, and each hewed down his horse to the Gods, but the two War-dukes slew the tenth and fairest: and the blood was caught in the bowls, and Agni took a sprinkler and went round about the ring of men, and cast the blood of the Gods'-gifts over the Folk, as was the custom of those days.

Then they cut up the carcases and burned on the altar the share of the Gods, and Agni and the War-dukes tasted thereof, and the rest they bore off to the Daylings' abode for the feast to be holden that night.

Thiodolf Speaks

Then Otter and Thiodolf spake apart together for awhile, and presently went up again on to the Speech-Hill, and Thiodolf said:

O kindreds of the Markmen; to-morrow with the day
We shall wend up Mirkwood-water to bar our foes the way;
And there shall we make our Wain-burg on the edges of the wood,
Where in the days past over at last the aliens stood,
The Slaughter Tofts ye call it. There tidings shall we get
If the curse of the world is awakened, and the serpent crawleth yet
Amidst the Mirkwood thicket; and when the sooth we know,
Then bearing battle with us through the thicket shall we go,
The ancient Wood-wolf's children, and the People of the Shield,
And the Spear-kin and the Horse-kin, while the others keep the field
About the warded Wain-burg; for not many need we there
Where amidst of the thickets' tangle and the woodland net they fare,
And the hearts of the aliens falter and they curse the fight ne'er done,
And wonder who is fighting and which way is the sun.

Thus he spoke; then Agni took up the war-horn again, and blew a blast, and then he cried out:

Now sunder we the Folk-motel and the feast is for to-night,
And to-morrow the Wayfaring; But unnamed is the day of the fight;
O warriors, look ye to it that not long we need abide
'Twixt the hour of the word we have spoken, and our fair-fame's blooming-tide!

For then 'midst the toil and the turmoil shall we sow the seeds of peace,
And the Kindreds' long endurance, and the Gothfolk's great increase.

Then arose the last great shout, and soberly and in due order, kindred by kindred, they turned and departed from the Thing-stead and went their way through the wood to the abode of the Daylings.

9. THE ANCIENT MAN OF THE DAYLINGS

Thiodolf receives a veiled warning about the dangers of his dwarf-made Hauberk from Asmund, an old man known to be a seer. Others wonder what that warning means. Agni is skeptical of Asmund's warning, but Thiodolf will say nothing. He does, however, ponder whether he should wear the Hauberk.

There still hung the more part of the stay-at-homes round about the Roof. But on the plain beneath the tofts were all the wains of the host drawn up round about a square like the streets about a market-place; all these now had their tilts rigged over them, some white, some black, some red, some tawny of hue; and some, which were of the Beamings, green like the leafy tree.

The warriors of the host went down into this wain-town, which they had not fenced in any way, since they in no wise looked for any onset there; and there were their thralls dighting the feast for them, and a many of the Dayling kindred, both men and women, went with them; but some men did the Daylings bring into their Roof, for there was room for a good many besides their own folk. So they went over the Bridge of turf into the garth and into the Great Roof of the Daylings; and amongst these were the two War-dukes.

Asmund the Old's Warning

So when they came to the dais it was as fair all round about there as might well be; and there sat elders and ancient warriors to welcome the guests; and among them was the old carle [common laborer] who had sat on the edge of the burg to watch the faring of the host, and had shuddered back at the sight of the Wolfing Banner.

And when the old carle saw the guests, he fixed his eyes on Thiodolf, and presently came up and stood before him; and Thiodolf looked on the old man, and greeted him kindly and smiled on him; but the carle spake not till he had looked on him a while; and at last he fell a-trembling, and reached his hands out to Thiodolf's bare head, and handled his curls and caressed them, as a mother does with her son, even if he be a grizzled-haired man, when there is none by: and at last he said:

How dear is the head of the mighty, and the apple of the tree
That blooms with the life of the people which is and yet shall be!
It is helmed with ancient wisdom, and the long remembered thought,
That liveth when dead is the iron, and its very rust but nought.

Ah! were I but young as aforetime, I would fare to the battle-stead
And stand amidst of the spear-hail for the praise of the hand and the head!

Then his hands left Thiodolf's head, and strayed down to his shoulders and his breast, and he felt the cold rings of the Hauberk, and let his hands fall down to his side again; and the tears gushed out of his old eyes and again he spake:

O HOUSE OF THE HEART OF THE MIGHTY, O BREAST OF THE BATTLE-LORD
Why art thou coldly hidden from the flickering flame of the sword?
I know thee not, nor see thee; thou art as the fells afar
Where the Fathers have their dwelling, and the halls of Godhome are:
The wind blows wild betwixt us, and the cloud-rack flies along,
And high aloft enfoldeth the dwelling of the strong;
They are, as of old they have been, but their hearths flame not for me;
And the kindness of their feast-halls mine eyes shall never see.

Thiodolf's lips still smiled on the old man, but a shadow had come over his eyes and his brow; and the chief of the Daylings and their mighty guests stood by listening intently with the knit brows of anxious men; nor did any speak till the ancient man again betook him to words:

I CAME TO THE HOUSE OF THE FOEMAN WHEN HUNGER MADE ME A FOOL;
And the foeman said, 'Thou art weary, lo, set thy foot on the stool;'
And I stretched out my feet,—and was shackled: and he spake with a dastard's
   smile,
'O guest, thine hands are heavy; now rest them for a while!'
So I stretched out my hands, and the hand-gyves lay cold on either wrist:
And the wood of the wolf had been better than that feast-hall, had I wist
That this was the ancient pit-fall, and the long expected trap,
And that now for my heart's desire I had sold the world's goodhap.

Therewith the ancient man turned slowly away from Thiodolf, and departed sadly to his own place. Thiodolf changed countenance but little, albeit those about him looked strangely on him, as though if they durst they would ask him what these words might be, and if he from his hidden knowledge might fit a meaning to them. For to many there was a word of warning in them, and to some an evil omen of the days soon to be; and scarce anyone heard those words but he had a misgiving in his heart, for the ancient man was known to be foreseeing, and wild and strange his words seemed to them.

But Agni would make light of it, and he said: "Asmund the Old is of good will, and wise he is; but he hath great longings for the deeds of men, when he hath tidings of battle; for a great warrior and a red-hand hewer he hath been in times past; he loves the Kindred, and deems it ill if he may not fare afield with them; for the thought of dying in the straw is hateful to him."

"Yea," said another, "and moreover he hath seen sons whom he loved slain in battle; and when he seeth a warrior in his prime he becometh dear to him, and he feareth for him."

"Yet," said a third, "Asmund is foreseeing; and may be, Thiodolf, thou wilt wot of the drift of these words, and tell us thereof."

But Thiodolf spake nought of the matter, though in his heart he pondered it.

So the guests were led to table, and the feast began, within the hall and without it, and wide about the plain; and the Dayling maidens went in bands trimly decked out throughout all the host and served the warriors with meat and drink, and sang the overword to their lays, and smote the harp, and drew the bow over the fiddle till it laughed and wailed and chuckled, and were blithe and merry with all, and great was the glee on the eve of battle. And if Thiodolf's heart were overcast, his face showed it not, but he passed from hall to Wain-burg and from Wain-burg to hall again blithe and joyous with all men. And thereby he raised the hearts of men, and they deemed it good that they had gotten such a War-duke, meet to uphold all hearts of men both at the feast and in the fray.

10. That Carline Cometh to the Roof of the Wolfings

Back at the House of the Wolfing's, with most of the men gone, the women tire from all their labors. Wood-Sun, again disguised as an old woman comes in, and Hall-Sun encourages the other women to be kind to her.

Now it was three days after this that the women were gathering to the Women's-Chamber of the Roof of the Wolfings a little before the afternoon changes into evening. The hearts of most were somewhat heavy, for the doubt wherewith they had watched the departure of the fighting-men still hung about them; nor had they any tidings from the host (nor was it like that they should have). And as they were somewhat down-hearted, so it seemed by the aspect of all things that afternoon.

It was not yet the evening, as is aforesaid, but the day was worn and worsened, and all things looked weary. The sky was a little clouded, but not much; yet was it murky down in the south-east, and there was a threat of storm in it, and in the air close round each man's head, and in the very waving of the leafy boughs. There was by this time little doing in field and fold (for the kine were milked), and the women were coming up from the acres and the meadow and over the open ground anigh the Roof; there was the grass worn and dusty, and the women that trod it, their feet were tanned and worn, and dusty also; skin-dry and weary they looked, with the sweat dried upon them; their girt-up gowns grey and lightless, their half-unbound hair blowing about them in the dry wind, which had in it no morning freshness, and no evening coolness.

It was a time when toil was well-nigh done, but had left its aching behind it; a time for folk to sleep and forget for a little while, till the low sun should make it evening, and make all things fair with his level rays; no time for anxious thoughts concerning deeds doing, wherein the anxious ones could do nought to help. Yet such thoughts those stay-at-homes needs must have in the hour of their toil scarce over, their rest and mirth not begun.

Slowly one by one the women went in by the Women's-door, and the Hall-Sun sat on a stone hard by, and watched them as they passed; and she looked keenly at all persons and all things. She had been working in the acres, and her hand was yet on the hoe she had been using, and but for her face her body was as of one resting after toil: her dark blue gown was ungirded, her dark hair loose and floating, the flowers that had wreathed it, now faded, lying strewn upon the grass before her: her feet bare for coolness' sake, her left hand lying loose and open upon her knee.

Yet though her body otherwise looked thus listless, in her face was no listlessness, nor rest: her eyes were alert and clear, shining like two stars in the heavens of dawn-tide; her lips were set close, her brow knit, as of one striving to shape thoughts hard to understand into words that all might understand.

So she sat noting all things, as woman by woman went past her into the hall, till at last she slowly rose to her feet; for there came two young women leading between them that same old carline with whom she had talked on the Hill-of-Speech. She looked on the carline steadfastly, but gave no token of knowing her; but the ancient woman spoke when she came near to the Hall-Sun, and old as her semblance was, yet did her speech sound sweet to the Hall-Sun, and indeed to all those that heard it: and she said: "May we be here to-night, O Hall-Sun, thou lovely Seeress of the mighty Wolfings? may a wandering woman sit amongst you and eat the meat of the Wolfings?"

Then spake the Hall-Sun in a sweet measured voice: "Surely mother: all men who bring peace with them are welcome guests to the Wolfings: nor will any ask thine errand, but we will let thy tidings flow from thee as thou wilt. This is the custom of the kindred, and no word of mine own; I speak to thee because thou hast spoken to me, but I have no authority here, being myself but an alien. Albeit I serve the House of the Wolfings, and I love it as the hound loveth his master who feedeth him, and his master's children who play with him. Enter, mother, and be glad of heart, and put away care from thee."

Then the old woman drew nigher to her and sat down in the dust at her feet, for she was now sitting down again, and took her hand and kissed it and fondled it, and seemed loth to leave handling the beauty of the Hall-Sun; but she looked kindly on the carline, and smiled on her, and leaned down to her, and kissed her mouth, and said: "Damsels, take care of this poor woman, and make her good cheer; for she is wise of wit, and a friend of the Wolfings; and I have seen her before, and spoken with her; and she loveth us. But as for me I must needs be alone in the meads for a while; and it may be that when I come to you again, I shall have a word to tell you."

Now indeed it was in a manner true that the Hall-Sun had no authority in the Wolfing House; yet was she so well beloved for her wisdom and beauty and her sweet speech, that all hastened to do her will in small matters and in great, and now as they looked at her after the old woman had caressed her, it seemed to them that her fairness grew under their eyes, and that they had never seen her so fair; and the sight of her seemed so good to them, that the outworn day and its weariness changed to them, and it grew as pleasant as the first hours of the sunlight, when men arise happy from their rest, and look on the day that lieth hopeful before them with all its deeds to be.

So they grew merry, and they led the carline into the Hall with them, and set her down in the Women's-Chamber, and washed her feet, and gave her meat and drink, and bade her rest and think of nothing troublous, and in all wise made her good cheer; and she was merry with them, and praised their fairness and their deftness, and asked them many questions about their weaving and spinning and carding; (howbeit the looms were idle as then because it was midsummer, and the men gone to the war). And this they deemed strange, as it seemed to them that all women should know of such things; but they thought it was a token that she came from far away.

But afterwards she sat among them, and told them pleasant tales of past times and far countries, and was blithe to them and they to her and the time wore on toward nightfall in the Women's-Chamber.

11. THE HALL-SUN SPEAKETH

Hall-Sun goes down to the Mirkwood-water to swim and returns to the House of the Wolfings, entering by the Man's door. She changes and calls the women and the old woman to join the men in the hall hear the vision she has about the coming battle.

B ut for the Hall-Sun; she sat long on that stone by the Women's-door; but when the evening was now come, she arose and went down through the cornfields and into the meadow, and wandered away as her feet took her.

Night was falling by then she reached that pool of Mirkwood-water, whose eddies she knew so well. There she let the water cover her in the deep stream, and she floated down and sported with the ripples where the river left that deep to race over the shallows; and the moon was casting shadows by then she came up the bank again by the shallow end bearing in her arms a bundle of the blue-flowering mouse-ear. Then she clad herself at once, and went straight as one with a set purpose toward the Great Roof, and entered by the Man's-door; and there were few men within and they but old and heavy with the burden of years and the coming of night-tide; but they wondered and looked to each other and nodded their heads as she passed them by, as men who would say, There is something toward.

So she went to her sleeping-place, and did on fresh raiment, and came forth presently clad in white and shod with gold and having her hair wreathed about with the herb of wonder, the blue-flowering mouse-ear of Mirkwood-water. Thus she passed through the Hall, and those elders were stirred in their hearts when they beheld her beauty. But she opened the door of the Women's-Chamber, and stood on the threshold; and lo, there sat the carline amidst a ring of the Wolfing women, and she telling them tales of old time such as they had not yet heard; and her eyes were glittering, and the sweet words were flowing from her mouth; but she sat straight up like a young woman; and at whiles it seemed to those who hearkened, that she was no old and outworn woman, but fair and strong, and of much avail. But when she heard the Hall-Sun she turned and saw her on the threshold, and her speech fell suddenly, and all that might and briskness faded from her, and she fixed her eyes on the Hall-Sun and looked wistfully and anxiously on her.

Hall-Sun Speaks
Then spake the Hall-Sun standing in the doorway:

> HEAR YE A MATTER, MAIDENS, AND YE WOLFING WOMEN ALL,
> And thou alien guest of the Wolfings! But come ye up the hall,
> That the ancient men may hearken: for methinks I have a word
> Of the battle of the Kindreds, and the harvest of the sword.

Then all arose up with great joy, for they knew that the tidings were good, when they looked on the face of the Hall-Sun and beheld the pride of her beauty unmarred by doubt or pain.

She led them forth to the dais, and there were the sick and the elders gathered and some ancient men of the thralls: so she stepped lightly up to her place, and stood under her namesake, the wondrous lamp of ancient days. And thus she spake:

> ON MY SOUL THERE LIES NO BURDEN, AND NO TANGLE OF THE FIGHT
> In plain or dale or wild-wood enmeshes now my sight.
> I see the Markmen's Wain-burg, and I see their warriors go
> As men who wait for battle and the coming of the foe.
> And they pass 'twixt the wood and the Wain-burg within earshot of the horn,
> But over the windy meadows no sound thereof is borne,
> And all is well amongst them. To the burg I draw anigh
> And I see all battle-banners in the breeze of morning fly,
> But no Wolfings round their banner and no warrior of the Shield,
> No Geiring and no Hrossing in the burg or on the field.

She held her peace for a little while, and no one dared to speak; then she lifted up her head and spake:

> NOW I GO BY THE LIP OF THE WILD-WOOD AND A SOUND WITHAL I HEAR,
> As of men in the paths of the thicket, and a many drawing anear.
> Then, muffled yet by the tree-boles, I hear the Shielding song,
> And warriors blithe and merry with the battle of the strong.
> Give back a little, Markmen, make way for men to pass

To your ordered battle-dwelling o'er the trodden meadow-grass,
For alive with men is the wild-wood and shineth with the steel,
And hath a voice most merry to tell of the Kindreds' weal
'Twixt each tree a warrior standeth come back from the spear-strewn way,
And forth they come from the wild-wood and a little band are they.

Then again was she silent; but her head sank not, as of one thinking, as before it did, but she looked straight forward with bright eyes and smiling, as she said:

Lo, NOW THE GUESTS THEY ARE BRINGING THAT YE HAVE NOT SEEN BEFORE;
Yet guests but ill-entreated; for they lack their shields of war,
No spear in the hand they carry and with no sax are girt.
Lo, these are the dreaded foemen, these once so strong to hurt;
The men that all folk fled from, the swift to drive the spoil,
The men that fashioned nothing but the trap to make men toil.
They drew the sword in the cities, they came and struck the stroke
And smote the shield of the Markmen, and point and edge they broke.
They drew the sword in the war-garth, they swore to bring aback
God's gifts from the Markmen houses where the tables never lack.
O Markmen, take the God-gifts that came on their own feet
O'er the hills through the Mirkwood thicket the Stone of Tyr to meet!

Again she stayed her song, which had been loud and joyous, and they who heard her knew that the Kindreds had gained the day, and whilst the Hall-Sun was silent they fell to talking of this fair day of battle and the taking of captives. But presently she spread out her hands again and they held their peace, and she said:

I SEE, O WOLFING women, and many a thing I see,
But not all things, O elders, this eve shall ye learn of me,
For another mouth there cometh: the thicket I behold
And the Sons of Tyr amidst it, and I see the oak-trees old,
And the war-shout ringing round them; and I see the battle-lord
Unhelmed amidst of the mighty; and I see his leaping sword;
Strokes struck and warriors falling, and the streaks of spears I see,
But hereof shall the other tell you who speaketh after me.
For none other than the Shieldings from out the wood have come,
And they shift the turn with the Daylings to drive the folk-spear home,
And to follow with the Wolfings and thrust the war-beast forth.
And so good men deem the tidings that they bid them journey north
On the feet of a Shielding runner, that Gisli hath to name;
And west of the water he wendeth by the way that the Wolfings came;
Now for sleep he tarries never, and no meat is in his mouth
Till the first of the Houses hearkeneth the tidings of the south;

Lo, he speaks, and the mead-sea sippeth, and the bread by the way doth eat,
And over the Geiring threshold and outward pass his feet;
And he breasts the Burg of the Daylings and saith his happy word,
And stayeth to drink for a minute of the waves of Battle-ford.
Lone then by the stream he runneth, and wendeth the wild-wood road,
And dasheth through the hazels of the Oselings' fair abode,
And the Elking women know it, and their hearts are glad once more,
And ye—yea, hearken, Wolfings, for his feet are at the door.

12. TIDINGS OF THE BATTLE IN MIRKWOOD

A messenger named Gisili of the Shieldings arrives from the Markmen wanting to receive a vision from Hall-Sun. He tells them of the battle and of their victory over the Romans. Notice in particular that he says Thiodolf, as he went to into battle, was "unhelmed and bore no shield, nor had he any coat of fence; nought but a deer-skin frock." Thiodolf is not wearing the dwarf-made Hauberk. Wood-Sun, disguised as an old woman, hears that and Hall-Sun notices her response. Messengers are sent out to tell other tribes of their victory. Notice that swords often have names, as in Tolkien.

As the Hall-Sun made an end they heard in good sooth the feet of the runner on the hard ground without the hall, and presently the door opened and he came leaping over the threshold, and up to the table, and stood leaning on it with one hand, his breast heaving with his last swift run. Then he spake presently: "I am Gisli of the Shieldings: Otter sendeth me to the Hall-Sun; but on the way I was to tell tidings to the Houses west of the Water: so have I done. Now is my journey ended; for Otter saith: 'Let the Hall-Sun note the tidings and send word of them by four of the lightest limbed of the women, or by lads a-horseback, both west and east of the Water; let her send the word as it seemeth to her, whether she hath seen it or not. I will drink a short draught since my running is over."

Then a damsel brought him a horn of mead and let it come into his hand, and he drank sighing with pleasure, while the damsel for pleasure of him and his tidings laid her hand on his shoulder.

Gisli Tells of Victory in Battle

Then he set down the horn and spake: "We, the Shieldings, with the Geirings, the Hrossings, and the Wolfings, three hundred warriors and more, were led into the Wood by Thiodolf the War-duke, beside whom went Fox, who hath seen the Romans. We were all afoot; for there is no wide way through the Wood, nor would we have it otherwise, lest the foe find the thicket easy. But many of us know the thicket and its ways; so we made not the easy hard. I was near the War-duke, for I know the thicket and am light-foot: I am a bowman. **I saw Thiodolf that he was unhelmed and bore no shield, nor had he any coat of fence; nought but a deer-skin frock.**"

As he said that word, the carline, who had drawn very near to him and was looking hard at his face, turned and looked on the Hall-Sun and stared at her till she reddened under those keen eyes: for in her heart began to gather some knowledge of the tale of her mother and what her will was.

But Gisli went on: "Yet by his side was his mighty sword, and we all knew it for Throng-plough, and were glad of it and of him and the unfenced breast of the dauntless. Six hours we went spreading wide through the thicket, not always seeing one another, but knowing one another to be nigh; those that knew the thicket best led, the others followed on. So we went till it was high noon on the plain and glimmering dusk in the thicket, and we saw nought, save here and there a roe, and here and there a sounder of swine, and coneys where it was opener, and the sun shone and the grass grew for a little space. "

"So came we unto where the thicket ended suddenly, and there was a long glade of the wild-wood, all set about with great oak-trees and grass thereunder, which I knew well; and thereof the tale tells that it was a holy place of the folk who abided in these parts before the Sons of the Goths. Now will I drink."

So he drank of the horn and said: "It seemeth that Fox had a deeming of the way the Romans should come; so now we abided in the thicket without that glade and lay quiet and hidden, spreading ourselves as much about that lawn of the oak-trees as we might, the while Fox and three others crept through the wood to espy what might be toward: not long had they been gone ere we heard a war-horn blow, and it was none of our horns: it was a long way off, but we looked to our weapons: for men are eager for the foe and the death that cometh, when they lie hidden in the thicket.

"A while passed, and again we heard the horn, and it was nigher and had a marvelous voice; then in a while was a little noise of men, not their voices, but footsteps going warily through the brake to the south, and twelve men came slowly and warily into that oak-lawn, and lo, one of them was Fox; but he was clad in the raiment of the dastard of the Goths whom he had slain. I tell you my heart beat, for I saw that the others were Roman men, and one of them seemed to be a man of authority, and he held Fox by the shoulder, and pointed to the thicket where we lay, and something he said to him, as we saw by his gesture and face, but his voice we heard not, for he spake soft.

"Then of those ten men of his he sent back two, and Fox going between them, as though he should be slain if he misled them; and he and the eight abided there wisely and warily, standing silently some six feet from each other, moving scarce at all, but looking like images fashioned of brown copper and iron; holding their casting-spears (which be marvelous heavy weapons) and girt with the sax.

"As they stood there, not out of earshot of a man speaking in his wonted voice, our War-duke made a sign to those about him, and we spread very quietly to the right hand and the left of him once more, and we drew as close as might be to the thicket's edge, and those who had bows the nighest thereto. Thus then we abided a while again; and again came the horn's voice; for belike they had no mind to come their ways covertly because of their pride.

"Soon therewithal comes Fox creeping back to us, and I saw him whisper into the ear of the War-duke, but heard not the word he said. I saw that he had hanging to him two Roman saxes, so I deemed he had slain those two, and so escaped the Romans. Maidens, it were well that ye gave me to drink again, for I am weary and my journey is done."

So again they brought him the horn, and made much of him; and he drank, and then spake on. "Now heard we the horn's voice again quite close, and it was sharp and shrill, and nothing like to the roar of our battle-horns: still was the wood and no wind abroad, not even down the oak-lawn; and we heard now the tramp of many men as they thrashed through the small wood and bracken of the thicket-way; and those eight men and their leader came forward, moving like one, close up to the thicket where I lay, just where the path passed into the thicket beset by the Sons of the Goths: so near they were that I could see the dints upon their armour, and the strands of the wire on their sax-handles. Down then bowed the tall bracken on the further side of the wood-lawn, the thicket crashed before the march of men, and on they strode into the lawn, a goodly band, wary, alert, and silent of cries.

"But when they came into the lawn they spread out somewhat to their left hands, that is to say on the west side, for that way was the clear glade; but on the east the thicket came close up to them and edged them away. Therein lay the Goths.

"There they stayed awhile, and spread out but a little, as men marching, not as men fighting. A while we let them be; and we saw their captain, no big man, but dight with very fair armour and weapons; and there drew up to him certain Goths armed, the dastards of the folk, and another unarmed, an old man bound and bleeding. With these Goths had the captain some converse, and presently he cried out two or three words of Welsh [Latin] in a loud voice, and the nine men who were ahead shifted them somewhat away from us to lead down the glade westward. The prey had come into the net, but they had turned their faces toward the mouth of it.

"Then turned Thiodolf swiftly to the man behind him who carried the war-horn, and every man handled his weapons: but that man understood, and set the little end to his mouth, and loud roared the horn of the Markmen, and neither friend nor foe misdoubted the tale thereof. Then leaped every man to his feet, all bow-strings twanged and the cast-spears flew; no man forebore to shout; each as he might leapt out of the thicket and fell on with sword and axe and spear, for it was from the bowmen but one shaft and no more.

"Then might you have seen Thiodolf as he bounded forward like the wild-cat on the hare, how he had no eyes for any save the Roman captain. Foemen enough he had round about him after the two first bounds from the thicket; for the Romans were doing their best to spread, that they might handle those heavy cast-spears, though they might scarce do it, just come out of the thicket as they were, and thrust together by that onslaught of the kindreds falling on from two sides and even somewhat from behind. To right and left flashed Throng-plough, while Thiodolf himself scarce seemed to guide it: men fell before him at once, and close at his heels poured the Wolfing kindred into the gap, and in a minute of time was he amidst of the throng and face to face with the gold-dight captain.

"What with the sweep of Throng-plough and the Wolfing onrush, there was space about him for a great stroke; he gave a side-long stroke to his right and hewed down a tall Burgundian, and then up sprang the white blade, but ere its edge fell he turned his wrist, and drove the point through that Captain's throat just above the ending of his hauberk, so that he fell dead amidst of his folk.

"All the four kindreds were on them now, and amidst them, and needs must they give way: but stoutly they fought; for surely no other warriors might have withstood that onslaught of the Markmen for the twinkling of an eye: but had the Romans had but the space to have spread themselves out there, so as to handle their shot-weapons, many a woman's son of us had fallen; for no man shielded himself in his eagerness, but let the swiftness of the Onset of point-and-edge shield him; which, sooth to say, is often a good shield, as here was found.

"So those that were unslain and unhurt fled west along the glade, but not as dastards, and had not Thiodolf followed hard in the chase according to his wont, they might even yet have made a fresh stand and spread from oak-tree to oak-tree across the glade: but as it befel, they might not get a fair offing so as to disentangle themselves and array themselves in good order side by side; and whereas the Markmen were fleet of foot, and in the woods they knew, there were a many aliens slain in the chase or taken alive unhurt or little hurt: but the rest fled this way and that way into the thicket, with whom were some of the Burgundians; so there they abide now as outcasts and men unholy, to be slain as wild-beasts one by one as we meet them.

"Such then was the battle in Mirkwood. Give me the mead-horn that I may drink to the living and the dead, and the memory of the dead, and the deeds of the living that are to be."

So they brought him the horn, and he waved it over his head and drank again and spake: "Sixty and three dead men of the Romans we counted there up and down that oak-glade; and we cast earth over them; and three dead dastards of the Goths, and we left them for the wolves to deal with. And twenty-five men of the Romans we took alive to be for hostages if need should be, and these did we Shielding men, who are not very many, bring aback to the Wain-burg; and the Daylings, who are a great company, were appointed to enter the wood and be with Thiodolf; and me did Otter bid to bear the tidings, even as I have told you. And I have not loitered by the way."

Great then was the joy in the Hall; and they took Gisli, and made much of him, and led him to the bath, and clad him in fine raiment taken from the coffer which was but seldom opened, because the cloths it held were precious; and they set a garland of green wheat-ears on his head. Then they fell to and spread the feast in the hall; and they ate and drank and were merry.

But as for speeding the tidings, the Hall-Sun sent two women and two lads, all a-horseback, to bear the words: the women to remember the words which she taught them carefully, the lads to be handy with the horses, or in the ford, or the swimming of the deeps, or in the thicket. So they went their ways, down the water: one pair went on the western side, and the other crossed Mirkwood-water at the shallows (for being Midsummer the water was but small), and went along the east side, so that all the kindred might know of the tidings and rejoice.

Great was the glee in the Hall, though the warriors of the House were away, and many a song and lay they sang: but amidst the first of the singing they bethought them of the old woman, and would have bidden her tell them some tale of times past, since she was so wise in the ancient lore. But when they sought for her on all sides she was not to be found, nor could anyone remember seeing her depart from the Hall. But this had they no call to heed, and the feast ended, as it began, in great glee.

Albeit the Hall-Sun was troubled about the carline, both that she had come, and that she had gone: and she determined that the next time she met her she would strive to have of her a true tale of what she was, and of all that was toward.

13. THE HALL-SUN SAITH ANOTHER WORD

The next evening at the House of the Wolfings, Hall-Sun speaks again of a vision of victory in battle but closes with sad and confusing words.

It was no later than the next night, and a many of what thralls were not with the host were about in the feast-hall with the elders and lads and weaklings of the House; for last night's tidings had drawn them thither. Gisli had gone back to his kindred and the Wain-burg in the Upper-mark, and the women were sitting, most of them, in the Women's-Chamber, some of them doing what little summer work needed doing about the looms, but more resting from their work in field and acre.

Then came the Hall-Sun forth from her room clad in glittering raiment, and summoned no one, but went straight to her place on the dais under her namesake the Lamp, and stood there a little without speaking. Her face was pale now, her lips a little open, her eyes set and staring as if they saw nothing of all that was round about her.

Hall-Sun Speaks

Now went the word through the Hall and the Women's-Chamber that the Hall-Sun would speak again, and that great tidings were toward; so all folk came flock-meal to the dais, both thralls and free; and scarce were all gathered there, ere the Hall-Sun began speaking, and said:

THE DAYS OF THE WORLD THRUST ONWARD, AND MEN ARE BORN THEREIN
A many and a many, and divers deeds they win
In the fashioning of stories for the kindreds of the earth,

A garland interwoven of sorrow and of mirth.
To the world a warrior cometh; from the world he passeth away,
And no man then may sunder his good from his evil day.
By the Gods hath he been tormented, and been smitten by the foe:
He hath seen his maiden perish, he hath seen his speech-friend go:
His heart hath conceived a joyance and hath brought it unto birth:
But he hath not carried with him his sorrow or his mirth.
He hath lived, and his life hath fashioned the outcome of the deed,
For the blossom of the people, and the coming kindreds' seed.

Thus-wise the world is fashioned, and the new sun of the morn
Where earth last night was desert beholds a kindred born,
That to-morrow and to-morrow blossoms all gloriously
With many a man and maiden for the kindreds yet to be,
And fair the Goth-folk groweth. And yet the story saith
That the deeds that make the summer make too the winter's death,
That summer-tides unceasing from out the grave may grow
And the spring rise up unblemished from the bosom of the snow.

Thus as to every kindred the day comes once for all
When yesterday it was not, and to-day it builds the hall,
So every kindred bideth the night-tide of the day,
Whereof it knoweth nothing, e'en when noon is past away.
E'en thus the House of the Wolfings 'twixt dusk and dark doth stand,
And narrow is the pathway with the deep on either hand.
On the left are the days forgotten, on the right the days to come,
And another folk and their story in the stead of the Wolfing home.
Do the shadows darken about it, is the even here at last?
Or is this but a storm of the noon-tide that the wind is driving past?

Unscathed as yet it standeth; it bears the stormy drift,
Nor bows to the lightening flashing adown from the cloudy lift.
I see the hail of battle and the onslaught of the strong,
And they go adown to the folk-mote that shall bide there over long.
I see the slain-heaps rising and the alien folk prevail,
And the Goths give back before them on the ridge o'er the treeless vale.
I see the ancient fallen, and the young man smitten dead,
And yet I see the War-duke shake Throng-plough o'er his head,
And stand unhelmed, unbyrnied before the alien host,
And the hurt men rise around him to win back battle lost;
And the wood yield up her warriors, and the whole host rushing on,
And the swaying lines of battle until the lost is won.

Then forth goes the cry of triumph, as they ring the captives round
And cheat the crow of her portion and heap the warriors' mound.
There are faces gone from our feast-hall not the least beloved nor worst,
But the wane of the House of the Wolfings not yet the world hath cursed.
The sun shall rise to-morrow on our cold and dewy roof,
For they that longed for slaughter were slaughtered far aloof.

She ceased for a little, but her countenance, which had not changed during her song, changed not at all now: so they all kept silence although they were rejoicing in this new tale of victory; for they deemed that she was not yet at the end of her speaking. And in good sooth she spake again presently, and said:

I WOT NOT WHAT HATH BEFALLEN NOR WHERE MY SOUL MAY BE,
For confusion is within me and but dimly do I see,
As if the thing that I look on had happed a while ago.
They stand by the tofts of a war-garth, a captain of the foe,
And a man that is of the Goth-folk, and as friend and friend they speak,
But I hear no word they are saying, though for every word I seek.
And now the mist flows round me and blind I come aback
To the House-roof of the Wolfings and the hearth that hath no lack.

Her voice grew weaker as she spake the last words, and she sank backward on to her chair: her clenched hands opened, the lids fell down over her bright eyes, her breast heaved no more as it had done, and presently she fell asleep.

The folk were doubtful and somewhat heavy-hearted because of those last words of hers; but they would not ask her more, or rouse her from her sleep, lest they should grieve her; so they departed to their beds and slept for what was yet left of the night.

14. THE HALL-SUN IS CAREFUL CONCERNING THE PASSES OF THE WOOD

The next morning at the House of the Wolfings, they prepare for the harvest. Hall-Sun asks them to make her their leader and they agree. She then warns them that traitors will lead the Romans to attack the House of the Wolfings with its treasures through an unguarded path. She sends out ten strong women led by Hrosshild to watch for this attack. Then Egil, a messenger from the Markmen arrives. He bears the same warning that Hall-Sun has just given and calls all of them to the Speech-Hill.

In the morning early folk arose; and the lads and women who were not of the night-shift got them ready to go to the mead and the acres; for the sunshine had been plenty these last days and the wheat was done blossoming, and all must be got ready for harvest. So they broke their fast, and got their tools into their hands: but they were somewhat heavy-hearted because of those last words of the Hall-Sun, and the doubt of last night still hung about them, and they were scarcely as merry as men are wont to be in the morning.

As for the Hall-Sun, she was afoot with the earliest, and was no less, but mayhap more merry than her wont was, and was blithe with all, both old and young. But as they were at the point of going she called to them, and said: "Tarry a little, come ye all to the dais and hearken to me."

So they all gathered thereto, and she stood in her place and spake. "Women and elders of the Wolfings, is it so that I spake somewhat of tidings last night?"

"Yea," said they all.

She said, "And was it a word of victory?"

They answered "yea" again.

"Good is that," she said; "doubt ye not! there is nought to unsay. But hearken! I am nothing wise in war like Thiodolf or Otter of the Laxings, or as Heriulf the Ancient was, though he was nought so wise as they be. Nevertheless ye shall do well to take me for your captain, while this House is bare of warriors."

"Yea, yea," they said, "so will we."

And an old warrior, hight [named] Sorli, who sat in his chair, no longer quite way-worthy, said: "Hall-Sun, this we looked for of thee; since thy wisdom is not wholly the wisdom of a spae-wife [a woman who can foretell the future], but rather is of the children of warriors: and we know thine heart to be high and proud, and that thy death seemeth to thee a small matter beside the life of the Wolfing House."

Then she smiled and said, "Will ye all do my bidding?"

And they all cried out heartily, "Yea, Hall-Sun, that will we."

She said: "Hearken then; ye all know that east of Mirkwood-water, when ye come to the tofts of the Bearings, and their Great Roof, the thicket behind them is close, but that there is a wide way cut through it; and often have I gone there: if ye go by that way, in a while ye come to the thicket's end and to bare places where the rocks crop up through the gravel and the woodland loam. There breed the coneys [rabbits] without number; and wild-cats haunt the place for that sake, and foxes; and the wood-wolf walketh there in summer-tide, and hard by the she-wolf hath her litter of whelps, and all these have enough; and the bald-head erne [eagle] hangeth over it and the kite [bird of prey], and also the kestril [falcon], for shrews and mice abound there. Of these things there is none that feareth me, and none that maketh me afraid.

Beyond this place for a long way the wood is nowise thick, for first grow ash-trees about the clefts of the rock and also quicken-trees, but not many of either; and here and there a hazel brake easy to thrust through; then comes a space of oak-trees scattered about the lovely wood-lawn, and then at last the beech-wood close above but clear beneath. This I know well, because I myself have gone so far and further; and by this easy way have I gone so far to the south, that I have come out into the fell country, and seen afar off the snowy mountains beyond the Great Water.

Preparing for a Surprise Attack

"Now fear ye not, but pluck up a heart! For either I have seen it or dreamed it, or thought it, that by this road easy to wend the Romans should come into the Mark. For shall not those dastards and traitors that wear the raiment and bodies of the Goths over the hearts and the lives of foemen, tell them hereof? And will they not have heard of our Thiodolf, and this my holy namesake?

"Will they not therefore be saying to themselves, 'Go to now, why should we wrench the hinges off the door with plenteous labour, when another door to the same chamber standeth open before us? This House of the Wolfings is the door to the treasure chamber of the Markmen; let us fall on that at once rather than have many battles for other lesser matters, and then at last have to fight for this also: for having this we have all, and they shall be our thralls, and we may slaughter what we will, and torment what we will and deflower what we will, and make our souls glad with their grief and anguish, and take aback with us to the cities what we will of the thralls, that their anguish and our joy may endure the longer.'

"Thus will they say: therefore is it my rede that the strongest and hardiest of you women take horse, a ten of you and one to lead besides, and ride the shallows to the Bearing House, and tell them of our rede; which is to watch diligently the ways of the wood; the outgate to the Mark, and the places where the wood is thin and easy to travel on: and ye shall bid them give you of their folk as many as they deem fittest thereto to join your company, so that ye may have a chain of watchers stretching far into the wilds; but two shall lie without the wood, their horses ready for them to leap on and ride on the spur to the Wain-burg in the Upper-mark if any tidings befal. Now of these eleven I ordain Hrosshild to be the leader and captain, and to choose for her fellows the stoutest-limbed and heaviest-handed of all the maidens here: art thou content Hrosshild?"

Then stood Hrosshild forth and said nought, but nodded yea; and soon was her choice made amid jests and laughter, for this seemed no hard matter to them. So the ten got together, and the others fell off from them, and there stood the ten maidens with Hrosshild, well nigh as strong as men, clean-limbed and tall, tanned with sun and wind; for all these were unwearied afield, and oft would lie out a-nights, since they loved the lark's song better than the mouse's squeak; but as their kirtles [dress] shifted at neck and wrist, you might see their skins as white as privet-flower where they were wont to be covered.

Then said the Hall-Sun: "Ye have heard the word, see ye to it, Hrosshild, and take this other word also: Bid the Bearing stay-at-homes bide not the sword and the torch at home if the Romans come, but hie them over hither, to hold the Hall or live in the wild-wood with us, as need may be; for might bides with many.

"But ye maidens, take this counsel for yourselves; do ye each bear with you a little keen knife, and if ye be taken, and it seem to you that ye may not bear the smart of the Roman torments (for they be wise in tormenting), but will speak and betray us under them, then thrust this little edge tool into the place of your bodies where the life lieth closest, and so go to the Gods with a good tale in your mouths: so may the Almighty God of Earth speed you, and the fathers of the kindred!"

So she spoke; and they made no delay but each one took what axe or spear or sword she liked best, and two had their bows and quivers of arrows; and so all folk went forth from the Hall.

Soon were the horses saddled and bridled, and the maidens bestrode them joyously and set forth on their way, going down the lanes of the wheat, and rode down speedily toward the shallows of the water, and all cried good speed after them. But the others would turn to their day's work, and would go about their divers errands. But even as they were at point to sunder, they saw a swift runner passing by those maidens just where the acres joined the meadow, and he waved his hand aloft and shouted to them, but stayed not his running for them, but came up the lanes of the wheat at his swiftest: so they knew at once that this was again a messenger from the host, and they stood together and awaited his coming; and as he drew near they knew him for Egil, the swiftest-footed of the Wolfings; and he gave a great shout as he came among them; and he was dusty and wayworn, but eager; and they received him with all love, and would have brought him to the Hall to wash him and give him meat and drink, and cherish him in all ways.

But he cried out, "To the Speech-Hill first, to the Speech-Hill first! But even before that, one word to thee, Hall-Sun! Saith Thiodolf, Send ye watchers to look to the entrance into Mid-mark, which is by the Bearing dwelling; and if aught untoward befalleth let one ride on the spur with the tidings to the Wain-burg. For by that way also may peril come."

Then smiled some of the bystanders, and the Hall-Sun said: "Good is it when the thought of a friend stirreth betimes in one's own breast. The thing is done, Egil; or sawest thou not those ten women, and Hrosshild the eleventh, as thou camest up into the acres?"

Said Egil; "Fair fall thine hand, Hall-Sun! thou art the Wolfings' Ransom. Wend we now to the Speech-Hill."

So did they, and every thrall that was about the dwellings, man, woman, and child fared with them, and stood about the Speech-Hill: and the dogs went round about the edge of that assembly, wandering in and out, and sometimes looking hard on some one whom they knew best, if he cried out aloud.

But the men-folk gave all their ears to hearkening, and stood as close as they might. Then Egil clomb the Speech-Hill, and said.

15. They Hear Tell of the Battle on the Ridge

Egil tells them of the Battle on the Ridge, a long and brutal one during which many Markmen died. Note Thiodolf still fights without the Hauberk Wood-Sun gave him.

Ye have heard how the Daylings were appointed to go to help Thiodolf in driving the folk-spear home to the heart of the Roman host. So they went; but six hours thereafter comes one to Otter bidding him send a great part of the kindreds to him; for that he had had tidings that a great host of Romans were drawing near the wood-edge, but were not entered therein, and that fain would he meet them in the open field.

"So the kindreds drew lots, and the lot fell first to the Elkings, who are a great company, as ye know; and then to the Hartings, the Beamings, the Alftings, the Vallings (also a great company), the Galtings, (and they no lesser) each in their turn; and last of all to the Laxings; and the Oselings prayed to go with the Elkings, and this Otter deemed good, whereas a many of them be bowmen.

"All these then to the number of a thousand or more entered the wood; and I was with them, for in sooth I was the messenger. No delay made we in the wood, nor went we over warily, trusting to the warding of the wood by Thiodolf; and there were men with us who knew the paths well, whereof I was one; so we speedily came through into the open country.

"Shortly we came upon our folk and the War-duke lying at the foot of a little hill that went up as a buttress to a long ridge high above us, whereon we set a watch; and a little brook came down the dale for our drink.

"Night fell as we came thither; so we slept for a while, but abode not the morning, and we were afoot (for we had no horses with us) before the moon grew white. We took the road in good order, albeit our folk-banners we had left behind in the burg; so each kindred raised aloft a shield of its token to be for a banner. So we went forth, and some swift footmen, with Fox, who hath seen the Roman war-garth, had been sent on before to spy out the ways of the foemen.

Romans Camped on a Ridge

"Two hours after sunrise cometh one of these, and telleth how he hath seen the Romans, and how that they are but a short mile hence breaking their fast, not looking for any onslaught; 'but,' saith he, 'they are on a high ridge whence they can see wide about, and be in no danger of ambush, because the place is bare for the most part, nor is there any cover except here and there down in the dales a few hazels and blackthorn bushes, and the rushes of the becks in the marshy bottoms, wherein a snipe may hide, or a hare, but scarce a man; and note that there is no way up to that ridge but by a spur thereof as bare as my hand; so ye will be well seen as ye wend up thereto.'

"So spake he in my hearing. But Thiodolf bade him lead on to that spur, and old Heriulf, who was standing nigh, laughed merrily and said: 'Yea, lead on, and speedily, lest the day wane and nothing done save the hunting of snipes.'

"So on we went, and coming to the hither side of that spur beheld those others and Fox with them; and he held in his hand an arrow of the aliens, and his face was all astir with half-hidden laughter, and he breathed hard, and pointed to the ridge, and somewhat low down on it we saw a steel cap and three spear-heads showing white from out a little hollow in its side, but the men hidden by the hollow: so we knew that Fox had been chased, and that the Romans were warned and wary.

"No delay made the War-duke, but led us up that spur, which was somewhat steep; and as we rose higher we saw a band of men on the ridge, a little way down it, not a many; archers and slingers mostly, who abode us till we were within shot, and then sent a few shots at us, and so fled. But two men were hurt with the sling-plummets, and one, and he not grievously, with an arrow, and not one slain.

"Thus we came up on to the ridge, so that there was nothing between us and the bare heavens; thence we looked south-east and saw the Romans wisely posted on the ridge not far from where it fell down steeply to the north; but on the south, that is to say on their left hands, and all along the ridge past where we were stayed, the ground sloped gently to the south-west for a good way, before it fell, somewhat steeply, into another long dale. Looking north we saw the outer edge of Mirkwood but a little way from us, and we were glad thereof; because ere we left our sleeping-place that morn Thiodolf had sent to Otter another messenger bidding him send yet more men on to us in case we should be hard-pressed in the battle; for he had had a late rumour that the Romans were many. And now when he had looked on the Roman array and noted how wise it was, he sent three swift-foot ones to take stand on a high knoll which we had passed on the way, that they might take heed where our folk came out from the wood and give signal to them by the horn, and lead them to where the battle should be.

"So we stood awhile and breathed us, and handled our weapons some half a furlong from the alien host. They had no earth rampart around them, for that ridge is water-less, and they could not abide there long, but they had pitched sharp pales [wooden stakes] in front of them and they stood in very good order, as if abiding an onslaught, and moved not when they saw us; for that band of shooters had joined themselves to them already. Taken one with another we deemed them to be more than we were; but their hauberked footmen with the heavy cast-spears not so many as we by a good deal.

"Now we were of mind to fall on them ere they should fall on us; so all such of us as had shot-weapons spread out from our company and went forth a little; and of the others Heriulf stood foremost along with the leaders of the Beamings and the Elkings; but as yet Thiodolf held aback and led the midmost company, as his wont was, and the more part of the Wolfings were with him.

Battle Begins

"Thus we ordered ourselves, and awaited a little while yet what the aliens should do; and presently a war-horn blew amongst them, and from each flank of their mailed footmen came forth a many bowmen and slingers and a band of horsemen; and drew within bowshot, the shooters in open array yet wisely, and so fell to on us, and the horsemen hung aback a little as yet.

"Their arrow-shot was of little avail, their bowmen fell fast before ours; but deadly was their sling-shot, and hurt and slew many and some even in our main battle; for they slung round leaden balls and not stones, and they aimed true and shot quick; and the men withal were so light and lithe, never still, but crouching and creeping and bounding here and there, that they were no easier to hit than coneys amidst of the fern, unless they were very nigh.

"Howbeit when this storm had endured a while, and we moved but little, and not an inch aback, and gave them shot for shot, then was another horn winded from amongst the aliens; and thereat the bowmen cast down their bows, and the slingers wound their slings about their heads, and they all came on with swords and short spears and feathered darts, running and leaping lustily, making for our flanks, and the horsemen set spurs to their horses and fell on in the very front of our folk like good and valiant men-at-arms.

"That saw Heriulf and his men, and they set up the war-whoop, and ran forth to meet them, axe and sword aloft, terribly yet maybe somewhat unwarily. The archers and slingers never came within sword-stroke of them, but fell away before them on all sides; but the slingers fled not far, but began again with their shot, and slew a many. Then was a horn winded, as if to call back the horsemen, who, if they heard, heeded not, but rode hard on our kindred like valiant warriors who feared not death. Sooth to say, neither were the horses big or good, nor the men fit for the work, saving for their hardihood; and their spears were short withal and their bucklers unhandy to wield.

"Now could it be seen how the Goths gave way before them to let them into the trap, and then closed around again, and the axes and edge weapons went awork hewing as in a wood; and Heriulf towered over all the press, and the Wolf's-sister flashed over his head in the summer morning.

"Soon was that storm over, and we saw the Goths tossing up their spears over the slain, and horses running loose and masterless adown over the westward-lying slopes, and a few with their riders still clinging to them. Yet some, sore hurt by seeming, galloping toward the main battle of the Romans.

"Unwarily then fared the children of Tyr that were with Heriulf; for by this time they were well nigh within shot of the spears of those mighty footmen of the Romans: and on their flanks were the slingers, and the bowmen, who had now gotten their bows again; and our bowmen, though they shot well and strong, were too few to quell them; and indeed some of them had cast by their bows to join in Heriulf's storm. Also the lie of the ground was against us, for it sloped up toward the Roman array at first very gently, but afterwards steeply enough to breathe a short-winded man. Also behind them were we of the other kindreds, whom Thiodolf had ordered into the wedge-array; and we were all ready to move forward, so that had they abided somewhat, all had been well and better.

"So did they not, but straightway set up the Victory-whoop and ran forward on the Roman host. And these were so ordered that, as aforesaid, they had before them sharp piles stuck into the earth and pointed against us, as we found afterwards to our cost; and within these piles stood the men some way apart from each other, so as to handle their casting spears, and in three ranks were they ordered and many spears could be cast at once, and if any in the front were slain, his fellow behind him took his place.

"So now the storm of war fell at once upon our folk, and swift and fierce as was their onslaught yet were a many slain and hurt or ever they came to the piles aforesaid. Then saw they death before them and heeded it nought, but tore up the piles and dashed through them, and fell in on those valiant footmen. Short is the tale to tell: whereso-ever a sword or spear of the Goths was upraised there were three upon him, and saith Toti of the Beamings, who was hurt and crawled away and yet lives, that on Heriulf there were six at first and then more; and he took no thought of shielding himself, but raised up the Wolf's-sister and hewed as the woodman in the thicket, when night cometh and hunger is on him. There fell Heriulf the Ancient and many a man of the Beamings and the Elkings with him, and many a Roman.

"But amidst the slain and the hurt our wedge-array moved forward slowly now, warily shielded against the plummets and shafts on either side; and when the Romans saw our unbroken array, and Thiodolf the first with Throng-plough naked in his hand, they chased not such men of ours unhurt or little hurt, as drew aback from before them: so these we took amongst us, and when we had gotten all we might, and held a grim face to the foe, we drew aback little by little, still facing them till we were out of shot of their spears, though the shot of the arrows and the sling-plummets ceased not wholly from us. Thus ended Heriulf's Storm."

Then he rested from his speaking for a while, and none said aught, but they gazed on him as if he bore with him a picture of the battle, and many of the women wept silently for Heriulf, and yet more of the younger ones were wounded to the heart when they thought of the young men of the Elkings, and the Beamings, since with both those houses they had affinity; and they lamented the loves that they had lost, and would have asked concerning their own speech-friends had they durst. But they held their peace till the tale was told out to an end.

Then Egil spake again: "No long while had worn by in Heriulf's Storm, and though men's hearts were nothing daunted, but rather angered by what had befallen, yet would Thiodolf wear away the time somewhat more, since he hoped for succour from the Wain-burg and the Wood; and he would not that any of these Romans should escape us, but would give them all to Tyr, and to be a following to Heriulf the Old and the Great. **So there we abided a while moving nought, and Thiodolf stood with Throng-plough on his shoulder, unhelmed, unbyrnied [no Hauberk], as though he trusted to the kindred for all defence.** Nor for their part did the Romans dare to leave their vantage-ground, when they beheld what grim countenance we made them.

"Albeit, when we had thrice made as if we would fall on, and yet they moved not, whereas it trieth a man sorely to stand long before the foeman, and do nought but endure, and whereas many of our bowmen were slain or hurt, and the rest too few to make head against the shot-weapons of the aliens, then at last we began to draw nearer and a little nearer, not breaking the wedge-array; and at last, just before we were within shot of the cast-spears of their main battle, loud roared our war-horn: then indeed we broke the wedge-array, but orderly as we knew how, spreading out from right and left of the War-duke till we were facing them in a long line: one minute we abode thus, and

Tolkien Warriors—The House of the Wolfings

then ran forth through the spear-storm: and even therewith we heard, as it were, the echo of our own horn, and whoso had time to think betwixt the first of the storm and the handstrokes of the Romans deemed that now would be coming fresh kindreds for our helping.

"Not long endured the spear-rain, so swift we were, neither were we in one throng as betid in Heriulf's Storm, but spread abroad, each trusting in the other that none thought of the backward way. Though we had the ground against us we dashed like fresh men at their pales, and were under the weapons at once. Then was the battle grim; they could not thrust us back, nor did we break their array with our first storm; man hewed at man as if there were no foes in the world but they two: sword met sword, and sax met sax; it was thrusting and hewing with point and edge, and no long-shafted weapons were of any avail; there we fought hand to hand and no man knew by eyesight how the battle went two yards from where he fought, and each one put all his heart in the stroke he was then striking, and thought of nothing else.

"Yet at the last we felt that they were faltering and that our work was easier and our hope higher; then we cried our cries and pressed on harder, and in that very nick of time there arose close behind us the roar of the Markmen's horn and the cries of the kindreds answering ours. Then such of the Romans as were not in the very act of smiting, or thrusting, or clinging or shielding, turned and fled, and the whoop of victory rang around us, and the earth shook, and past the place of the slaughter rushed the riders of the Goths; for they had sent horsemen to us, and the paths were grown easier for our much treading of them. Then I beheld Thiodolf, that he had just slain a foe, and clear was the space around him, and he rushed sideways and caught hold of the stirrup of Angantyr of the Bearings, and ran ten strides beside him, and then bounded on afoot swifter than the red horses of the Bearings, urging on the chase, as his wont was.

"But we who were wearier, when we had done our work, stood still between the living and the dead, between the freemen of the Mark and their war-thralls. And in no long while there came back to us Thiodolf and the chasers, and we made a great ring on the field of the slain, and sang the Song of Triumph; and it was the Wolfing Song that we sang. Thus then ended Thiodolf's Storm."

Many Dead

When he held his peace there was but little noise among the stay-at-homes, for still were they thinking about the deaths of their kindred and their lovers. But Egil spoke again. "Yet within that ring lay the sorrow of our hearts; for Odin had called a many home, and there lay their bodies; and the mightiest was Heriulf; and the Romans had taken him up from where he fell, and cast him down out of the way, but they had not stripped him, and his hand still gripped the Wolf's-sister. His shield was full of shafts of arrows and spears; his byrny was rent in many places, his helm battered out of form. He had been grievously hurt in the side and in the thigh by cast-spears or ever he came to hand-blows with the Romans, but moreover he had three great wounds from the point of the sax, in the throat, in the side, in the belly, each enough for his bane. His face was yet fair to look on, and we deemed that he had died smiling.

"At his feet lay a young man of the Beamings in a gay green coat, and beside him was the head of another of his House, but his green-clad body lay some yards aloof. There lay of the Elkings a many. Well may ye weep, maidens, for them that loved you. Now fare they to the Gods a goodly company, but a goodly company is with them.

"Seventy and seven of the Sons of the Goths lay dead within the Roman battle, and fifty-four on the slope before it; and to boot there were twenty-four of us slain by the arrows and plummets of the shooters, and a many hurt withal.

"But there were no hurt men inside the Roman array or before it. All were slain outright, for the hurt men either dragged themselves back to our folk, or onward to the Roman ranks, that they might die with one more stroke smitten.

"Now of the aliens the dead lay in heaps in that place, for grim was the slaughter when the riders of the Bearings and the Wormings fell on the aliens; and a many of the foemen scorned to flee, but died where they stood, craving no peace; and to few of them was peace given. There fell of the Roman footmen five hundred and eighty and five, and the remnant that fled was but little: but of the slingers and bowmen but eighty and six were slain, for they were there to shoot and not to stand; and they were nimble and fleet of foot, men round of limb, very dark-skinned, but not foul of favour."

Then he said:

THERE ARE MEN THROUGH THE DUSK A-FARING, OUR SPEECH-FIENDS AND OUR
KIN,
No more shall they crave our helping, nor ask what work to win;
They have done their deeds and departed when they had holpen the House,
So high their heads are holden, and their hurts are glorious
With the story of strokes stricken, and new weapons to be met,
And new scowling of foes' faces, and new curses unknown yet.
Lo, they dight the feast in Godhome, and fair are the tables spread,
Late come, but well-beloved is every war-worn head,
And the God-folk and the Fathers, as these cross the tinkling bridge,
Crowd round and crave for stories of the Battle on the Ridge.

Therewith he came down from the Speech-Hill and the women-folk came round about him, and they brought him to the Hall, and washed him, and gave him meat and drink; and then would he sleep, for he was weary.

Howbeit some of the women could not refrain themselves, but must needs ask after their speech-friends who had been in the battle; and he answered as he could, and some he made glad, and some sorry; and as to some, he could not tell them whether their friends were alive or dead. So he went to his place and fell asleep and slept long, while the women went down to acre and meadow, or saw to the baking of bread or the sewing of garments, or went far afield to tend the neat and the sheep.

Howbeit the Hall-Sun went not with them; but she talked with that old warrior, Sorli, who was now halt and grown unmeet for the road, but was a wise man; and she and he together with some old carlines and a few young lads fell to work, and saw to many matters about the Hall and the garth that day; and they got together what weapons there were both for shot and for the hand-play, and laid them where they were handy to come at, and they saw to the meal in the hall that there was provision for many days; and they carried up to a loft above the Women's-Chamber many great vessels of water, lest the fire should take the Hall; and they looked everywhere to the entrances and windows and had fastenings and bolts and bars fashioned and fitted to them; and saw that all things were trim and stout. And so they abided the issue.

16. HOW THE DWARF-WROUGHT HAUBERK WAS BROUGHT AWAY FROM THE HALL OF THE DAYLINGS

Early the next morning, someone calling himself, Thorkettle, in appearance a Wolfing warrior, arrives at the House of the Wolfings on horseback. With Thiodolf's ring to confirm his authority, he asks for the dwarf-made Hauberk (here called "the Treasure of the World") that was in the House's treasury. An old woman brings it to him and he departs. Notice that the two aged warriors who played a prominent role at the Folkmote have returned to the House. In the next chapter we learn that Thiodolv had left the Haubeck in in Roof of the Daylings. It seems likely that Asmund, who had warned of its dangers, or Agni, who was less worried, had brought it back to the House of the Wolfings. Asmund, the old man who warned Thiodolf about the Hauberk in Chapter 9, is also now back at the House. He watches Thorkettle depart and fears that evil will come from it. At the end, we discover the true identity of Thorkettle.

Now it must be told that early in the morning, after the night when Gisli had brought to the Wolfing Stead the tidings of the Battle in the Wood, a man came riding from the south to the Dayling abode. It was just before sunrise, and but few folk were stirring about the dwellings. He rode up to the Hall and got off his black horse, and tied it to a ring in the wall by the Man's-door, and went in clashing, for he was in his battle-gear, and had a great wide-rimmed helm on his head.

Folk were but just astir in the Hall, and there came an old woman to him, and looked on him and saw by his attire that he was a man of the Goths and of the Wolfing kindred; so she greeted him kindly: but he said: "Mother, I am come hither on an errand, and time presses."

Said she: "Yea, my son, or what tidings bearest thou from the south? for by seeming thou art new-come from the host."

Said he: "The tidings are as yesterday, save that Thiodolf will lead the host through the wild-wood to look for the Romans beyond it: therefore will there soon be battle again. See ye, Mother, hast thou here one that knoweth this ring of Thiodolf's, if perchance men doubt me when I say that I am sent on my errand by him?"

"Yea," she said, "Agni will know it; since he knoweth all the chief men of the Mark; but what is thine errand, and what is thy name?"

"It is soon told," said he, "I am a Wolfing hight Thorkettle, and I come to have away for Thiodolf the Treasure of the World, the dwarf-wrought Hauberk, which he left with you when we fared hence to the south three days ago. Now let Agni come, that I may have it, for time presses sorely."

There were three or four gathered about them now, and a maiden of them said: "Shall I bring Agni hither, mother?"

"What needeth it?" said the carline, "he sleepeth, and shall be hard to awaken; and he is old, so let him sleep. I shall go fetch the Hauberk, for I know where it is, and my hand may come on it as easily as on mine own girdle."

So she went her ways to the treasury where were the precious things of the kindred; the woven cloths were put away in fair coffers to keep them clean from the whirl of the Hall-dust and the reek; and the vessels of gold and some of silver were standing on the shelves of a cupboard before which hung a veil of needlework: but the weapons and war-gear hung upon pins along the wall, and many of them had much fair work on them, and were dight with gold and gems: but amidst them all was the wondrous Hauberk clear to see, dark grey and thin, for it was so wondrously wrought that it hung in small compass. So the carline took it down from the pin, and handled it, and marveled at it, and said:

"Strange are the hands that have passed over thee, sword-rampart, and in strange places of the earth have they dwelt! For no smith of the kindreds hath fashioned thee, unless he had for his friend either a God or a foe of the Gods. Well shalt thou wot of the tale of sword and spear ere thou comest back hither! For Thiodolf shall bring thee where the work is wild."

Then she went with the Hauberk to the new-come warrior, and made no delay, but gave it to him, and said: "When Agni awaketh, I shall tell him that Thorkettle of the Wolfings hath borne aback to Thiodolf the Treasure of the World, the dwarf-wrought Hauberk."

Then Thorkettle took it and turned to go; but even therewith came old Asmund from out of his sleeping-place, and gazed around the Hall, and his eyes fell on the shape of the Wolfing as he was going out of the door, and he asked the carline. "What doeth he here? What tidings is there from the host? For my soul was nought unquiet last night."

"It is a little matter," she said; "the War-duke hath sent for the wondrous Byrny that he left in our treasury when he departed to meet the Romans. Belike there shall be a perilous battle, and few hearts need a stout sword-wall more than Thiodolf's."

As she spoke, Thorkettle had passed the door, and got into his saddle, and sat his black horse like a mighty man as he slowly rode down the turf bridge that led into the plain. And Asmund went to the door and stood watching him till he set spurs to his horse, and departed a great gallop to the south. Then said Asmund:

WHAT THEN ARE THE GODS DEVISING, WHAT WONDERS DO THEY WILL?
What mighty need is on them to work the kindreds ill,
That the seed of the Ancient Fathers and a woman of their kin
With her all unfading beauty must blend herself therein?
Are they fearing lest the kindreds should grow too fair and great,
And climb the stairs of God-home, and fashion all their fate,
And make all earth so merry that it never wax the worse,
Nor need a gift from any, nor prayers to quench the curse?
Fear they that the Folk-wolf, growing as the fire from out the spark
Into a very folk-god, shall lead the weaponed Mark
From wood to field and mountain, to stand between the earth
And the wrights that forge its thraldom and the sword to slay its mirth?
Fear they that the sons of the wild-wood the Loathly Folk shall quell,
And grow into Gods thereafter, and aloof in God-home dwell?

Therewith he turned back into the Hall, and was heavy-hearted and dreary of aspect; for he was somewhat foreseeing; and it may not be hidden that this seeming Thorkettle was no warrior of the Wolfings, but the Wood-Sun in his likeness; for she had the power and craft of shape-changing.

17. THE WOOD-SUN SPEAKETH WITH THIODOLF

Tired, Thiodof leaves his fellow warriors to sleep alone. He wakes just before dawn to see Wood-Sun in front of him. She tries to charm him into wearing the dwarf-made Hauberk. He resists, fearing some "doom" attached to it. We now discover that, after being warned by Asmund, he left it under the Roof of the Daylings. He fears that if he wears it, he will live and his people die. If he does not, he will die in glory but his people will live. Despite those protests, she charms him into putting it on. There's a small mistake in the first paragraph that's probably from Morris himself. A 'howe' is a Middle English/Scottish word for a hole, hollow or valley. The first use in the first sentence fits with that meaning, but the second does not. Read it as saying that the Markmen "heaped a mighty mound over him," much like the mounds built for the kings of Rohan in *The Lord of the Rings*. And much like Rohan, they show little regard for the bodies of their foes. These are lightly covered with earth and left to the wolves. Morris makes this same mistake with "howe" elsewhere. These ancient words were no more a part of his daily speech than they are of ours.

Now the Markmen laid Heriulf in howe on the ridge-crest where he had fallen, and heaped a mighty howe over him that could be seen from far, and round about him they laid the other warriors of the kindreds. For they deemed it was fittest that they should lie on the place whose story they had fashioned. But they cast earth on the foemen lower down on the westward-lying bents.

The sun set amidst their work, and night came on; and Thiodolf was weary and would fain rest him and sleep: but he had many thoughts, and pondered whitherward he should lead the folk, so as to smite the Romans once again, and he had a mind to go apart and be alone for rest and slumber; so he spoke to a man of the kindred named Solvi in whom he put all trust, and then he went down from the ridge, and into a little dale on the southwest side thereof, a furlong from the place of the battle. A beck [mountain stream] ran down that dale, and the further end of it was closed by a little wood of yew trees, low, but growing thick together, and great grey stones were scattered up and down on the short grass of the dale.

Thiodolf went down to the brook-side, and to a place where it trickled into a pool, whence it ran again in a thin thread down the dale, turning aside before it reached the yew-wood to run its ways under low ledges of rock into a wider dale. He looked at the pool and smiled to himself as if he had thought of something that pleased him; then he drew a broad knife from his side, and fell to cutting up turfs till he had what he wanted; and then he brought stones to the place, and built a dam across the mouth of the pool, and sat by on a great stone to watch it filling.

Thiodolf Plans Battle and Sleeps

As he sat he strove to think about the Roman host and how he should deal with it; but despite himself his thoughts wandered, and made for him pictures of his life that should be when this time of battle was over; so that he saw nothing of the troubles that were upon his hands that night, but rather he saw himself partaking in the deeds of the life of man. There he was between the plough-stilts in the acres of the kindred when the west wind was blowing over the promise of early spring; or smiting down the ripe wheat in the hot afternoon amidst the laughter and merry talk of man and maid; or far away over Mirkwood-water watching the edges of the wood against the prowling wolf and lynx, the stars just beginning to shine over his head, as now they were; or wending the windless woods in the first frosts before the snow came, the hunter's bow or javelin in hand: or coming back from the wood with the quarry on the sledge across the snow, when winter was deep, through the biting icy wind and the whirl of the drifting snow, to the lights and music of the Great Roof, and the merry talk therein and the smiling of the faces glad to see the hunting-carles come back; and the full draughts of mead, and the sweet rest a night-tide when the north wind was moaning round the ancient home.

All seemed good and fair to him, and whiles he looked around him, and saw the long dale lying on his left hand and the dark yews in its jaws pressing up against the rock-ledges of the brook, and on his right its windings as the ground rose up to the buttresses of the great ridge. The moon was rising over it, and he heard the voice of the brook as it tinkled over the stones above him; and the whistle of the plover and the laugh of the whimbrel [a wading bird] came down the dale sharp and clear in the calm evening; and sounding far away, because the great hill muffled them, were the voices of his fellows on the ridge, and the songs of the warriors and the high-pitched cries of the watch. And this also was a part of the sweet life which was, and was to be; and he smiled and was happy and loved the days that were coming, and longed for them, as the young man longs for the feet of his maiden at the try sting-place.

So as he sat there, the dreams wrapping him up from troublous thoughts, at last slumber overtook him, and the great warrior of the Wolfings sat nodding like an old carle in the chimney ingle, and he fell asleep, his dreams going with him, but all changed and turned to folly and emptiness.

He woke with a start in no long time; the night was deep, the wind had fallen utterly, and all sounds were stilled save the voice of the brook, and now and again the cry of the watchers of the Goths. The moon was high and bright, and the little pool beside him glittered with it in all its ripples; for it was full now and trickling over the lip of his dam. So he arose from the stone and did off his war-gear, casting Throng-plough down into the grass beside him, for he had been minded to bathe him, but the slumber was still on him, and he stood musing while the stream grew stronger and pushed off first one of his turfs and then another, and rolled two or three of the stones over, and then softly thrust all away and ran with a gush down the dale, filling all the little bights by the way for a minute or two; he laughed softly thereat, and stayed the undoing of his kirtle, and so laid himself down on the grass beside the stone looking down the dale, and fell at once into a dreamless sleep.

Wood-Sun Comes to Thiodolf

When he awoke again, it was yet night, but the moon was getting lower and the first beginnings of dawn were showing in the sky over the ridge; he lay still a moment gathering his thoughts and striving to remember where he was, as is the wont of men waking from deep sleep; then he leapt to his feet, and lo, he was face to face with a woman, and she who but the Wood-Sun? And he wondered not, but reached out his hand to touch her, though he had not yet wholly cast off the heaviness of slumber or remembered the tidings of yesterday.

She drew aback a little from him, and his eyes cleared of the slumber, and he saw her that she was scantily clad in black raiment, barefoot, with no gold ring on her arms or necklace on her neck, or crown about her head. But she looked so fair and lovely even in that end of the night-tide, that he remembered all her beauty of the day and the sunshine, and he laughed aloud for joy of the sight of her, and said: "What aileth thee, O Wood-Sun, and is this a new custom of thy kindred and the folk of God-home that their brides array themselves like thralls new-taken, and as women who have lost their kindred and are outcast? Who then hath won the Burg of the Anses, and clomb the rampart of God-home?"

But she spoke from where she stood in a voice so sweet, that it thrilled to the very marrow of his bones.

I HAVE DWELT A WHILE WITH SORROW SINCE WE MET, WE TWAIN, IN THE WOOD:
I have mourned, while thou hast been merry, who deemest the war-play good.
For I know the heart of the wilful and how thou wouldst cast away
The rampart of thy life-days, and the wall of my happy day.

Yea I am the thrall of Sorrow; she hath stripped my raiment off
And laid sore stripes upon me with many a bitter scoff.
Still bidding me remember that I come of the God-folk's kin,
And yet for all my godhead no love of thee may win.

Then she looked longingly at him a while and at last could no longer refrain her, but drew nigh him and took his hands in hers, and kissed his mouth, and said as she caressed him:

O where are thy wounds, beloved? How turned the spear from thy
    breast,
When the storm of war blew strongest, and the best men met the best?
Lo, this is the tale of to-day: but what shall to-morrow tell?
That Thiodolf the Mighty in the fight's beginning fell;
That there came a stroke ill-stricken, there came an aimless thrust,
And the life of the people's helper lay quenched in the summer dust.

He answered nothing, but smiled as though the sound of her voice and the touch of her hand were pleasant to him, for so much love there was in her, that her very grief was scarcely grievous. But she said again:

Thou sayest it: I am outcast; for a God that lacketh mirth
Hath no more place in God-home and never a place on earth.
A man grieves, and he gladdens, or he dies and his grief is gone;
But what of the grief of the Gods, and the sorrow never undone?
Yea verily I am the outcast. When first in thine arms I lay
On the blossoms of the woodland my godhead passed away;
Thenceforth unto thee was I looking for the light and the glory of life
And the Gods' doors shut behind me till the day of the uttermost strife.
And now thou hast taken my soul, thou wilt cast it into the night,
And cover thine head with the darkness, and turn thine eyes from the light.
Thou wouldst go to the empty country where never a seed is sown
And never a deed is fashioned, and the place where each is alone;
But I thy thrall shall follow, I shall come where thou seemest to lie,
I shall sit on the howe that hides thee, and thou so dear and nigh!
A few bones white in their war-gear that have no help or thought,
Shall be Thiodolf the Mighty, so nigh, so dear—and nought.

His hands strayed over her shoulders and arms, caressing them, and he said softly and lovingly:

I am Thiodolf the Mighty: but as wise as I may be
No story of that grave-night mine eyes can ever see,
But rather the tale of the Wolfings through the coming days of earth,
And the young men in their triumph and the maidens in their mirth;

And morn's promise every evening, and each day the promised morn,
And I amidst it ever reborn and yet reborn.
This tale I know, who have seen it, who have felt the joy and pain,
Each fleeing, each pursuing, like the links of the draw-well's chain:
But that deedless tide of the grave-mound, and the dayless nightless day,
E'en as I strive to see it, its image wanes away.
What say'st thou of the grave-mound? shall I be there at all
When they lift the Horn of Remembrance, and the shout goes down the hall,
And they drink the Mighty War-duke and Thiodolf the old?
Nay rather; there where the youngling that longeth to be bold
Sits gazing through the hall-reek and sees across the board
A vision of the reaping of the harvest of the sword,
There shall Thiodolf be sitting; e'en there shall the youngling be
That once in the ring of the hazels gave up his life to thee.

She laughed as he ended, and her voice was sweet, but bitter was her laugh. Then she said:

NAY THOU SHALT BE DEAD, O WARRIOR, THOU SHALT NOT SEE THE HALL
Nor the children of thy people 'twixt the dais and the wall.
And I, and I shall be living; still on thee shall waste my thought:
I shall long and lack thy longing; I shall pine for what is nought.

But he smiled again, and said:

NOT ON EARTH SHALL I LEARN THIS WISDOM; AND HOW SHALL I LEARN IT THEN
When I lie alone in the grave-mound, and have no speech with men?
But for thee,—O doubt it nothing that my life shall live in thee,
And so shall we twain be loving in the days that yet shall be.

It was as if she heard him not; and she fell aback from him a little and stood silently for a while as one in deep thought; and then turned and went a few paces from him, and stooped down and came back again with something in her arms (and it was the Hauberk once more), and said suddenly:

O THIODOLF, NOW TELL ME FOR WHAT CAUSE THOU WOULDST NOT BEAR
This grey wall of the hammer in the tempest of the spear?
Didst thou doubt my faith, O Folk-wolf, or the counsel of the Gods,
That thou needs must cast thee naked midst the flashing battle-rods,
Or is thy pride so mighty that it seemed to thee indeed
That death was a better guerdon than the love of the God-head's seed?

But Thiodolf said: "O Wood-Sun, this thou hast a right to ask of me, why I have not worn in the battle thy gift, the Treasure of the World, the dwarf-wrought Hauberk! And what is this that thou sayest? I doubt not thy faith towards me and thine abundant love: and as for the rede of the Gods, I know it not, nor may I know it, nor turn it this way nor that: and as for thy love and that I would choose death sooner, I know not what thou meanest; I will not say that I love thy love better than life itself; for these two, my life and my love, are blended together and may not be sundered.

Thiodolf Fears about the Hauberk

"Hearken therefore as to the Hauberk: I wot well that it is for no light matter that thou wouldst have me bear thy gift, the wondrous Hauberk, into battle; I deem that some doom is wrapped up in it; maybe that I shall fall before the foe if I wear it not; and that if I wear it, somewhat may betide me which is unmeet to betide a warrior of the Wolfings. Therefore will I tell thee why I have fought in two battles with the Romans with unmailed body, and why I left the Hauberk, (which I see that thou bearest in thine arms) in the Roof of the Daylings. For when I entered therein, clad in the Hauberk, there came to meet me an ancient man, one of the very valiant of days past, and he looked on me with the eyes of love, as though he had been the very father of our folk, and I the man that was to come after him to carry on the life thereof. But when he saw the Hauberk and touched it, then was his love smitten cold with sadness and he spoke words of evil omen; so that putting this together with thy words about the gift, and that thou didst in a manner compel me to wear it, I could not but deem that this mail is for the ransom of a man and the ruin of a folk.

"Wilt thou say that it is not so? then will I wear the Hauberk, and live and die happy. But if thou sayest that I have deemed aright, and that a curse goeth with the Hauberk, then either for the sake of the folk I will not wear the gift and the curse, and I shall die in great glory, and because of me the House shall live; or else for thy sake I shall bear it and live, and the House shall live or die as may be, but I not helping, nay I no longer of the House nor in it. How sayest thou?"

Then she said:

HAIL BE THY MOUTH, BELOVED, FOR THAT LAST WORD OF THINE,
And the hope that thine heart conceiveth and the hope that is born in mine.
Yea, for a man's deliverance was the Hauberk born indeed
That once more the mighty warrior might help the folk at need.
And where is the curse's dwelling if thy life be saved to dwell
Amidst the Wolfing warriors and the folk that loves thee well
And the house where the high Gods left thee to be cherished well therein?

YEA MORE: I have told thee, beloved, that thou art not of the kin;
The blood in thy body is blended of the wandering Elking race,
And one that I may not tell of, who in God-home hath his place,
And who changed his shape to beget thee in the wild-wood's leafy roof.
How then shall the doom of the Wolfings be woven in the woof
Which the Norns for thee have shuttled? Or shall one man of war
Cast down the tree of the Wolfings on the roots that spread so far?

O friend, thou art wise and mighty, but other men have lived
Beneath the Wolfing roof-tree whereby the folk has thrived.

He reddened at her word; but his eyes looked eagerly on her. She cast down the
Hauberk, and drew one step nigher to him. She knitted her brows, her face waxed terrible, and her stature seemed to grow greater, as she lifted up her gleaming right arm,
and cried out in a great voice.

Thou Thiodolf the Mighty! Hadst thou will to cast the net
And tangle the House in thy trouble, it is I would slay thee yet;
For 'tis I and I that love them, and my sorrow would I give,
And thy life, thou God of battle, that the Wolfing House might live.

Therewith she rushed forward, and cast herself upon him, and threw her arms
about him, and strained him to her bosom, and kissed his face, and he, her in likewise,
for there was none to behold them, and nought but the naked heaven was the roof
above their heads.

And now it was as if the touch of her face and her body, and the murmuring of
her voice changed and soft close to his ear, as she murmured mere words of love to
him, drew him away from the life of deeds and doubts and made a new world for him,
wherein he beheld all those fair pictures of the happy days that had been in his musings
when first he left the field of the dead. So they sat down on the grey stone together
hand in hand, her head laid upon his shoulder, no otherwise than if they had been two
lovers, young and without renown in days of deep peace.

So as they sat, her foot smote on the cold hilts of the sword, which Thiodolf had
laid down in the grass; and she stooped and took it up, and laid it across her knees and
his as they sat there; and she looked on Throng-plough as he lay still in the sheath, and
smiled on him, and saw that the peace-strings were not yet wound about his hilts. So
she drew him forth and raised him up in her hand, and he gleamed white and fearful
in the growing dawn, for all things had now gotten their colours again, whereas amidst
their talking had the night worn, and the moon low down was grown white and pale.

But she leaned aside, and laid her cheek against Thiodolf's, and he took the sword
out of her hand and set it on his knees again, and laid his right hand on it, and said:

Two things by these blue edges in the face of the dawning I swear;
And first this warrior's ransom in the coming fight to bear,
And evermore to love thee who hast given me second birth.
And by the sword I swear it, and by the Holy Earth,
To live for the House of the Wolfings, and at last to die for their need.
For though I trow thy saying that I am not one of their seed,
Nor yet by the hand have been taken and unto the Father shown
As a very son of the Fathers, yet mid them hath my body grown;
And I am the guest of their Folk-Hall, and each one there is my friend.
So with them is my joy and sorrow, and my life, and my death in the end.

Now whatso doom hereafter my coming days shall bide,
Thou speech-friend, thou deliverer, thine is this dawning-tide.

She spoke no word to him; but they rose up and went hand in hand down the dale, he still bearing his naked sword over his shoulder, and thus they went together into the yew-copse at the dale's end. There they abode till after the rising of the sun, and each to each spake many loving words at their departure; and the Wood-Sun went her ways at her will.

But Thiodolf went up the dale again, and set Throng-plough in his sheath, and wound the peace-strings round him. Then he took up the Hauberk from the grass whereas the Wood-Sun had cast it, and did it on him, as it were of the attire he was wont to carry daily. So he girt Throng-plough to him, and went soberly up to the ridge-top to the folk, who were just stirring in the early morning.

18. Tidings Brought to the Wain-Burg

In the evening two days after the Battle of the Ridge, the Markmen are eager for battle and fear the Romans will withdraw. Then Hrosshild of the Wolfings arrives and asks for Otter the War-duke. She warns him that the Romans are about to attack the Mid-Mark. Otter orders his men to prepare to march. She tells how Hall-Sun had anticipated the attack and set women to watch for it. She describes how the Romans were discovered and Otter plans to intercept them close to the Battleford. He also sends Geirbald and Viglund to find Thiodolf and tell him not to chase after the Romans.

Now it must be told of Otter and they of the Wain-burg how they had the tidings of the overthrow of the Romans on the Ridge, and that Egil had left them on his way to Wolfstead. They were joyful of the tale, as was like to be, but eager also to strike their stroke at the foe-men, and in that mood they abode fresh tidings.

It has been told how Otter had sent the Bearings and the Wormings to the aid of Thiodolf and his folk, and these two were great kindreds, and they being gone, there abode with Otter, one man with another, thralls and freemen, scant three thousand men: of these many were bowmen good to fight from behind a wall or fence, or some such cover, but scarce meet to withstand a shock in the open field. However it was deemed at this time in the Wain-burg that Thiodolf and his men would soon return to them; and in any case, they said, he lay between the Romans and the Mark, so that they had but little doubt; or rather they feared that the Romans might draw aback from the Mark before they could be met in battle again, for as aforesaid they were eager for the fray.

Now it was in the cool of the evening two days after the Battle on the Ridge, that the men, both freemen and thralls, had been disporting themselves in the plain ground without the Burg in casting the spear and putting the stone, and running races a-foot and a-horseback, and now close on sunset three young men, two of the Laxings and one of the Shieldings, and a grey old thrall of that same House, were shooting a match with the bow, driving their shafts at a rushen roundel (a disk made of rushes) hung on a pole which the old thrall had dight.

Men were peaceful and happy, for the time was fair and calm, and, as aforesaid, they dreaded not the Roman Host any more than if they were Gods dwelling in God-home. The shooters were deft men, and they of the Burg were curious to note their deftness, and many were breathed with the games wherein they had striven, and thought it good to rest, and look on the new sport: so they sat and stood on the grass about the shooters on three sides, and the mead-horn went briskly from man to man; for there was no lack of meat and drink in the Burg, whereas the kindreds that lay nighest to it had brought in abundant provision, and women of the kindreds had come to them, and not a few were there scattered up and down among the carles.

Now the Shielding man, Geirbald by name, had just loosed at the mark, and had shot straight and smitten the roundel in the midst, and a shout went up from the onlookers thereat; but that shout was, as it were, lined with another, and a cry that a messenger was riding toward the Burg: thereat most men looked round toward the wood, because their minds were set on fresh tidings from Thiodolf's company, but as it happened it was from the north and the side toward Mid-mark that they on the outside of the throng had seen the rider coming; and presently the word went from man to man that so it was, and that the new comer was a young man on a grey horse, and would speedily be amongst them; so they wondered what the tidings might be, but yet they did not break up the throng, but abode in their places that they might receive the messenger more orderly; and as the rider drew near, those who were nighest to him perceived that it was a woman.

So men made way before the grey horse, and its rider, and the horse was much spent and travel-worn. So the woman rode right into the ring of warriors, and drew rein there, and lighted down slowly and painfully, and when she was on the ground could scarce stand for stiffness; and two or three of the swains drew near her to help her, and knew her at once for Hrosshild of the Wolfings, for she was well-known as a doughty woman.

Hrosshild's Warning

Then she said: "Bring me to Otter the War-duke; or bring him hither to me, which were best, since so many men are gathered together; and meanwhile give me to drink; for I am thirsty and weary."

So while one went for Otter, another reached to her the mead-horn, and she had scarce done her draught, ere Otter was there, for they had found him at the gate of the Burg. He had many a time been in the Wolfing Hall, so he knew her at once and said: "Hail, Hrosshild! How farest thou?"

She said: "I fare as the bearer of evil tidings. Bid thy folk do on their war-gear and saddle their horses, and make no delay; for now presently shall the Roman host be in Mid-mark!"

Then cried Otter: "Blow up the war-horn! Get ye all to your weapons and be ready to leap on your horses, and come ye to the Thing in good order kindred by kindred: later on ye shall hear Hrosshild's story as she shall tell it to me!"

Therewith he led her to a grassy knoll that was hard by, and set her down thereon and himself beside her, and said: "Speak now, damsel, and fear not! For now shall one fate go over us all, either to live together or die together as the free children of Tyr, and friends of the Almighty God of the Earth. How camest thou to meet the Romans and know of their ways and to live thereafter?"

She said: "Thus it was: the Hall-Sun bethought her how that the eastern ways into Mid-mark that bring a man to the thicket behind the Roof of the Bearings are nowise hard, even for an host; so she sent ten women, and me the eleventh to the Bearing dwelling and the road through the thicket aforesaid; and we were to take of the Bearing stay-at-homes whomso we would that were handy, and then all we to watch the ways for fear of the Romans. And methinks she has had some vision of their ways, though mayhap not altogether clear.

"Anyhow we came to the Bearing dwellings, and they gave us of their folk eight doughty women and two light-foot lads, and so we were twenty and one in all.

"So then we did as the Hall-Sun bade us, and ordained a chain of watchers far up into the waste; and these were to sound a point of war upon their horns each to each till the sound thereof should come to us who lay with our horses hoppled ready beside us in the fair plain of the Mark outside the thicket.

"To be short, the horns waked us up in the midst of yesternight, and of the watches also came to us the last, which had heard the sound amidst the thicket, and said that it was certainly the sound of the Goths' horn, and the note agreed on. Therefore I sent a messenger at once to the Wolfing Roof to say what was toward; but to thee I would not ride until I had made surer of the tidings; so I waited awhile, and then rode into the wild-wood; and a long tale I might make both of the waiting and the riding, had I time thereto; but this is the end of it; that going warily a little past where the thicket thinneth and the road endeth, I came on three of those watches or links in the chain we had made, and half of another watch or link; that is to say six women, who were come together after having blown their horns and fled (though they should rather have abided in some lurking-place to espy whatever might come that way) and one other woman, who had been one of the watch much further off, and had spoken with the furthest of all, which one had seen the faring of the Roman Host, and that it was very great, and no mere band of pillagers or of scouts. And, said this fleer (who was indeed half wild with fear), that while they were talking together, came the Romans upon them, and saw them; and a band of Romans beat the wood for them when they fled, and she, the fleer, was at point to be taken, and saw two taken indeed, and haled off by the Roman scourers of the wood. But she escaped and so came to the others on the skirts of the thicket, having left of her skin and blood on many a thornbush and rock by the way.

"Now when I heard this, I bade this fleer get her home to the Bearings as swiftly as she might, and tell her tale; and she went away trembling, and scarce knowing whether

her feet were on earth or on water or on fire; but belike failed not to come there, as no Romans were before her. But for the others, I sent one to go straight to Wolf-stead on the heels of the first messenger, to tell the Hall-Sun what had befallen, and other five I set to lurk in the thicket, whereas none could lightly lay hands on them, and when they had new tidings, to flee to Wolf-stead as occasion might serve them; and for myself I tarried not, but rode on the spur to tell thee hereof.

"But my last word to thee, Otter, is that by the Hall-Sun's bidding the Bearings will not abide fire and steel at their own stead, but when they hear true tidings of the Romans being hard at hand, will take with them all that is not too hot or too heavy to carry, and go their ways unto Wolf-stead: and the tidings will go up and down the Mark on both sides of the water, so that whatever is of avail for defence will gather there at our dwelling, and if we fall, goodly shall be the howe heaped over us, even if ye come not in time.

"Now have I told thee what I needs must and there is no need to question me more, for thou hast it all—do thou what thou hast to do!"

With that word she cast herself down on the grass by the mound-side, and was presently asleep, for she was very weary.

Otter Marches for Battle

But all the time she had been telling her tale had the horn been sounding, and there were now a many warriors gathered and more coming in every moment: so Otter stood up on the mound after he had bidden a man of his House to bring him his horse and war-gear, and abided a little, till, as might be said, the whole host was gathered: then he bade cry silence, and spake:

"Sons of Tyr, now hath an Host of the Romans gotten into the Mark; a mighty host, but not so mighty that it may not be met. Few words are best: let the Steerings, who are not many, but are men well-tried in war and wisdom abide in the Burg along with the fighting thralls: but let the Burg be broken up and moved from the place, and let its warders wend towards Mid-mark, but warily and without haste, and each night let them make the wain-garth and keep good watch.

"But know ye that the Romans shall fall with all their power on the Wolfing dwellings, deeming that when they have that, they shall have all that is ours with ourselves also. For there is the Hall-Sun under the Great Roof, and there hath Thiodolf, our War-duke, his dwelling-place; therefore shall all of us, save those that abide with the wains, take horse, and ride without delay, and cross the water at Battleford, so that we may fall upon the foe before they come west of the water; for as ye know there is but one ford whereby a man wending straight from the Bearings may cross Mirkwood-water, and it is like that the foe will tarry at the Bearing stead long enough to burn and pillage it.

"So do ye order yourselves according to your kindreds, and let the Shieldings lead. Make no more delay! But for me I will now send a messenger to Thiodolf to tell him of the tidings, and then speedily shall he be with us. Geirbald, I see thee; come hither!"

Now Geirbald stood amidst the Shieldings, and when Otter had spoken, he came forth bestriding a white horse, and with his bow slung at his back. Said Otter: "Geirbald, thou shalt ride at once through the wood, and find Thiodolf; and tell him the tidings, and that in nowise he follow the Roman fleers away from the Mark, nor to heed anything but the trail of the foemen through the south-eastern heaths of Mirkwood, whether other Romans follow him or not: whatever happens let him lead the Goths by that road, which for him is the shortest, towards the defence of the Wolfing dwellings. Lo thou, my ring for a token! Take it and depart in haste. Yet first take thy fellow Viglund the Woodman with thee, lest if perchance one fall, the other may bear the message. Tarry not, nor rest till thy word be said!"

Then turned Geirbald to find Viglund who was anigh to him, and he took the ring, and the twain went their ways without more ado, and rode into the wild-wood.

But about the Wain-burg was there plenteous stir of men till all was ordered for the departure of the host, which was no long while, for there was nothing to do but on with the war-gear and up on to the horse.

Forth then they went duly ordered in their kindreds towards the head of the Upper-mark, riding as swiftly as they might without breaking their array.

19. THOSE MESSENGERS COME TO THIODOLF

As Geirbad and Viglund ride to Thiodolf, they meet Asbiorn, who bears news that Thiodolf suspects the Romans on the ridge was a diversion and that they will attack the Mid-Mark by surprise. Both armies of Markmen now intend to intercept the Romans. The three agree that Geirbald and Viglund will continue to ride to Thiodolf to urge him to march faster, while Asbiorn rides to Otter to tell him of Thiodolf's plans. After riding all night, they reach Thiodolf and discover he has also heard from one of Hall-Sun's messengers. Thiodolf gives a speech and his men march away.

Of Geirbald and Viglund the tale tells that they rode the woodland paths as speedily as they might. They had not gone far, and were winding through a path amidst of a thicket mingled of the hornbeam and holly, betwixt the openings of which the bracken grew exceeding tall, when Viglund, who was very fine-eared, deemed that he heard a horse coming to meet them: so they lay as close as they might, and drew back their horses behind a great holly-bush lest it should be some one or more of the foes who had fled into the wood when the Romans were scattered in that first fight.

But as the sound drew nearer, and it was clearly the footsteps of a great horse, they deemed it would be some messenger from Thiodolf, as indeed it turned out: for as the new-comer fared on, somewhat unwarily, they saw a bright helm after the fashion of the Goths amidst of the trees, and then presently they knew by his attire that he was of the Bearings, and so at last they knew him to be Asbiorn of the said House, a doughty man; so they came forth to meet him and he drew rein when he saw armed men, but presently beholding their faces he knew them and laughed on them, and said: "Hail fellows! What tidings are toward?"

"These," said Viglund, "that thou art well met, since now shalt thou turn back and bring us to Thiodolf as speedily as may be."

But Asbiorn laughed and said: "Nay rather turn about with me; or why are ye so grim of countenance?"

"Our errand is no light one," said Geirbald, "but thou, why art thou so merry?"

"I have seen the Romans fall," said he, "and belike shall soon see more of that game: for I am on an errand to Otter from Thiodolf: the War-duke, when he had questioned some of those whom we took on the Day of the Ridge, began to have a deeming that the Romans had beguiled us, and will fall on the Mark by the way of the south-east heaths: so now is he hastening to fetch a compass and follow that road either to overtake them or prevent them; and he biddeth Otter tarry not, but ride hard along the water to meet them if he may, or ever they have set their hands to the dwellings of my House. And belike when I have done mine errand to Otter I shall ride with him to look on these burners and slayers once more; therefore am I merry. Now for your tidings, fellows."

Said Geirbald: "Our tidings are that both our errands are prevented, and come to nought: for Otter hath not tarried, but hath ridden with all his folk toward the stead of thine House. So shalt thou indeed see these burners and slayers if thou ridest hard; since we have tidings that the Romans will by now be in Mid-mark. And as for our errand, it is to bid Thiodolf do even as he hath done. Hereby may we see how good a pair of War-dukes we have gotten, since each thinketh of the same wisdom. Now take we counsel together as to what we shall do; whether we shall go back to Otter with thee, or thou go back to Thiodolf with us; or else each go the road ordained for us."

Said Asbiorn: "To Otter will I ride as I was bidden, that I may look on the burning of our roof, and avenge me of the Romans afterwards; and I bid you, fellows, ride with me, since fewer men there are with Otter, and he must be the first to bide the brunt of battle."

"Nay," said Geirbald, "as for me ye must even lose a man's aid; for to Thiodolf was I sent, and to Thiodolf will I go: and bethink thee if this be not best, since Thiodolf hath but a deeming of the ways of the Romans and we wot surely of them. Our coming shall make him the speedier, and the less like to turn back if any alien band shall follow after him. What sayest thou, Viglund?"

Said Viglund: "Even as thou, Geirbald: but for myself I deem I may well turn back with Asbiorn. For I would serve the House in battle as soon as may be; and maybe we shall slaughter these kites of the cities, so that Thiodolf shall have no work to do when he cometh."

Said Asbiorn; "Geirbald, knowest thou right well the ways through the wood and on the other side thereof, to the place where Thiodolf abideth? For ye see that night is at hand."

"Nay, not over well," said Geirbald.

Said Asbiorn: "Then I rede thee take Viglund with thee; for he knoweth them yard by yard, and where they be hard and where they be soft. Moreover it were best indeed that ye meet Thiodolf betimes; for I deem not but that he wendeth leisurely, though always warily, because he deemeth not that Otter will ride before to-morrow morning. Hearken, Viglund! Thiodolf will rest to-night on the other side of the water, nigh to where the hills break off into the sheer cliffs that are called the Kites' Nest, and the water runneth under them, coming from the east: and before him lieth the easy ground of the eastern heaths where he is minded to wend to-morrow betimes in the morning: and if ye do your best ye shall be there before he is upon the road, and sure it is that your tidings shall hasten him."

"Thou sayest sooth," saith Geirbald, "tarry we no longer; here sunder our ways; farewell!"

"Farewell," said he, "and thou, Viglund, take this word in parting, that belike thou shalt yet see the Romans, and strike a stroke, and maybe be smitten. For indeed they be most mighty warriors."

The Riders Part

Then made they no delay but rode their ways either side. And Geirbald and Viglund rode over rough and smooth all night, and were out of the thick wood by day-dawn: and whereas they rode hard, and Viglund knew the ways well, they came to Mirkwood-water before the day was old, and saw that the host was stirring, but not yet on the way. And or ever they came to the water's edge, they were met by Wolfkettle of the Wolfings, and Hiarandi of the Elkings, and three others who were but just come from the place where the hurt men lay down in a dale near the Great Ridge; there had Wolfkettle and Hiarandi been tending Toti of the Beamings, their fellow-in-arms, who had been sorely hurt in the battle, but was doing well, and was like to live. So when they saw the messengers, they came up to them and hailed them, and asked them if the tidings were good or evil.

"That is as it may be," said Geirbald, "but they are short to tell; the Romans are in Mid-mark, and Otter rideth on the spur to meet them, and sendeth us to bid Thiodolf wend the heaths to fall in on them also. Nor may we tarry one minute ere we have seen Thiodolf."

Said Wolfkettle, "We will lead you to him; he is on the east side of the water, with all his host, and they are hard on departing."

So they went down the ford, which was not very deep; and Wolfkettle rode the ford behind Geirbald, and another man behind Viglund; but Hiarandi went afoot with the others beside the horses, for he was a very tall man. But as they rode amidst the clear water Wolfkettle lifted up his voice and sang:

WHITE HORSE, WITH WHAT ARE YE LADEN AS YE WADE THE SHALLOWS WARM,
But with tidings of the battle, and the fear of the fateful storm?
What loureth now behind us, what pileth clouds before,
On either hand what gathereth save the stormy tide of war?

Now grows midsummer mirky, and fallow falls the morn,
And dusketh the Moon's Sister, and the trees look overworn;
God's Ash tree shakes and shivers, and the sheer cliff standeth white
As the bones of the giants' father when the Gods first fared to fight.

And indeed the morning had grown mirky and grey and threatening, and from far away the thunder growled, and the face of the Kite's Nest showed pale and awful against a dark steely cloud; and a few drops of rain pattered into the smooth water before them from a rag of the cloud-flock right over head. They were in mid stream now, for the water was wide there; on the eastern bank were the warriors gathering, for they had beheld the faring of those men, and the voice of Wolfkettle came to them across the water, so they deemed that great tidings were toward, and would fain know on what errand those were come.

Then the waters of the ford deepened till Hiarandi was wading more than waist-deep, and the water flowed over Geirbald's saddle; then Wolfkettle laughed, and turning as he sat, dragged out his sword, and waved it from east to west and sang:

O SUN, PALE UP IN HEAVEN, SHRINK FROM US IF THOU WILT,
And turn thy face from beholding the shock of guilt with guilt!
Stand still, O blood of summer! and let the harvest fade,
Till there be nought but fallow where once was bloom and blade!
O day, give out but a glimmer of all thy flood of light,
If it be but enough for our eyen to see the road of fight!
Forget all else and slumber, if still ye let us wake,
And our mouths shall make the thunder, and our swords shall the lightening make,
And we shall be the storm-wind and drive the ruddy rain,
Till the joy of our hearts in battle bring back the day again.

As he spake that word they came up through the shallow water dripping on to the bank, and they and the men who abode them on the bank shouted together for joy of fellowship, and all tossed aloft their weapons. The man who had ridden behind Viglund slipped off on to the ground; but Wolfkettle abode in his place behind Geirbald.

Thiodolf with the Hauberk

So the messengers passed on, and the others closed up round about them, and all the throng went up to where Thiodolf was sitting on a rock beneath a sole ash-tree, the face of the Kite's Nest rising behind him on the other side of a bight [bend] of the river. There he sat unhelmed with the dwarf-wrought Hauberk about him, holding Throng-plough in its sheath across his knees, while he gave word to this and that man concerning the order of the host.

So when they were come thither, the throng opened that the messengers might come forward; for by this time had many more drawn near to hearken what was toward. There they sat on their horses, the white and the grey, and Wolfkettle stood by Geirbald's bridle rein, for he had now lighted down; and a little behind him, his head towering over the others, stood Hiarandi great and gaunt. The ragged cloud had drifted down south-east now and the rain fell no more, but the sun was still pale and clouded.

THEN THIODOLF LOOKED GRAVELY ON THEM, AND SPAKE:
What do ye sons of the War-shield? what tale is there to tell?
Is the kindred fallen tangled in the grasp of the fallow Hell?
Crows the red cock over the homesteads, have we met the foe too late?
For meseems your brows are heavy with the shadowing o'er of fate.

But Geirbald answered:

STILL COLD WITH DEW IN THE MORNING the SHIELDING ROOF-RIDGE STANDS,
Nor yet hath grey Hell bounden the Shielding warriors' hands;
But lo, the swords, O War-duke, how thick in the wind they shake,
Because we bear the message that the battle-road ye take,
Nor tarry for the thunder or the coming on of rain,
Or the windy cloudy night-tide, lest your battle be but vain.
And this is the word that Otter yestre'en hath set in my mouth;
Seek thou the trail of the Aliens of the Cities of the South,
And thou shalt find it leading o'er the heaths to the beechen-wood,
And thence to the stony places where the foxes find their food;
And thence to the tangled thicket where the folkway cleaves it through,
To the eastern edge of Mid-mark where the Bearings deal and do.

Then said Thiodolf in a cold voice, "What then hath befallen Otter?"
Said Geirbald:

WHEN LAST I LOOKED UPON OTTER, ALL ARMED HE RODE THE PLAIN,
With his whole host clattering round him like the rush of the summer rain;
To the right or the left they looked not but they rode through the dusk and the dark
Beholding nought before them but the dream of the foes in the Mark.
So he went; but his word fled from him and on my horse it rode,
And again it saith, O War-duke seek thou the Bear's abode,
And tarry never a moment for ought that seems of worth,
For there shall ye find the sword-edge and the flame of the foes of the earth.

"Tarry not, Thiodolf, nor turn aback though a new foe followeth on thine heels. No need to question me more; I have no more to tell, save that a woman brought these tidings to us, whom the Hall-Sun had sent with others to watch the ways: and some of them had seen the Romans, who are a great host and no band stealing forth to lift the herds."

Now all those round about him heard his words, for he spake with a loud voice; and they knew what the bidding of the War-duke would be; so they loitered not, but each man went about his business of looking to his war-gear and gathering to the appointed place of his kindred. And even while Geirbald had been speaking, had Hiarandi brought up the man who bore the great horn, who when Thiodolf leapt to his feet to find him, was close at hand. So he bade him blow the war-blast, and all men knew the meaning of that voice of the horn, and every man armed him in haste, and they who had horses (and these were but the Bearings and the Warnings), saddled them, and mounted, and from mouth to mouth went the word that the Romans were gotten into Mid-mark, and were burning the Bearing abodes. So speedily was the whole host ready for the way, the Wolfings at the head of all. Then came forth Thiodolf from the midst of his kindred, and they raised him upon a great war-shield upheld by many men, and he stood thereon and spake:

O sons of Tyr, ye have vanquished, and sore hath been your pain;
But he that smiteth in battle must ever smite again;
And thus with you it fareth, and the day abideth yet
When ye shall hold the Aliens as the fishes in the net.
On the Ridge ye slew a many; but there came a many more
From their strongholds by the water to their new-built garth of war,
And all these have been led by dastards o'er the way our feet must tread
Through the eastern heaths and the beechwood to the door of the Bearing stead,
Now e'en yesterday I deemed it, but I durst not haste away
Ere the word was borne to Otter and 'tis he bids haste to-day;
So now by day and by night-tide it behoveth us to wend
And wind the reel of battle and weave its web to end.
Had ye deemed my eyes foreseeing, I would tell you of my sight,
How I see the folk delivered and the Aliens turned to flight,
While my own feet wend them onwards to the ancient Father's Home.
But belike these are but the visions that to many a man shall come
When he goeth adown to the battle, and before him riseth high
The wall of valiant foemen to hide all things anigh.
But indeed I know full surely that no work that we may win
To-morrow or the next day shall quench the Markmen's kin.
On many a day hereafter shall their warriors carry shield;
On many a day their maidens shall drive the kine afield,
On many a day their reapers bear sickle in the wheat
When the golden wind-wrought ripple stirs round the feast-hall's feet.
Lo, now is the day's work easy—to live and overcome,
Or to die and yet to conquer on the threshold of the Home.

And therewith he gat him down and went a-foot to the head of the Wolfing band, a great shout going with him, which was mingled with the voice of the war-horn that bade away.

So fell the whole host into due array, and they were somewhat over three thousand warriors, all good and tried men and meet to face the uttermost of battle in the open field; so they went their ways with all the speed that footmen may, and in fair order; and the sky cleared above their heads, but the distant thunder still growled about the world. Geirbald and Viglund joined themselves to the Wolfings and went a-foot along with Wolfkettle; but Hiarandi went with his kindred who were second in the array.

20. OTTER AND HIS FOLK COME INTO MID-MARK

Otter and his men reach the Mid-mark and see in the distance Roman fires. Notice how disciplined they are. Although furious at this attack on their homes, they take care not to exhaust themselves or their horses. As they ride, small number of hastily armed locals join them. When they reach the Roman army, one much larger than their own, both sides skirmish but delay the main battle to the next day. Notice that the motives of the two sides differ. While the Markmen fight for their people and homes, the Roman general wants fame, loot and slaves. He is unaware that the other Roman army has been defeated at the ridge, freeing Thiodolf to join the fighting in the Mid-mark.

Otter and his folk rode their ways along Mirkwood-water, and made no stay, except now and again to breathe their horses, till they came to Battleford in the early morning; there they baited their horses, for the grass was good in the meadow, and the water easy to come at.

So after they had rested there a short hour, and had eaten what was easy for them to get, they crossed the ford, and wended along Mirkwood-water between the wood and the river, but went slower than before lest they should weary their horses; so that it was high-noon before they had come out of the woodland way into Mid-mark; and at once as soon as the whole plain of the Mark opened out before them, they saw what most of them looked to see (since none doubted Hrosshild's tale), and that was a column of smoke rising high and straight up into the air, for the afternoon was hot and windless.

Great wrath rose in their hearts thereat, and many a strong man trembled for anger, though none for fear, as Otter raised his right hand and stretched it out towards that token of wrack and ruin; yet they made no stay, nor did they quicken their pace much; because they knew that they should come to Bearham before night-fall, and they would not meet the Romans way-worn and haggard; but they rode on steadily, a terrible company of wrathful men.

They passed by the dwellings of the kindreds, though save for the Galtings the houses on the east side of the water between the Bearings and the wild-wood road were but small; for the thicket came somewhat near to the water and pinched the meadows. But the Galtings were great hunters and trackers of the wild-wood, and they of the Geddings, the Erings and the Withings, which were smaller Houses, lived somewhat on the take of fish from Mirkwood-water (as did the Laxings also of the Nether-mark), for thereabout were there goodly pools and eddies, and sun-warmed shallows therewithal for the spawning of the trouts; as there were eyots in the water, most of which tailed off into a gravelly shallow at their lower ends.

Now as the riders of the Goths came over against the dwellings of the Withings, they saw people, mostly women, driving up the beasts from the meadow towards the garth; but upon the tofts about their dwellings were gathered many folk, who had their eyes turned toward the token of ravage that hung in the sky above the fair plain; but when these beheld the riding of the host, they tossed up their arms to them and whatever they bore in them, and the sound of their shrill cry (for they were all women and young lads) came down the wind to the ears of the riders.

But down by the river on a swell of the ground were some swains and a few thralls, and among them some men armed and a-horseback; and these, when they perceived the host coming on turned and rode to meet them; and as they drew near they shouted as men overjoyed to meet their kindred; and indeed the fighting-men of their own House were riding in the host. And the armed men were three old men, and one very old with marvelous long white hair, and four long lads of some fifteen winters, and four stout carles of the thralls bearing bows and bucklers, and these rode behind the swains; so they found their own kindred and rode amongst them.

But when they were all jingling and clashing on together, the dust arising from the sun-dried turf, the earth shaking with the thunder of the horse-hoofs, then the heart of the long-hoary one stirred within him as he bethought him of the days of his youth, and to his old nostrils came the smell of the horses and the savour of the sweat of warriors riding close together knee to knee adown the meadow. So he lifted up his voice and sang:

RIDETH lovely along
The strong by the strong;
Soft under his breath
Singeth sword in the sheath,
And shield babbleth oft
Unto helm-crest aloft;
How soon shall their words rise mid wrath of the battle
Into wrangle unheeded of clanging and rattle,
And no man shall note then the gold on the sword
When the runes have no meaning, the mouth-cry no word,
When all mingled together, the war-sea of men
Shall toss up the steel-spray round fourscore and ten.

Now AS MAIDS burn the weed
Betwixt acre and mead,
So the Bearings' Roof
Burneth little aloof,
And red gloweth the hall
Betwixt wall and fair wall,

Where often the mead-sea we sipped in old days,
When our feet were a-weary with wending the ways;
When the love of the lovely at even was born,
And our hands felt fair hands as they fell on the horn.
There round about standeth the ring of the foe
Tossing babes on their spears like the weeds o'er the low.

RIDE, RIDE THEN! nor spare
The red steeds as ye fare!
Yet if daylight shall fail,
By the fire-light of bale
Shall we see the bleared eyes
Of the war-learned, the wise.
In the acre of battle the work is to win,
Let us live by the labour, sheaf-smiting therein;
And as oft o'er the sickle we sang in time past
When the crake that long mocked us fled light at the last,
So sing o'er the sword, and the sword-hardened hand
Bearing down to the reaping the wrath of the land.

So he sang; and a great shout went up from his kindred and those around him, and it was taken up all along the host, though many knew not why they shouted, and the whole host quickened its pace, and went a great trot over the smooth meadow. So in no long while were they come over against the stead of the Erings, and thereabouts were no beasts a-field, and no women, for all the neat were driven into the garth of the House; but all they who were not war-fit were standing without doors looking down the Mark towards the reek of the Bearing dwellings, and these also sent a cry of welcome toward the host of their kindred. But along the river-bank came to meet the host an armed band of two old men, two youths who were their sons, and twelve thralls who were armed with long spears; and all these were a-horseback: so they fell in with their kindred and the host made no stay for them, but pressed on over-running the meadow. And still went up that column of smoke, and thicker and blacker it grew a-top, and ruddier amidmost.

So came they by the abode of the Geddings, and there also the neat and sheep were close in the home-garth: but armed men were lying or standing about the river bank, talking or singing merrily none otherwise than though deep peace were on the land; and when they saw the faring of the host they sprang to their feet with a shout and gat to their horses at once: they were more than the other bands had been, for the Geddings were a greater House; they were seven old men, and ten swains, and ten thralls bearing long spears like to those of the Erings; and no sooner had they fallen in with their kindred, than the men of the host espied a greater company yet coming to meet them: and these were of the folk of the Galtings; and amongst them were ten warriors in their prime, because they had but of late come back from the hunting in the wood and had been belated from the muster of the kindreds; and with them were eight old men and fifteen lads, and eighteen thralls; and the swains and thralls all bore bows besides the swords that they were girt withal, and not all of them had horses, but they who had none rode behind the others: so they joined themselves to the host, shouting aloud; and they had with them a great horn that they blew on till they had taken their place in the array; and whereas their kindred was with Thiodolf, they followed along with the hinder men of the Shieldings.

So now all the host went on together, and when they had passed the Galting abodes, there was nothing between them and Bearham, nor need they look for any further help of men; there were no beasts afield nor any to herd them, and the stay-at-homes were within doors dighting them for departure into the wild-wood if need should be: but a little while after they had passed these dwellings came into the host two swains of about twenty winters, and a doughty [brave and resolute] maid, their sister, and they bare no weapons save short spears and knives; they were wet and dripping with the water, for they had just swum Mirkwood-water. They were of the Wolfing House, and had been shepherding a few sheep on the west side of the water, when they saw the host faring to battle, and might not refrain them, but swam their horses across the swift deeps to join their kindred to live and die with them. The tale tells that they three fought in the battles that followed after, and were not slain there, though they entered them unarmed, but lived long years afterwards: of them need no more be said.

Now, when the host was but a little past the Galting dwellings men began to see the flames mingled with the smoke of the burning, and the smoke itself growing thinner, as though the fire had over-mastered everything and was consuming itself with its own violence; and somewhat afterwards, the ground rising, they could see the Bearing meadow and the foemen thereon: yet a little further, and from the height of another swelling of the earth they could see the burning houses themselves and the array of the Romans; so there they stayed and breathed their horses a while.

And they beheld how of the Romans a great company was gathered together in close array betwixt the ford and the Bearing Hall, but nigher unto the ford, and these were a short mile from them; but others they saw streaming out from the burning dwellings, as if their work were done there, and they could not see that they had any captives with them. Other Romans there were, and amongst them men in the attire of the Goths, busied about the river banks, as though they were going to try the ford.

But a little while abode Otter in that place, and then waved his arm and rode on and all the host followed; and as they drew nigher, Otter, who was wise in war, beheld the Romans and deemed them a great host, and the very kernel and main body of them many more than all his company; and moreover they were duly and well arrayed as men waiting a foe; so he knew that he must be wary or he would lose himself and all his men.

So he stayed his company when they were about two furlongs from them, and the main body of the foe stirred not, but horsemen and slingers came forth from its sides and made on toward the Goths, and in three or four minutes were within bowshot of them. Then the bowmen of the Goths slipped down from their horses and bent their bows and nocked their arrows and let fly, and slew and hurt many of the horsemen, who endured their shot but for a minute or two and then turned rein and rode back slowly to their folk, and the slingers came not on very eagerly whereas they were dealing with men a-horseback, and the bowmen of the Goths also held them still.

Now turned Otter to his folk and made them a sign, which they knew well, that they should get down from their horses; and when they were afoot the leaders of tens and hundreds arrayed them, into the wedge-array, with the bowmen on either flank: and Otter smiled as he beheld this adoing and that the Romans meddled not with them, belike because they looked to have them good cheap, since they were but a few wild men.

But when they were all arrayed he sat still on his horse and spake to them short and sharply, saying: "Men of the Goths, will ye mount your horses again and ride into the wood and let it cover you, or will ye fight these Romans?" They answered him with a great shout and the clashing of their weapons on their shields. "That is well," quoth Otter, "since we have come so far; for I perceive that the foe will come to meet us, so that we must either abide their shock or turn our backs. Yet must we fight wisely or we are undone, and Thiodolf in risk of undoing; this have we to do if we may, to thrust in between them and the ford, and if we may do that, there let us fight it out, till we fall one over another. But if we may not do it, then will we not throw our lives away but do the foemen what hurt we may without mingling ourselves amongst them, and so abide the coming of Thiodolf; for if we get not betwixt them and the ford we may in no case hinder them from crossing. And all this I tell you that ye may follow me wisely, and refrain your wrath that ye may live yet to give it the rein when the time comes."

So he spake and got down from his horse and drew his sword and went to the head of the wedge-array and began slowly to lead forth; but the thralls and swains had heed of the horses, and they drew aback with them towards the wood which was but a little way from them.

But for Otter he led his men down towards the ford, and when the Romans saw that, their main body began to move forward, faring slant-wise, as a crab, down toward the ford; then Otter hastened somewhat, as he well might, since his men were well learned in war and did not break their array; but now by this time were those burners of the Romans come up with the main battle, and the Roman captain sent them at once against the Goths, and they advanced boldly enough, a great cloud of men in loose array who fell to with arrows and slings on the wedge-array and slew and hurt many; yet did not Otter stay his folk; but it was ill going for them, for their unshielded sides were turned to the Romans, nor durst Otter scatter his bowmen out from the wedge-array, lest the Romans, who were more than they, should enter in amongst them.

A Brief Battle

Ever he gazed earnestly on the main battle of the Romans, and what they were doing, and presently it became clear to him that they would outgo him and come to the ford, and then he wotted well that they would set on him just when their light-armed were on his flank and his rearward, and then it would go hard but they would break their array and all would be lost: therefore he slacked his pace and went very slowly and the Romans went none the slower for that; but their light-armed grew bolder and drew more together as they came nigher to the Goths, as though they would give them an onset; but just at that nick of time Otter passed the word down the ranks, and, waving his sword, turned sharply to the right and fell with all the wedge-array on the clustering throng of the light-armed, and his bowmen spread out now from the right flank of the wedge-array, and shot sharp and swift and the bowmen on the left flank ran forward swiftly till they had cleared the wedge-array and were on the flank of the light-armed Romans; and they, what between the onset of the swordsmen and spearmen of the Goths, and their sharp arrows, knew not which way to turn, and a great slaughter befell amongst them, and they of them were the happiest who might save themselves by their feet.

Now after this storm, and after these men had been thrust away, Otter stayed not, but swept round about the field toward the horses; and indeed he looked to it that the main-battle of the Romans should follow him, but they did not, but stayed still to receive the fleers of their light-armed. And this indeed was the goodhap of the Goths; for they were somewhat disordered by their chase of the light-armed, and they smote and spared not, their hearts being full of bitter wrath, as might well be; for even as they turned on the Romans, they beheld the great roof of the Bearings fall in over the burned hall, and a great shower of sparks burst up from its fall, and there were the ragged gables left standing, licked by little tongues of flame which could not take hold of them because of the clay which filled the spaces between the great timbers and was daubed over them. And they saw that all the other houses were either alight or smouldering, down to the smallest cot of a thrall, and even the barns and booths both great and little.

The Roman Captain

Therefore, whereas the Markmen were far fewer in all than the Roman main-battle, and whereas this same host was in very good array, no doubt there was that the Markmen would have been grievously handled had the Romans fallen on; but the Roman Captain would not have it so: for though he was a bold man, yet was his boldness that of the wolf, that falleth on when he is hungry and skulketh when he is full. He was both young and very rich, and a mighty man among his townsmen, and well had he learned that ginger is hot in the mouth, and though he had come forth to the war for the increasing of his fame, he had no will to die among the Markmen, either for the sake of the city of Rome, or of any folk whatsoever, but was liefer [ready] to live for his own sake.

Therefore was he come out to vanquish easily, that by his fame won he might win more riches and dominion in Rome; and he was well content also to have for his own whatever was choice amongst the plunder of these wild-men (as he deemed them), if it were but a fair woman or two. So this man thought, It is my business to cross the ford and come to Wolfstead, and there take the treasure of the tribe, and have a stronghold there, whence we may slay so many of these beasts with little loss to us that we may march away easily and with our hands full, even if Maenius with his men come not to our aid, as full surely he will: therefore as to these angry men, who be not without might and conduct in battle, let us remember the old saw that saith 'a bridge of gold to a fleeing foe,' and let them depart with no more hurt of Romans, and seek us afterwards when we are fenced into their stead, which shall then be our stronghold: even so spake he to his Captains about him.

For it must be told that he had no tidings of the overthrow of the Romans on the Ridge; nor did he know surely how many fighting-men the Markmen might muster, except by the report of those dastards of the Goths; and though he had taken those two women in the wastes, yet had he got no word from them, for they did as the Hall-Sun bade them, when they knew that they would be questioned with torments, and smiting themselves each with a little sharp knife, so went their ways to the Gods.

Thus then the Roman Captain let the Markmen go their ways, and turned toward the ford, and the Markmen went slowly now toward their horses. Howbeit there were many of them who murmured against Otter, saying that it was ill done to have come so far and ridden so hard, and then to have done so little, and that were to-morrow come, they would not be led away so easily: but now they said it was ill; for the Romans would cross the water, and make their ways to Wolfstead, none hindering them, and would burn the dwellings and slay the old men and thralls, and have away the women and children and the Hall-Sun the treasure of the Markmen. In sooth, they knew not that a band of the Roman light-armed had already crossed the water, and had fallen upon the dwellings of the Wolfings; but that the old men and younglings and thralls of the House had come upon them as they were entangled amidst the tofts and the garths, and had overcome them and slain many.

Watching through the Night

Thus went Otter and his men to their horses when it was now drawing toward sunset (for all this was some while adoing), and betook them to a rising ground not far from the wood-side, and there made what sort of a garth they might, with their horses and the limbs of trees and long-shafted spears; and they set a watch and abode in the garth right warily, and lighted no fires when night fell, but ate what meat they had with them, which was but little, and so sleeping and watching abode the morning. But the main body of the Romans did not cross the ford that night, for they feared lest they might go astray therein, for it was an ill ford to those that knew not the water: so they abode on the bank nigh to the water's edge, with the mind to cross as soon as it was fairly daylight.

Now Otter had lost of his men some hundred and twenty slain or grievously hurt, and they had away with them the hurt men and the bodies of the slain. The tale tells not how many of the Romans were slain, but a many of their light-armed had fallen, since the Markmen had turned so hastily upon them, and they had with them many of the best bowmen of the Mark.

21. They Bicker about the Ford

Ali, a messenger from Hall-Sun arrives and Otter tells him he hopes to delay the battle until Thiodolf arrives. The two, he hopes, will be strong enough to stop the Romans at the ford. Otter sends word to her that he will distract the Romans with feigned attacks long enough for those in the House of the Wolfings to flee into the woods. In turn, Ali warns Otter that the Romans appear to be planning to cross the ford early that day. Notice that the Romans are being aided by "dastards" [traitors] from among the Goths. When the Romans prepare to fight, Otter withdraws, refusing to be drawn into a trap. Harried by the attacks and afraid the House of the Wolfings is strongly defended, the Roman captain crosses the ford but moves slowly and carefully.

In the grey of the morning was Otter afoot with the watchers, and presently he got on his horse and peered over the plain, but the mist yet hung low on it, so that he might see nought for a while; but at last he seemed to note something coming toward the host from the upper water above the ford, so he rode forward to meet it, and lo, it was a lad of fifteen winters, naked save his breeches, and wet from the river; and Otter drew rein, and the lad said to him: "Art thou the War-duke?" "Yea," said Otter.

Said the lad, "I am Ali, the son of Grey, and the Hall-Sun hath sent me to thee with this word: 'Are ye coming? Is Thiodolf at hand? For I have seen the Roof-ridge red in the sunlight as if it were painted with cinnabar.'"

Said Otter, "Art thou going back to Wolfstead, son?"

"Yea, at once, my father," said Ali.

"Then tell her," said Otter, "that Thiodolf is at hand, and when he cometh we shall both together fall upon the Romans either in crossing the ford or in the Wolfing meadow; but tell her also that I am not strong enough to hinder the Romans from crossing."

"Father," said Ali, "the Hall-Sun saith: Thou art wise in war; now tell us, shall we hold the Hall against the Romans that ye may find us there? For we have discomfited their vanguard already, and we have folk who can fight; but belike the main battle of the Romans shall get the upper hand of us ere ye come to our helping: belike it were better to leave the hall, and let the wood cover us."

Hall-Sun to Flee into the Wood

"Now is this well asked," said Otter; "get thee back, my son, and bid the Hall-Sun trust not to warding of the Hall, for the Romans are a mighty host: and this day, even when Thiodolf cometh hither, shall be hard for the Gothfolk: let her hasten lest these thieves come upon her hastily; let her take the Hall-Sun her namesake, and the old men and children and the women, and let those fighting folk she hath be a guard to all this in the wood. And hearken moreover; it will, maybe, be six hours ere Thiodolf cometh; tell her I will cast the dice for life or death, and stir up these Romans now at once, that they may have other things to think of than burning old men and women and children in their dwellings; thus may she reach the wood unhindered. Hast thou all this in thine head? Then go thy ways."

But the lad lingered, and he reddened and looked on the ground and then he said: "My father, I swam the deeps, and when I reached this bank, I crept along by the mist and the reeds toward where the Romans are, and I came near to them, and noted what they were doing; and I tell thee that they are already stirring to take the water at the ford. Now then do what thou wilt." Therewith he turned about, and went his way at once, running like a colt which has never felt halter or bit.

But Otter rode back hastily and roused certain men in whom he trusted, and bid them rouse the captains and all the host and bid men get to horse speedily and with as little noise as might be. So did they, and there was little delay, for men were sleeping with one eye open, as folk say, and many were already astir. So in a little while they were all in the saddle, and the mist yet stretched low over the meadow; for the morning was cool and without wind. Then Otter bade the word be carried down the ranks that they should ride as quietly as may be and fare through the mist to do the Romans some hurt, but in nowise to get entangled in their ranks, and all men to heed well the signal of turning and drawing aback; and therewith they rode off down the meadow led by men who could have led them through the dark night.

But for the Romans, they were indeed getting ready to cross the ford when the mist should have risen; and on the bank it was thinning already and melting away; for a little air of wind was beginning to breathe from the north-east and the sunrise, which was just at hand; and the bank, moreover, was stonier and higher than the meadow's face, which fell away from it as a shallow dish from its rim: thereon yet lay the mist like a white wall.

So the Romans and their friends the dastards of the Goths had well nigh got all ready, and had driven stakes into the water from bank to bank to mark out the safe ford, and some of their light-armed and most of their Goths were by now in the water or up on the Wolfing meadow with the more part of their baggage and wains; and the rest of the host was drawn up in good order, band by band, waiting the word to take the water, and the captain was standing nigh to the river bank beside their God the chief banner of the Host.

Otter's Sudden Attack

Of a sudden one of the dastards of the Goths who was close to the Captain cried out that he heard horse coming; but because he spake in the Gothic tongue, few heeded; but even therewith an old leader of a hundred cried out the same tidings in the Roman tongue, and all men fell to handling their weapons; but before they could face duly toward the meadow, came rushing from out of the mist a storm of shafts that smote many men, and therewithal burst forth the sound of the Markmen's war-horn, like the roaring of a hundred bulls mingled with the thunder of horses at the gallop; and then dark over the wall of mist showed the crests of the riders of the Mark, though scarce were their horses seen till their whole war-rank came dark and glittering into the space of the rising-ground where the mist was but a haze now, and now at last smitten athwart by the low sun just arisen.

Therewith came another storm of shafts, wherein javelins and spears cast by the hand were mingled with the arrows: but the Roman ranks had faced the meadow and the storm which it yielded, swiftly and steadily, and they stood fast and threw their spears, albeit not with such good aim as might have been, because of their haste, so that few were slain by them.

And the Roman Captain still loth [unwilling] to fight with the Goths in earnest for no reward, and still more and more believing that this was the only band of them that he had to look to, bade those who were nighest the ford not to tarry for the onset of a few wild riders, but to go their ways into the water; else by a sudden onrush might the Romans have entangled Otter's band in their ranks, and so destroyed all. As it was the horsemen fell not on the Roman ranks full in face, but passing like a storm athwart the ranks to the right, fell on there where they were in thinnest array (for they were gathered to the ford as aforesaid), and slew some and drave some into the deeps and troubled the whole Roman host.

So now the Roman Captain was forced to take new order, and gather all his men together, and array his men for a hard fight; and by now the mist was rolling off from the face of the whole meadow and the sun was bright and hot. His men serried their ranks, and the front rank cast their spears, and slew both men and horses of the Goths as those rode along their front casting their javelins, and shooting here and there from behind their horses if occasion served, or making a shift to send an arrow even as they sat a-horseback; then the second rank of the Romans would take the place of the first, and cast in their turn, and they who had taken the water turned back and took their place behind the others, and many of the light-armed came with them, and all the mass of them flowed forward together, looking as if it might never be broken. But Otter would not abide the shock, since he had lost men and horses, and had no mind to be caught in the sweep of their net; so he made the sign, and his Company drew off to right and left, yet keeping within bow-shot, so that the bowmen still loosed at the Romans.

But they for their part might not follow afoot men on untired horses, and their own horse was on the west side with the baggage, and had it been there would have been but of little avail, as the Roman Captain knew. So they stood awhile making grim countenance, and then slowly drew back to the ford under cover of their light-armed who shot at the Goths as they rode forward, but abode not their shock.

But Otter and his folk followed after the Romans again, and again did them some hurt, and at last drew so nigh, that once more the Romans stormed forth, and once more smote a stroke in the air; nor even so would the Markmen cease to meddle with them, though never would Otter suffer his men to be mingled with them. At the last the Romans, seeing that Otter would not walk into the open trap, and growing weary of this bickering, began to take the water little by little, while a strong Company kept face to the Markmen; and now Otter saw that they would not be hindered any longer, and he had lost many men, and even now feared lest he should be caught in the trap, and so lose all.

And on the other hand it was high noon by now, so that he had given respite to the stay-at-homes of the Wolfings, so that they might get them into the wood. So he drew out of bowshot and bade his men breathe their horses and rest themselves and eat something; and they did so gladly, since they saw that they might not fall upon the Romans to live and die for it until Thiodolf was come, or until they knew that he was not coming.

But the Romans crossed the ford in good earnest and were soon all gathered together on the western bank making them ready for the march to Wolfstead. And it must be told that the Roman Captain was the more deliberate about this because after the overthrow of his light-armed there the morning before, he thought that the Roof was held by warriors of the kindreds, and not by a few old men, and women, and lads. Therefore he had no fear of their escaping him. Moreover it was this imagination of his, to wit that a strong band of warriors was holding Wolf-stead, that made him deem there were no more worth thinking about of the warriors of the Mark save Otter's Company and the men in the Hall of the Wolfings.

22. OTTER FALLS ON AGAINST HIS WILL

After the Romans cross the ford, their captain leaves it unguarded, allowing Otter and his men to cross unopposed. Thus far the Romans have killed few and not taken many captives. Otter is criticized for not going into battle, but says that attacking before reinforcements arrived would waste lives. The riders of the Bearings and the Wormings, however, choose to attack before Thiodolf and his men arrive, and to prevent their defeat, Otter also attacks. The two armies ride together, filled with the 'joy of battle.'

It was with the same imagination working in him belike that the Roman Captain set none to guard the ford on the westward side of Mirkwood-water. The Romans tarried there but a little hour, and then went their ways; but Otter sent a man on a swift horse to watch them, and when they were clean gone for half an hour, he bade his folk to horse, and they departed, all save a handful of the swains and elders, who were left to tell the tidings to Thiodolf when he should come into Mid-mark.

So Otter and his folk crossed the ford, and drew up in good order on the westward bank, and it was then somewhat more than three hours after noon. He had been there but a little while before he noted a stir in the Bearing meadow, and lo, it was the first of Thiodolf's folk, who had gotten out of the wood and had fallen in with the men whom he had left behind. And these first were the riders of the Bearings, and the Wormings, (for they had out-gone the others who were afoot). It may well be thought how fearful was their anger when they set eyes on the smouldering ashes of the dwellings; nor even when those folk of Otter had told them all they had to tell could some of them refrain them from riding off to the burnt houses to seek for the bodies of their kindred. But when they came there, and amidst the ashes could find no bones, their hearts were lightened, and yet so mad wroth they were, that some could scarce sit their horses, and great tears gushed from the eyes of some, and pattered down like hail-stones, so eager were they to see the blood of the Romans.

So they rode back to where they had left their folk talking with them of Otter; and the Bearings were sitting grim upon their horses and somewhat scowling on Otter's men. Then the foremost of those who had come back from the houses waved his hand toward the ford, but could say nought for a while; but the captain and chief of the Bearings, a grizzled man very big of body, whose name was Arinbiorn, spake to that man and said; "What aileth thee Sweinbiorn the Black? What hast thou seen?"
He said:

Now red and grey is the pavement of the Bearings' house of old:
Red yet is the floor of the dais, but the hearth all grey and cold.
I knew not the house of my fathers; I could not call to mind
The fashion of the building of that Warder of the Wind.
O wide were grown the windows, and the roof exceeding high!
For nought there was to look on 'twixt the pavement and the sky.
But the tie-beam lay on the dais, and methought its staining fair;
For rings of smoothest charcoal were round it here and there,
And the red flame flickered o'er it, and never a staining wight
Hath red earth in his coffer so clear and glittering bright,
And still the little smoke-wreaths curled o'er it pale and blue
Yea, fair is our hall's adorning for a feast that is strange and new.

Said Arinbiorn: "What sawest thou therein, O Sweinbiorn, where sat thy grandsire at the feast? Where were the bones of thy mother lying?"
Said Sweinbiorn:

We sought the feast-hall over, and nought we found therein
Of the bones of the ancient mothers, or the younglings of the kin.
The men are greedy, doubtless, to lose no whit of the prey,
And will try if the hoary elders may yet outlive the way
That leads to the southland cities, till at last they come to stand
With the younglings in the market to be sold in an alien land.

Arinbiorn's brow lightened somewhat; but ere he could speak again an ancient thrall of the Galtings spake and said: "True it is, O warriors of the Bearings, that we might not see any war-thralls being led away by the Romans when they came away from the burning dwellings; and we deem it certain that they crossed the water before the coming of the Romans, and that they are now with the stay-at-homes of the Wolfings in the wild-wood behind the Wolfing dwellings, for we hear tell that the War-duke would not that the Hall-Sun should hold the Hall against the whole Roman host."

Then Sweinbiorn tossed up his sword into the air and caught it by the hilts as it fell, and cried out: "On, on to the meadow, where these thieves abide us!" Arinbiorn spake no word, but turned his horse and rode down to the ford, and all men followed him;

and of the Bearings there were an hundred warriors save one, and of the Wormings eighty and seven.

So rode they over the meadow and into the ford and over it, and Otter's company stood on the bank to meet them, and shouted to see them; but the others made but little noise as they crossed the water. So when they were on the western bank Arinbiorn came among them of Otter, and cried out: "Where then is Otter, where is the War-duke, is he alive or dead?"

And the throng opened to him and Otter stood facing him; and Arinbiorn spake and said: "Thou art alive and unhurt, War-duke, when many have been hurt and slain; and methinks thy company is little minished though the kindred of the Bearings lacketh a roof; and its elders and women and children are gone into captivity. What is this? Was it a light thing that gangrel thieves should burn and waste in Mid-mark and depart unhurt, that ye stand here with clean blades and cold bodies?"

Said Otter: "Thou grievest for the hurt of thine House, Arinbiorn; but this at least is good, that though ye have lost the timber of your house ye have not lost its flesh and blood; the shell is gone, but the kernel is saved: for thy folk are by this time in the wood with the Wolfing stay-at-homes, and among these are many who may fight on occasion, so they are safe as for this time: the Romans may not come at them to hurt them."

Arinbiorn Argues with Otter

Said Arinbiorn: "Had ye time to learn all this, Otter, when ye fled so fast before the Romans, that the father tarried not for the son, nor the son for the father?"

He spoke in a loud voice so that many heard him, and some deemed it evil; for anger and dissension between friends seemed abroad; but some were so eager for battle, that the word of Arinbiorn seemed good to them, and they laughed for pride and anger.

Then Otter answered meekly, for he was a wise man and a bold: "We fled not, Arinbiorn, but as the sword fleeth, when it springeth up from the iron helm to fall on the woollen coat. Are we not now of more avail to you, O men of the Bearings, than our dead corpses would have been?"

Arinbiorn answered not, but his face waxed red, as if he were struggling with a weight hard to lift: then said Otter: "But when will Thiodolf and the main battle be with us?"

Arinbiorn answered calmly: "Maybe in a little hour from now, or somewhat more."

Said Otter: "My rede is that we abide him here, and when we are all met and well ordered together, fall on the Romans at once: for then shall we be more than they; whereas now we are far fewer, and moreover we shall have to set on them in their ground of vantage."

Arinbiorn answered nothing; but an old man of the Bearings, one Thorbiorn, came up and spake: "Warriors, here are we talking and taking counsel, though this is no Hallowed Thing to bid us what we shall do, and what we shall forbear; and to talk thus is less like warriors than old women wrangling over the why and wherefore of a broken crock. Let the War-duke rule here, as is but meet and right. Yet if I might speak and not break the peace of the Goths, then would I say this, that it might be better for us to fall on these Romans at once before they have cast up a dike about them, as Fox telleth is their wont, and that even in an hour they may do much."

As he spake there was a murmur of assent about him, but Otter spake sharply, for he was grieved. "Thorbiorn, thou art old, and shouldest not be void of prudence. Now it had been better for thee to have been in the wood to-day to order the women and the swains according to thine ancient wisdom than to egg on my young warriors to fare unwarily. Here will I abide Thiodolf."

Then Thorbiorn reddened and was wroth; but Arinbiorn spake: "What is this to-do? Let the War-duke rule as is but right: but I am now become a man of Thiodolf's company; and he bade me haste on before to help all I might. Do thou as thou wilt, Otter: for Thiodolf shall be here in an hour's space, and if much diking shall be done in an hour, yet little slaying, forsooth, shall be done, and that especially if the foe is all armed and slayeth women and children. Yea if the Bearing women be all slain, yet shall not Tyr make us new ones out of the stones of the waste to wed with the Galtings and the fish-eating Houses?—this is easy to be done forsooth. Yea, easier than fighting the Romans and overcoming them!"

And he was very wrath, and turned away; and again there was a murmur and a hum about him. But while these had been speaking aloud, Sweinbiorn had been talking softly to some of the younger men, and now he shook his naked sword in the air and spake aloud and sang:

> YE TARRY, BEARS OF BATTLE! YE LINGER, SONS OF THE WORM!
> Ye crouch adown, O kindreds, from the gathering of the storm!
> Ye say, it shall soon pass over and we shall fare afield
> And reap the wheat with the war-sword and winnow in the shield.
> But where shall be the corner wherein ye then shall abide,
> And where shall be the woodland where the whelps of the bears shall hide
> When 'twixt the snowy mountains and the edges of the sea
> These men have swept the wild-wood and the fields where men may be
> Of every living sword-blade, and every quivering spear,
> And in the southland cities the yoke of slaves ye bear?
> Lo ye! whoever follows I fare to sow the seed
> Of the days to be hereafter and the deed that comes of deed.

Arinbiorn Goes into Battle

Therewith he waved his sword over his head, and made as if he would spur onward. But Arinbiorn thrust through the press and outwent him and cried out: "None goeth before Arinbiorn the Old when the battle is pitched in the meadows of the kindred. Come, ye sons of the Bear, ye children of the Worm! And come ye, whosoever hath a will to see stout men die!"

Then on he rode nor looked behind him, and the riders of the Bearings and the Wormings drew themselves out of the throng, and followed him, and rode clattering over the meadow towards Wolfstead. A few of the others rode with them, and yet but a few. For they remembered the holy Folk-mote and the oath of the War-duke, and how they had chosen Otter to be their leader. Howbeit, man looked askance at man, as if in shame to be left behind.

But Otter bethought him in the flash of a moment, "If these men ride alone, they shall die and do nothing; and if we ride with them it may be that we shall overthrow the Romans, and if we be vanquished, it shall go hard but we shall slay many of them, so that it shall be the easier for Thiodolf to deal with them."

Then he spake hastily, and bade certain men abide at the ford for a guard; then he drew his sword and rode to the front of his folk, and cried out aloud to them: "Now at last has come the time to die, and let them of the Markmen who live hereafter lay us in howe. Set on, Sons of Tyr, and give not your lives away, but let them be dearly earned of our foemen."

Then all shouted loudly and gladly; nor were they otherwise than exceeding glad; for now had they forgotten all other joys of life save the joy of fighting for the kindred and the days to be.

So Otter led them forth, and when he heard the whole company clattering and thundering on the earth behind him and felt their might enter into him, his brow cleared, and the anxious lines in the face of the old man smoothed themselves out, and as he rode along the soul so stirred within him that he sang out aloud:

TIME WAS WHEN HOT WAS THE SUMMER AND I WAS YOUNG ON THE EARTH,
And I grudged me every moment that lacked its share of mirth.
I woke in the morn and was merry and all the world methought
For me and my heart's deliverance that hour was newly wrought.
I have passed through the halls of manhood, I have reached the doors of eld,
And I have been glad and sorry, but ever have upheld
My heart against all trouble that none might call me sad,
But ne'er came such remembrance of how my heart was glad
In the afternoon of summer 'neath the still unwearied sun
Of the days when I was little and all deeds were hopes to be won,
As now at last it cometh when e'en in such-like tide,
For the freeing of my trouble o'er the fathers' field I ride.

Many men perceived that he sang, and saw that he was merry, howbeit few heard his very words, and yet all were glad of him.

Fast they rode, being wishful to catch up with the Bearings and the Wormings, and soon they came anigh them, and they, hearing the thunder of the horse-hoofs, looked and saw that it was the company of Otter, and so slacked their speed till they were all joined together with joyous shouting and laughter. So then they ordered the ranks anew and so set forward in great joy without haste or turmoil toward Wolfstead and the Romans. For now the bitterness of their fury and the sourness of their abiding wrath were turned into the mere joy of battle; even as the clear red and sweet wine comes of the ugly ferment and rough trouble of the must.

23. Thiodolf Meeteth the Romans in the Wolfing Meadow

In about an hour, Thiodolf and his men approach the ford, meeting some of Otter's men, who tell them that the battle with the Romans is going badly and Otter's men are falling back. Thiodolf leads his men toward the fighting. As he goes into battle, he is clad in the Hauberk without a shield or helmet. As they approach, they find Otter and his men surrounded by Romans. Thiodolf's men attack in a wedge formation. Half the Romans turn to face them. Half continue to battle Otter's men. Then as Thiodolf waves his sword, he falls to the ground unconscious. Thiodolf's men lay him under an old oak tree, where Thiodolf dreams of his childhood. Then Thiodolf awakes and sees that he is in the middle of a battle. To look for wounds, his men had removed the Hauberk. Thiodolf rushes into battle, an old man chasing after him with the Hauberk.

It was scarce an hour after this that the footmen of Thiodolf came out of the thicket road on to the meadow of the Bearings; there saw they men gathered on a rising ground, and they came up to them and saw how some of them were looking with troubled faces towards the ford and what lay beyond it, and some toward the wood and the coming of Thiodolf. But these were they whom Otter had bidden abide Thiodolf there, and he had sent two messengers to them for Thiodolf's behoof that he might have due tidings so soon as he came out of the thicket: the first told how Otter had been compelled in a manner to fall on the Romans along with the riders of the Bearings and the Wormings, and the second who had but just then come, told how the Markmen had been worsted by the Romans, and had given back from the Wolfing dwellings, and were making a stand against the foemen in the meadow betwixt the ford and Wolfstead.

Now when Thiodolf heard of these tidings he stayed not to ask long questions, but led the whole host straightway down to the ford, lest the remnant of Otter's men should be driven down there, and the Romans should hold the western bank against him.

At the ford there was none to withstand them, nor indeed any man at all; for the men whom Otter had set there, when they heard that the battle had gone against their kindred, had ridden their ways to join them. **So Thiodolf crossed over the ford, he and his in good order all afoot, he like to the others; but for him he was clad in the dwarf-wrought Hauberk, but was unhelmeted and bare no shield.** Throng-plough was naked in his hand as he came up all dripping on to the bank and stood in the meadow of the Wolfings; his face was stern and set as he gazed straight onward to the place of the fray, but he did not look as joyous as his wont was in going down to the battle.

Now they had gone but a short way from the ford before the noise of the fight and the blowing of horns came down the wind to them, but it was a little way further before they saw the fray with their eyes; because the ground fell away from the river somewhat at first, and then rose and fell again before it went up in one slope toward the Wolfing dwellings. But when they were come to the top of the next swelling of the ground, they beheld from thence what they had to deal with; for there round about a ground of vantage was the field black with the Roman host, and in the midst of it was a tangle of struggling men and tossing spears, and glittering swords.

Thiodolf into Battle

So when they beheld the battle of their kindred they gave a great shout and hastened onward the faster; and they were ordered into the wedge-array and Thiodolf led them, as meet it was. And now even as they who were on the outward edge of the array and could see what was toward were looking on the battle with eager eyes, there came an answering shout down the wind, which they knew for the voice of the Goths amid the foemen, and then they saw how the ring of the Romans shook and parted, and their array fell back, and lo the company of the Markmen standing stoutly together, though sorely [de]minished; and sure it was that they had not fled or been scattered, but were ready to fall one over another in one band, for there were no men straggling towards the ford, though many masterless horses ran here and there about the meadow. Now, therefore, none doubted but that they would deliver their friends from the Romans, and overthrow the foemen.

But now befell a wonder, a strange thing to tell of. The Romans soon perceived what was adoing, whereupon the half of them turned about to face the new comers, while the other half still withstood the company of Otter: the wedge-array of Thiodolf drew nearer and nearer till it was hard on the place where it should spread itself out to storm down on the foe, and the Goths beset by the Romans made them ready to fall on from their side. **There was Thiodolf leading his host, and all men looking for the token and sign to fall on; but even as he lifted up Throng-plough to give that sign, a cloud came over his eyes and he saw nought of all that was before him, and he staggered back as one who hath gotten a deadly stroke, and so fell swooning to the earth, though none had smitten him.**

Then stayed was the wedge-array even at the very point of onset, and the hearts of the Goths sank, for they deemed that their leader was slain, and those who were nearest to him raised him up and bore him hastily aback out of the battle; and the Romans also had beheld him fall, and they also deemed him dead or sore hurt, and shouted for joy and loitered not, but stormed forth on the wedge-array like valiant men; for it must be told that they, who erst out-numbered the company of Otter, were now much out-numbered, but they deemed it might well be that they could dismay the Goths since they had been stayed by the fall of their leader; and Otter's company were wearied with sore fighting against a great host.

Nevertheless these last, who had not seen the fall of Thiodolf (for the Romans were thick between him and them) fell on with such exceeding fury that they drove the

Romans who faced them back on those who had set on the wedge-array, which also stood fast undismayed; for he who stood next to Thiodolf, a man big of body, and stout of heart, hight [named] Thorolf, hove up a great axe and cried out aloud: "Here is the next man to Thiodolf! Here is one who will not fall till some one thrusts him over, here is Thorolf of the Wolfings! Stand fast and shield you, and smite, though Thiodolf be gone untimely to the Gods!"

So none gave back a foot, and fierce was the fight about the wedge-array; and the men of Otter—but there was no Otter there, and many another man was gone, and Arinbiorn the Old led them—these stormed on so fiercely that they cleft their way through all and joined themselves to their kindred, and the battle was renewed in the Wolfing meadow. But the Romans had this gain, that Thiodolf's men had let go their occasion for falling on the Romans with their line spread out so that every man might use his weapons; yet were the Goths strong both in valiancy and in numbers, nor might the Romans break into their array, and as aforesaid the Romans were the fewer, for it was less than half of their host that had pursued the Goths when they had been thrust back from their fierce onset: nor did more than the half seem needed, so many of them had fallen along with Otter the War-duke and Sweinbiorn of the Bearings, that they seemed to the Romans but a feeble band easy to overcome.

Thiodolf Dreams

So fought they in the Wolfing meadow in the fifth hour after high-noon, and neither yielded to the other: but while these things were a-doing, men laid Thiodolf adown aloof from the battle under a doddered [ancient and feeble] oak half a furlong from where the fight was a-doing, round whose bole clung flocks of wool from the sheep that drew around it in the hot summer-tide and rubbed themselves against it, and the ground was trodden bare of grass round the bole, and close to the trunk was worn into a kind of trench. **There then they laid Thiodolf, and they wondered that no blood came from him, and that there was no sign of a shot-weapon in his body.**

But as for him, when he fell, all memory of the battle and what had gone before it faded from his mind, and he passed into sweet and pleasant dreams wherein he was a lad again in the days before he had fought with the three Hun-Kings in the hazelled field. And in these dreams he was doing after the manner of young lads, sporting in the meadows, backing unbroken colts, swimming in the river, going a-hunting with the elder carles.

And especially he deemed that he was in the company of one old man who had taught him both wood-craft and the handling of weapons: and fair at first was his dream of his doings with this man; he was with him in the forge smithying a sword-blade, and hammering into its steel the thin golden wires; and fishing with an angle along with him by the eddies of Mirkwood-water; and sitting with him in an ingle of the Hall, the old man telling a tale of an ancient warrior of the Wolfings hight Thiodolf also; then suddenly and without going there, they were in a little clearing of the woods resting after hunting, a roe-deer with an arrow in her lying at their feet, and the old man was talking, and telling Thiodolf in what wise it was best to go about to get the wind of a hart; but all the while there was going on the thunder of a great gale of wind through the woodland boughs, even as the drone of a bag-pipe cleaves to the tune.

Presently Thiodolf arose and would go about his hunting again, and stooped to take up his spear, and even therewith the old man's speech stayed, and Thiodolf looked up, and lo, his face was white like stone, and he touched him, and he was hard as flint, and like the image of an ancient god as to his face and hands, though the wind stirred his hair and his raiment, as they did before.

Therewith a great pang smote Thiodolf in his dream, and he felt as if he also were stiffening into stone, and he strove and struggled, and lo, the wild-wood was gone, and a white light empty of all vision was before him, and as he moved his head this became the Wolfing meadow, as he had known it so long, and thereat a soft pleasure and joy took hold of him, till again he looked, and saw there no longer the kine and sheep, and the herd-women tending them, but the rush and turmoil of that fierce battle, the confused thundering noise of which was going up to the heavens; for indeed he was now fully awake again.

So he stood up and looked about; and around him was a ring of the sorrowful faces of the warriors, who had deemed that he was hurt deadly, though no hurt could they find upon him. **But the dwarf-wrought Hauberk lay upon the ground beside him; for they had taken it off him to look for his hurts.** So he looked into their faces and said: "What aileth you, ye men? I am alive and unhurt; what hath betided?"

And one said: "Art thou verily alive, or a man come back from the dead? We saw thee fall as thou wentest leading us against the foe as if thou hadst been smitten by a thunder-bolt, and we deemed thee dead or grievously hurt. Now the carles are fighting stoutly, and all is well since thou livest yet."

So he said: "Give me the point and edges that I know, that I may smite myself therewith and not the foemen; for I have feared and blenched [drawn back] from the battle."

Said an old warrior: "If that be so, Thiodolf, wilt thou blench [flinch] twice? Is not once enough? Now let us go back to the hard handplay, and if thou wilt, smite thyself after the battle, when we have once more had a man's help of thee."

Therewith he held out Throng-plough to him by the point, and Thiodolf took hold of the hilts and handled it and said: "Let us hasten, while the Gods will have it so, and while they are still suffering me to strike a stroke for the kindred." And therewith he brandished Throng-plough, and went forth toward the battle, and the heart grew hot within him, and the joy of waking life came back to him, the joy which but erewhile he had given to a mere dream.

But the old man who had rebuked him stooped down and lifted the Hauberk from the ground, and cried out after him, "O Thiodolf, and wilt thou go naked into so strong a fight? and thou with this so goodly sword-rampart?"

Thiodolf stayed a moment, and even therewith they looked, and lo! The Romans giving back before the Goths and the Goths following up the chase, but slowly and steadily. Then Thiodolf heeded nothing save the battle, but ran forward hastily, and those warriors followed him, the old man [Jorund of the Wolfings] last of all holding the Hauberk in his hand, and muttering:

So fares hot blood to the glooming and the world beneath the grass;
And the fruit of the Wolfings' orchard in a flash from the world must pass.
Men say that the tree shall blossom in the garden of the folk,
And the new twig thrust him forward from the place where the old one broke,
And all be well as aforetime: but old and old I grow,
And I doubt me if such another the folk to come shall know.

And he still hurried forward as fast as his old body might go, so that he might wrap the safeguard of the Hauberk round Thiodolf's body.

24. The Goths Are Overthrown by the Romans

Distracted by the battle, Thiodolf puts the Hauberk back on. Soon his mind is in a fog and his men hang back, waiting for him to lead. Then Roman soldiers from the earlier battle on the ridge begin to arrive and drive the Markmen (Goths) back. Thiodolf revives and joins the battle, and then blacks out again. Led by Arinbiorn of the Bearings, the Markmen withdraw to a small hill near the ford. If the Roman general had attacked then, the battle would have been over, but he is cautious and withdraws.

Now rose up a mighty shout when Thiodolf came back to the battle of the kindreds, for many thought he had been slain; and they gathered round about him, and cried out to him joyously out of their hearts of good-fellowship, and the old man who had rebuked Thiodolf, and who was **Jorund of the Wolfings, came up to him and reached out to him the Hauberk, and he did it on scarce heeding**; for all his heart and soul was turned toward the battle of the Romans and what they were a-doing; and he saw that they were falling back in good order, as men out-numbered, but undismayed.

So he gathered all his men together and ordered them afresh; for they were somewhat disarrayed with the fray and the chase: and now he no longer ordered them in the wedge array, but in a line here three deep, here five deep, or more, for the foes were hard at hand, and outnumbered, and so far overcome, that he and all men deemed it a little matter to give these their last overthrow, and then onward to Wolf-stead to storm on what was left there and purge the house of the foemen.

Howbeit Thiodolf bethought him that succour might come to the Romans from their main-battle, as they needed not many men there, since there was nought to fear behind them: **but the thought was dim within him, for once more since he had gotten the Hauberk on him the earth was wavering and dream-like: he looked about him, and nowise was he as in past days of battle when he saw nought but the foe before him, and hoped for nothing save the victory.**

But now indeed the Wood-Sun seemed to him to be beside him, and not against his will, as one besetting and hindering him, but as though his own longing had drawn her thither and would not let her depart; and whiles it seemed to him that her beauty was clearer to be seen than the bodies of the warriors round about him. For the rest he seemed to be in a dream indeed, and, as men do in dreams, to be for ever striving to be doing something of more moment than anything which he did, but which he must ever leave undone.

And as the dream gathered and thickened about him the foe before him changed to his eyes, and seemed no longer the stern brown-skinned smooth-faced men under their crested iron helms with their iron-covered shields before them, but rather, big-headed men, small of stature, long-bearded, swart, crooked of body, exceeding foul of aspect. And he looked on and did nothing for a while, and his head whirled as though he had been grievously smitten.

Thus tarried the kindreds awhile, and they were bewildered and their hearts fell because Thiodolf did not fly on the foemen like a falcon on the quarry, as his wont was. But as for the Romans, they had now stayed, and were facing their foes again, and that on a vantage-ground, since the field sloped up toward the Wolfing dwelling; and they gathered heart when they saw that the Goths tarried and forbore them. But the sun was sinking, and the evening was hard at hand.

So at last Thiodolf led forward with Throng-plough held aloft in his right hand; but his left hand he held out by his side, as though he were leading someone along. And as he went, he muttered: "When will these accursed sons of the nether earth leave the way clear to us, that we may be alone and take pleasure each in each amidst of the flowers and the sun?"

Now as the two hosts drew near to one another, again came the sound of trumpets afar off, and men knew that this would be succour coming to the Romans from their main-battle, and the Romans thereon shouted for joy, and the host of the kindreds might no longer forbear, but rushed on fiercely against them; and for Thiodolf it was now come to this, that so entangled was he in his dream that he rather went with his men than led them. Yet had he Throng-plough in his right hand, and he muttered in his beard as he went, "Smite before! Smite behind! And smite on the right hand! But never on the left!"

Thus then they met, and as before, neither might the Goths sweep the Romans away, nor the Romans break the Goths into flight; yet were many of the kindred anxious and troubled, since they knew that aid was coming to the Romans, and they heard the trumpets sounding nearer and more joyous; and at last, as the men of the kindreds were growing a-wearied with fighting, they heard those horns as it were in their very ears, and the thunder of the tramp of footmen, and they knew that a fresh host of men was upon them; then those they had been fighting with opened before them, falling aside to the right and the left, and the fresh men passing between them, fell on the Goths like the waters of a river when a sluice-gate is opened. They came on in very good order, never breaking their ranks, but swift withal, smiting and pushing before them, and so brake through the array of the Goth-folk, and drave them this way and that way down the slopes.

Yet still fought the warriors of the kindred most valiantly, making stand and facing the foe again and again in knots of a score or two score, or maybe ten score; and though many a man was slain, yet scarce any one before he had slain or hurt a Roman; and some there were, and they the oldest, who fought as if they and the few about them were all the host that was left to the folk, and heeded not that others were driven back, or that the Romans gathered about them, cutting them off from all succour and aid, but went on smiting till they were felled with many strokes. Howbeit the array of the Goths was broken and many were slain, and perforce they must give back, and it seemed as if they would be driven into the river and all be lost.

But for Thiodolf, this befell him: that at first, when those fresh men fell on, he seemed, as it were, to wake unto himself again, and he cried aloud the cry of the Wolf, and thrust into the thickest of the fray, and slew many and was hurt of none, and for a moment of time there was an empty space round about him, such fear he cast even into the valiant hearts of the foemen. **But those who had time to see him as they stood by him noted that he was as pale as a dead man, and his eyes set and staring; and so of a sudden, while he stood thus threatening the ring of doubtful foemen, the weakness took him again, Throng-plough tumbled from his hand, and he fell to earth as one dead.**

Then of those who saw him some deemed that he had been striving against some secret hurt till he could do no more; and some that there was a curse abroad that had fallen upon him and upon all the kindreds of the Mark; some thought him dead and some swooning. But, dead or alive, the warriors would not leave their War-duke among the foemen, so they lifted him, and gathered about him a goodly band that held its own against all comers, and fought through the turmoil stoutly and steadily; and others gathered to them, till they began to be something like a host again, and the Romans might not break them into knots of desperate men any more.

Arinbiorn Leads

Thus they fought their way, Arinbiorn of the Bearings leading them now, with a mind to make a stand for life or death on some vantage-ground; and so, often turning upon the Romans, they came in array ever growing more solid to the rising ground looking one way over the ford and the other to the slopes where the battle had just been. There they faced the foe as men who may be slain, but will be driven no further; and what bowmen they had got spread out from their flanks and shot on the Romans, who had with them no light-armed, or slingers or bowmen, for they had left them at Wolf-stead.

So the Romans stood a while, and gave breathing-space to the Markmen, which indeed was the saving of them: for if they had fallen on hotly and held to it steadily, it is like that they would have passed over all the bodies of the Markmen: for these had lost their leader, either slain, as some thought, or, as others thought, banned from leadership by the Gods; and their host was heavy-hearted; and though it is like that they would have stood there till each had fallen over other, yet was their hope grown dim, and the whole folk brought to a perilous and fearful pass, for if these were slain or scattered there were no more but they, and nought between fire and the sword and the people of the Mark.

But once again the faint-heart folly of the Roman Captain saved his foes: for whereas he once thought that the whole power of the Markmen lay in Otter and his company, and deemed them too little to meddle with, so now he ran his head into the other hedge, and deemed that Thiodolf's company was but a part of the succour that was at hand for the Goths, and that they were over-big for him to meddle with.

True it is also that now dark night was coming on, and the land was unknown to the Romans, who moreover trusted not wholly to the dastards of the Goths who were their guides and scouts: furthermore the wood was at hand, and they knew not what it held; and with all this and above it all, it is to be said that over them also had fallen a dread of some doom anear; for those habitations amidst of the wild-woods were terrible to them as they were dear to the Goths; and the Gods of their foemen seemed to be lying in wait to fall upon them, even if they should slay every man of the kindreds.

So now having driven back the Goths to that height over the ford, which indeed was no stronghold, no mountain, scarce a hill even, nought but a gentle swelling of the earth, they forebore them; and raising up the whoop of victory drew slowly aback, picking up their own dead and wounded, and slaying the wounded Markmen. They had with them also some few captives, but not many; for the fighting had been to the death between man and man on the Wolfing Meadow.

25. The Host of the Markmen Cometh into the Wild-wood

Thiodolf revives but is sad and withdrawn. Even his sword Throng-plough is lost. Someone who says they are Ali the son of Grey arrives with a message from Hall-Sun that they are to come through the wood to the Thing-stead in Mid-Mark. (When Thiodolf's refers to Hall-Sun as "thy daughter" when talking to Ali, it hints that he knows the messenger is Wood-sun in disguise.) Hall-Sun has a private message for Thiodolf when he returns. The messenger also offers to guide them in the night. Afterward, Thiodolf tells Arinbiorn that he must lead their army. Arinbiorn tells his men to leave their fires burning (to deceive the Romans) and march. Ali leads them to the Thing-stead, which Hall-Sun has turned into a fortress. Hall-Sun greets them when they arrive. Speeches are made about the coming battle. After most have gone to sleep, Arinbiorn tells Thiodolf that he has been behaving strangely.

Yet though the Romans were gone, the Goth-folk were very hard bested. They had been overthrown, not sorely maybe if they had been in an alien land, and free to come and go as they would; yet sorely as things were, because the foeman was sitting in their own House, and they must needs drag him out of it or perish: and to many the days seemed evil, and the Gods fighting against them, and both the Wolfings and the other kindreds bethought them of the Hall-Sun and her wisdom and longed to hear of tidings concerning her.

But now the word ran through the host that Thiodolf was certainly not slain. Slowly he had come to himself, and yet was not himself, for he sat among his men gloomy and silent, clean contrary to his wont; for hitherto he had been a merry man, and a joyous fellow.

Amidst of the ridge whereon the Markmen now abode, there was a ring made of the chief warriors and captains and wise men who had not been slain or grievously hurt in the fray, and amidst them all sat Thiodolf on the ground, his chin sunken on his breast, looking more like a captive than the leader of a host amidst of his men; and that the more as his scabbard was empty; for when Throng-plough had fallen from his hand, it had been trodden under foot, and lost in the turmoil. There he sat, and the others in that ring of men looked sadly upon him; such as Arinbiorn of the Bearings, and Wolfkettle and Thorolf of his own House, and Hiarandi of the Elkings, and Geirbald the Shielding, the messenger of the woods, and Fox who had seen the Roman Garth, and many others.

It was night now, and men had lighted fires about the host, for they said that the Romans knew where to find them if they listed to seek; and about those fires were men eating and drinking what they might come at, but amidmost of that ring was the biggest fire, and men turned them towards it for counsel and help, for elsewhere none said, "What do we?" for they were heavy-hearted and redeless [without counsel or advice], since the Gods had taken the victory out of their hands just when they seemed at point to win it.

Wood-Sun Arrives as Ali, Son of Grey

But amidst all this there was a little stir outside that biggest ring, and men parted, and through them came a swain amongst the chiefs, and said, "Who will lead me to the War-duke?"

Thiodolf, who was close beside the lad, answered never a word; but Arinbiorn said; "This man here sitting is the War-duke: speak to him, for he may hearken to thee: but first who art thou?"

Said the lad; "My name is Ali the son of Grey, and I come with a message from the Hall-Sun and the stay-at-homes who are in the Woodland."

Now when he named the Hall-Sun Thiodolf started and looked up, and turning to his left-hand said, "And what sayeth thy daughter?"

Men did not heed that he said thy daughter, but deemed that he said my daughter, since he was wont as her would-be foster-father to call her so.

But Ali spake: "War-duke and ye chieftains, thus saith the Hall-Sun: 'I know that by this time Otter hath been slain and many another, and ye have been overthrown and chased by the Romans, and that now there is little counsel in you except to abide the foe where ye are and there to die valiantly. But now do my bidding and as I am bidden, and then whosoever dieth or liveth, the kindreds shall vanquish that they may live and grow greater. Do ye thus: the Romans think no otherwise but to find you here to-morrow or else departed across the water as broken men, and they will fall upon you with their whole host, and then make a war-garth after their manner at Wolf-stead and carry fire and the sword and the chains of thralldom into every House of the Mark. Now therefore fetch a compass and come into the wood on the north-west of the houses and make your way to the Thing-stead of the Mid-mark. For who knoweth but that to-morrow we may fall upon these thieves again? Of this shall ye hear more when we may speak together and take counsel face to face; for we stay-at-homes know somewhat closely of the ways of these Romans. Haste then! let not the grass grow over your feet! But to thee, Thiodolf, have I a word to say when we meet; for I wot that as now thou canst not hearken to my word.' Thus saith the Hall-Sun."

"Wilt thou speak, War-duke?" said Arinbiorn. But Thiodolf shook his head. Then said Arinbiorn; "Shall I speak for thee?" and Thiodolf nodded yea. Then said Arinbiorn: "Ali son of Grey, art thou going back to her that sent thee?"

"Yea," said the lad, "but in your company, for ye will be coming straightway and I know all the ways closely; and there is need for a guide through the dark night as ye will see presently."

The Wolfings Withdraw

Then stood up Arinbiorn and said: "Chiefs and captains, go ye speedily and array your men for departure: bid them leave all the fires burning and come their ways as silently as maybe; for now will we wend this same hour before moonrise into the Wild-wood and the Thing-stead of Mid-mark; thus saith the War-duke."

But when they were gone, and Arinbiorn and Thiodolf were left alone, Thiodolf lifted up his head and spake slowly and painfully: "Arinbiorn, I thank thee: and thou dost well to lead this folk: since as for me that is somewhat that weighs me down, and I know not whether it be life or death; therefore I may no longer be your captain, for twice now have I blenched from the battle. Yet command me, and I will obey, set a sword in my hand and I will smite, till the God snatches it out of my hand, as he did Throng-plough to-day."

"And that is well," said Arinbiorn, "it may be that ye shall meet that God to-morrow, and heave up sword against him, and either overcome him or go to thy fathers a proud and valiant man."

So they spake, and Thiodolf stood up and seemed of better cheer. But presently the whole host was afoot, and they went their ways warily with little noise, and wound little by little about the Wolfing meadow and about the acres towards the wood at the back of the Houses; and they met nothing by the way except an out-guard of the Romans, whom they slew there nigh silently, and bore away their bodies, twelve in number, lest the Romans when they sent to change the guard, should find the slain and have an inkling of the way the Goths were gone; but now they deemed that the

Romans might think their guard fled, or perchance that they had been carried away by the Gods of the woodland folk.

So came they into the wood, and Arinbiorn and the chiefs were for striking the All-men's road to the Thing-stead and so coming thither; but the lad Ali when he heard it laughed and said: "If ye would sleep to-night ye shall wend another way. For the Hall-Sun hath had us at work cumbering it against the foe with great trees felled with limbs, branches, and all. And indeed ye shall find the Thing-stead fenced like a castle, and the in-gate hard to find; yet will I bring you thither."

So did he without delay, and presently they came anigh the Thing-stead; and the place was fenced cunningly, so that if men would enter they must go by a narrow way that had a fence of tree-trunks on each side wending inward like the maze in a pleas-ance [a secluded place in a garden, with trees and walks]. Thereby now wended the host all afoot, since it was a holy place and no beast must set foot therein, so that the horses were left without it: so slowly and right quietly once more they came into the garth of the Thing-stead; and lo, a many folk there, of the Wolfings and the Bearings and other kindreds, who had gathered thereto; and albeit these were not warriors in their prime, yet were there none save the young children and the weaker of the women but had weapons of some kind; and they were well ordered, standing or sitting in ranks like folk awaiting battle.

At the Hill of Speech

There were booths of boughs and rushes set up for shelter of the feebler women and the old men and children along the edges of the fence, for the Hall-Sun had bid-den them keep the space clear round about the Doom-ring and the Hill of Speech as if for a mighty folk-mote, so that the warriors might have room to muster there and order their array. There were some cooking-fires lighted about the aforesaid booths, but neither many nor great, and they were screened with wattle from the side that lay toward the Romans; for the Hall-Sun would not that they should hold up lanterns for their foemen to find them by. Little noise there was in that stronghold, moreover, for the hearts of all who knew their right hands from their left were set on battle and the destruction of the foe that would destroy the kindreds.

Anigh the Speech-Hill, on its eastern side, had the bole of a slender beech tree been set up, and at the top of it a cross-beam was nailed on, and therefrom hung the wondrous lamp, the Hall-Sun, glimmering from on high, and though its light was but a glimmer amongst the mighty wood, yet was it also screened on three sides from the sight of the chance wanderer by wings of thin plank. But beneath her namesake as beforetime in the Hall sat the Hall-Sun, the maiden, on a heap of faggots, and she was wrapped in a dark blue cloak from under which gleamed the folds of the fair gold-en-broidered gown she was wont to wear at folk-motes, and her right hand rested on a naked sword that lay across her knees: beside her sat the old man Sorli, the Wise in War, and about her were slim lads and sturdy maidens and old carles of the thralls or freedmen ready to bear the commands that came from her mouth; for she and Sorli were the captains of the stay-at-homes.

Now came Thiodolf and Arinbiorn and other leaders into the ring of men before her, and she greeted them kindly and said: "Hail, Sons of Tyr! Now that I behold you again it seemeth to me as if all were already won: the time of waiting hath been weary, and we have borne the burden of fear every day from morn till even, and in the waking hour we presently remembered it. But now ye are come, even if this Thing-stead were lighted by the flames of the Wolfing Roof instead of by these moonbeams; even if we had to begin again and seek new dwellings, and another water and other meadows, yet great should grow the kindreds of the Men who have dwelt in the Mark, and nought should overshadow them: and though the beasts and the Romans were dwelling in their old places, yet should these kindreds make new clearings in the Wild-wood; and they with their deeds should cause other waters to be famous, that as yet have known no deeds of man; and they should compel the Earth to bear increase round about their dwelling-places for the welfare of the kindreds. O Sons of Tyr, friendly are your faces, and undismayed, and the Terror of the Nations has not made you afraid any more than would the onrush of the bisons that feed adown the grass hills. Happy is the eve, O children of the Goths, yet shall to-morrow morn be happier."

Many heard what she spake, and a murmur of joy ran through the ranks of men: for they deemed her words to forecast victory.

And now amidst her speaking, the moon, which had arisen on Mid-mark, when the host first entered into the wood, had overtopped the tall trees that stood like a green wall round about the Thing-stead, and shone down on that assembly, and flashed coldly back from the arms of the warriors. And the Hall-Sun cast off her dark blue cloak and stood up in her golden-broidered raiment, which flashed back the grey light like as it had been an icicle hanging from the roof of some hall in the midnight of Yule, when the feast is high within, and without the world is silent with the night of the ten-weeks' frost.

Then she spake again: "O War-duke, thy mouth is silent; speak to this warrior of the Bearings that he bid the host what to do; for wise are ye both, and dear are the minutes of this night and should not be wasted; since they bring about the salvation of the Wolfings, and the vengeance of the Bearings, and the hope renewed of all the kindreds."

Then Thiodolf abode a while with his head down cast; his bosom heaved, and he set his left hand to his swordless scabbard, and his right to his throat, as though he were sore troubled with something he might not tell of: but at last he lifted up his head and spoke to Arinbiorn, but slowly and painfully, as he had spoken before: "Chief of the Bearings, go up on to the Hill of Speech, and speak to the folk out of thy wisdom, and let them know that to-morrow early before the sun-rising those that may, and are not bound by the Gods against it, shall do deeds according to their might, and win rest for themselves, and new days of deeds for the kindreds."

Therewith he ceased, and let his head fall again, and the Hall-Sun looked at him askance. But Arinbiorn clomb the Speech-Hill and said: "Men of the kindreds, it is now a few days since we first met the Romans and fought with them; and whiles we have had the better, and whiles the worse in our dealings, as oft in war befalleth: for they are men, and we no less than men. But now look to it what ye will do; for we may no longer endure these outlanders in our houses, and we must either die or get our own again: and that is not merely a few wares stored up for use, nor a few head of neat, nor certain timbers piled up into a dwelling, but the life we have made in the land we have made. I show you no choice, for no choice there is. Here are we bare of everything in the wild-wood: for the most part our children are crying for us at home, our wives are longing for us in our houses, and if we come not to them in kindness, the Romans shall come to them in grimness.

"Down yonder in the plain, moreover, is our Wain-burg slowly drawing near to us, and with it is much livelihood of ours, which is a little thing, for we may get more; but also there are our banners of battle and the tokens of the kindred, which is a great thing. And between all this and us there lieth but little; nought but a band of valiant men, and a few swords and spears, and a few wounds, and the hope of death amidst the praise of the people; and this ye have to set out to wend across within two or three hours.

"I will not ask if ye will do so, for I wot that even so ye will; therefore when I have done, shout not, nor clash sword on shield, for we are no great way off that house of ours wherein dwells the foe that would destroy us. Let each man rest as he may, and sleep if he may with his war-gear on him and his weapons by his side, and when he is next awakened by the captains and the leaders of hundreds and scores, let him not think that it is night, but let him betake himself to his place among his kindred and be ready to go through the wood with as little noise as may be. Now all is said that the War-duke would have me say, and to-morrow shall those see him who are foremost in falling upon the foemen, for he longeth sorely for his seat on the days of the Wolfing Hall."

So he spake, and even as he bade them, they made no sound save a joyous murmur; and straightway the more part of them betook themselves to sleep as men who must busy themselves about a weighty matter; for they were wise in the ways of war.

So sank all the host to the ground save those who were appointed as watchers of the night, and Arinbiorn and Thiodolf and the Hall-Sun; they three yet stood together; and Arinbiorn said: "Now it seems to me not so much as if we had vanquished the foe and were safe and at rest, but rather as if we had no foemen and never have had. Deep peace is on me, though hitherto I have been deemed a wrathful man, and it is to me as if the kindreds that I love had filled the whole earth, and left no room for foemen: even so it may really be one day. To-night it is well, yet to-morrow it shall be better.

"What thine errand may be, Thiodolf, I scarce know; for something hath changed in thee, and thou art become strange to us. But as for mine errand, I will tell it thee; it is that I am seeking Otter of the Laxings, my friend and fellow, whose wisdom my foolishness drave under the point and edge of the Romans, so that he is no longer here; I am seeking him, and to-morrow I think I shall find him, for he hath not had time to travel far, and we shall be blithe and merry together. And now will I sleep; for I have bidden the watchers awaken me if any need be. Sleep thou also, Thiodolf! and wake up thine old self when the moon is low." Therewith he laid himself down under the lee of the pile of faggots, and was presently asleep.

26. Thiodolf Talketh with the Wood-Sun

In the night, Hall-Sun guides her father Thiodolf through the wood to a grief-stricken Wood-Sun. Read carefully her poetic speech to Wood-Sun in which she asks, "what shall it profit thee then, / That after the fashion of Godhead thou hast gotten thee a thrall / To be thine and never another's, whatso in the world may befall?" She goes on to warn Wood-Sun, "I shall bid my mighty father make choice of death in life, or life in death victorious and the crowned end of strife." Wood-Sun replies, telling of the "threat of the doom" she was trying to prevent and asking to be alone with Thiodolf. Note the conversation that follows between Thiodolf and Wood-Sun. What they discuss is the central dilemma of the book. Note also Wood-Sun's explanation of how the Hauberk became cursed.

Now were Thiodolf and the Hall-Sun left alone together standing by the Speech-Hill; and the moon was risen high in the heavens above the tree-tops of the wild-wood. Thiodolf scarce stirred, and he still held his head bent down as one lost in thought. Then said the Hall-Sun, speaking softly amidst the hush of the camp: "I have said that the minutes of this night are dear, and they are passing swiftly; and it may be that thou wilt have much to say and to do before the host is astir with the dawning. So come thou with me a little way, that thou mayst hear of new tidings, and think what were best to do amidst them."

And without more ado she took him by the hand and led him forth, and he went as he was led, not saying a word. They passed out of the camp into the wood, none hindering, and went a long way where under the beech-leaves there was but a glimmer of the moonlight, and presently Thiodolf's feet went as it were of themselves; for they had hit a path that he knew well and over-well.

Thiodolf Sits Beside Wood-Sun

So came they to that little wood-lawn where first in this tale Thiodolf met the Wood-Sun; and the stone seat there was not empty now any more than it was then; for thereon sat the Wood-Sun, clad once more in her glittering raiment. Her head was sunken down, her face hidden by her hands; neither did she look up when she heard their feet on the grass, for she knew who they were.

Thiodolf lingered not; for a moment it was to him as if all that past time had never been, and its battles and hurry and hopes and fears but mere shows, and the unspoken words of a dream. He went straight up to her and sat down by her side and put his arm about her shoulders, and strove to take her hand to caress it; but she moved but little, and it was as if she heeded him not. And the Hall-Sun stood before them and looked at them for a little while; and then she fell to speech; but at the first sound of her voice, it seemed that the Wood-Sun trembled, but still she hid her face. Said the Hall-Sun:

Two griefs I see before me in mighty hearts grown great;
And to change both these into gladness out-goes the power of fate.
Yet I, a lonely maiden, have might to vanquish one
Till it melt as the mist of the morning before the summer sun.
O Wood-Sun, thou hast borne me, and I were fain indeed
To give thee back thy gladness; but thou com'st of the Godhead's seed,
And herein my might avails not; because I can but show
Unto these wedded sorrows the truth that the heart should know
Ere the will hath wielded the hand; and for thee, I can tell thee nought
That thou hast not known this long while; thy will and thine hand have wrought,
And the man that thou lovest shall live in despite of Gods and of men,
If yet thy will endureth. But what shall it profit thee then
That after the fashion of Godhead thou hast gotten thee a thrall
To be thine and never another's, whatso in the world may befall?
Lo! yesterday this was a man, and to-morrow it might have been
The very joy of the people, though never again it were seen;
Yet a part of all they hoped for through all the lapse of years,
To make their laughter happy and dull the sting of tears;
To quicken all remembrance of deeds that never die,
And death that maketh eager to live as the days go by.
Yea, many a deed had he done as he lay in the dark of the mound;
As the seed-wheat plotteth of spring, laid under the face of the ground
That the foot of the husbandman treadeth, that the wind of the winter wears,
That the turbid cold flood hideth from the constant hope of the years.
This man that should leave in his death his life unto many an one
Wilt thou make him a God of the fearful who live lone under the sun?
And then shalt thou have what thou wouldedst when amidst of the hazelled field
Thou kissed'st the mouth of the helper, and the hand of the people's shield,
Shalt thou have the thing that thou wouldedst when thou broughtest me to birth,
And I, the soul of the Wolfings, began to look on earth?
Wilt thou play the God, O mother, and make a man anew,
A joyless thing and a fearful? Then I betwixt you two
'Twixt your longing and your sorrow will cast the sundering word,
And tell out all the story of that rampart of the sword!
I shall bid my mighty father make choice of death in life,
Or life in death victorious and the crowned end of strife.

Ere she had ended, the Wood-Sun let her hands fall down, and showed her face, which for all its unpaled beauty looked wearied and anxious; and she took Thiodolf's hand in hers, while she looked with eyes of love upon the Hall-Sun, and Thiodolf laid his cheek to her cheek, and though he smiled not, yet he seemed as one who is happy. At last the Wood-Sun spoke and said:

THOU SAYEST SOOTH, O DAUGHTER: I AM NO GOD OF MIGHT,
Yet I am of their race, and I think with their thoughts and see with their sight,
And the threat of the doom did I know of, and yet spared not to lie:
For I thought that the fate foreboded might touch and pass us by,
As the sword that heweth the war-helm and cleaveth a cantle away,
And the cunning smith shall mend it and it goeth again to the fray;
If my hand might have held for a moment, yea, even against his will,
The life of my beloved! But Weird is the master still:
And this man's love of my body and his love of the ancient kin
Were matters o'er mighty to deal with and the game withal to win.
Woe's me for the waning of all things, and my hope that needs must fade
As the fruitless sun of summer on the waste where nought is made!
And now farewell, O daughter, thou mayst not see the kiss
Of the hapless and the death-doomed when I have told of this;
Yet once again shalt thou see him, though I no more again,
Fair with the joy that hopeth and dieth not in vain.

Hall-Sun Leaves Them Alone

Then came the Hall-Sun close to her, and knelt down by her, and laid her head upon her knees and wept for love of her mother, who kissed her oft and caressed her; and Thiodolf's hand strayed, as it were, on to his daughter's head, and he looked kindly on her, though scarce now as if he knew her. Then she arose when she had kissed her mother once more, and went her ways from that wood-lawn into the woods again, and so to the Folk-mote of her people.

But when those twain were all alone again, the Wood-Sun spoke: "O Thiodolf canst thou hear me and understand?"

"Yea," he said, "when thou speakest of certain matters, as of our love together, and of our daughter that came of our love."

"Thiodolf," she said, "How long shall our love last?"

"As long as our life," he said.

"And if thou diest to-day, where then shall our love be?" said the Wood-Sun.

He said, "I must now say, I wot not; though time was I had said, It shall abide with the soul of the Wolfing Kindred."

She said: "And when that soul dieth, and the kindred is no more?"

"Time agone," quoth he, "I had said, it shall abide with the Kindreds of the Earth; but now again I say, I wot not."

"Will the Earth hide it," said she, "when thou diest and art borne to mound?"

"Even so didst thou say when we spake together that other night," said he; "and now I may say nought against thy word."

"Art thou happy, O Folk-wolf?" she said.

"Why dost thou ask me?" said he; "I know not; we were sundered and I longed for thee; thou art here; it is enough."

"And the people of thy Kindred?" she said, "dost thou not long for them?"

He said; "Didst thou not say that I was not of them? Yet were they my friends, and needed me, and I loved them: but by this evening they will need me no more, or but little; for they will be victorious over their foes: so hath the Hall-Sun foretold. What then! Shall I take all from thee to give little to them?"

"Thou art wise," she said; "Wilt thou go to battle to-day?"

"So it seemeth," said he.

She said: "And wilt thou bear the dwarf-wrought Hauberk? For if thou dost, thou wilt live, and if thou dost not, thou wilt die."

"I will bear it," said he, "that I may live to love thee."

"Thinkest thou that any evil goes with it?" said she.

There came into his face a flash of his ancient boldness as he answered: "So it seemed to me yesterday, when I fought clad in it the first time; and I fell unsmitten on the meadow, and was shamed, and would have slain myself but for thee. And yet it is not so that any evil goes with it; for thou thyself didst say that past night that there was no evil weird in it."

She said: "How then if I lied that night?"

Said he; "It is the wont of the Gods to lie, and be unashamed, and men-folk must bear with it."

"Ah! how wise thou art!" she said; and was silent for a while, and drew away from him a little, and clasped her hands together and wrung them for grief and anger. Then she grew calm again, and said:

"Wouldest thou die at my bidding?"

"Yea," said he, "not because thou art of the Gods, but because thou hast become a woman to me, and I love thee."

Then was she silent some while, and at last she said, "Thiodolf, wilt thou do off the Hauberk if I bid thee?"

"Yea, yea," said he, "and let us depart from the Wolfings, and their strife, for they need us not."

Thiodolf Removes the Hauberk

She was silent once more for a longer while still, and at last she said in a cold voice; "Thiodolf, I bid thee arise, and put off the Hauberk from thee."

He looked at her wondering, not at her words, but at the voice wherewith she spake them; but he arose from the stone nevertheless, and stood stark in the moonlight; he set his hand to the collar of the war-coat, and undid its clasps, which were of gold and blue stones, and presently he did the coat from off him and let it slide to the ground where it lay in a little grey heap that looked but a handful. Then he sat down on the stone again, and took her hand and kissed her and caressed her fondly, and she him again, and they spake no word for a while: but at the last he spake in measure and rhyme in a low voice, but so sweet and clear that it might have been heard far in the hush of the last hour of the night:

DEAR NOW ARE THIS DAWN-DUSK'S MOMENTS AS IS THE LAST OF THE LIGHT
When the foemen's ranks are wavering, and the victory feareth night;
And of all the time I have loved thee of these am I most fain,
When I know not what shall betide me, nor what shall be my gain.
But dear as they are, they are waning, and at last the time is come
When no more shall I behold thee till I wend to Odin's Home.
Now is the time so little that once hath been so long
That I fain would ask thee pardon wherein I have done thee wrong,
That thy longing might be softer, and thy love more sweet to have.
But in nothing have I wronged thee, there is nought that I may crave.
Strange too! as the minutes fail me, so do my speech-words fail,
Yet strong is the joy within me for this hour that crowns the tale.

Therewith he clipped her and caressed her, and she spake nothing for a while; and he said; "Thy face is fair and bright; art thou not joyous of these minutes?"

She said: "Thy words are sweet; but they pierce my heart like a sharp knife; for they tell me of thy death and the ending of our love."

Said he; "I tell thee nothing, beloved, that thou hast not known: is it not for this that we have met here once more?"

She answered after a while; "Yea, yea; yet mightest thou have lived."

He laughed, but not scornfully or bitterly and said: "So thought I in time past: but hearken, beloved; If I fall to-day, shall there not yet be a minute after the stroke hath fallen on me, wherein I shall know that the day is won and see the foemen fleeing, and wherein I shall once again deem I shall never die, whatever may betide afterwards, and though the sword lieth deep in my breast? And shall I not see then and know that our love hath no end?"

Bitter grief was in her face as she heard him. But she spake and said: "Lo here the Hauberk which thou hast done off thee, that thy breast might be the nearer to mine! Wilt thou not wear it in the fight for my sake?"

The Hauberk's Evil

He knit his brows somewhat, and said: "Nay, it may not be: true it is that thou saidest that no evil weird went with it, but hearken! Yesterday I bore it in the fight, and ere I mingled with the foe, before I might give the token of onset, a cloud came before my eyes and thick darkness wrapped me around, and I fell to the earth unsmitten; and so was I borne out of the fight, and evil dreams beset me of evil things, and the dwarfs that hate mankind.

"Then I came to myself, and the Hauberk was off me, and I rose up and beheld the battle, that the kindreds were pressing on the foe, and I thought not then of any past time, but of the minutes that were passing; and I ran into the fight straightway: but one followed me with that Hauberk, and I did it on, thinking of nought but the battle. Fierce then was the fray, yet I faltered in it; till the fresh men of the Romans came in upon us and broke up our array.

"Then my heart almost broke within me, and I faltered no more, but rushed on as of old, and smote great strokes all round about: no hurt I got, but once more came that ugly mist over my eyes, and again I fell unsmitten, and they bore me out of battle: then the men of our folk gave back and were overcome; and when I awoke from my evil dreams, we had gotten away from the fight and the Wolfing dwellings, and were on the mounds above the ford cowering down like beaten men. There then I sat shamed among the men who had chosen me for their best man at the Holy Thing, and lo I was their worst! Then befell that which never till then had befallen me, that life seemed empty and worthless and I longed to die and be done with it, and but for the thought of thy love I had slain myself then and there.

"Thereafter I went with the host to the assembly of the stay-at-homes and fleers, and sat before the Hall-Sun our daughter, and said the words which were put into my mouth. But now must I tell thee a hard and evil thing; that I loved them not, and was not of them, and outside myself there was nothing: within me was the world and nought without me. Nay, as for thee, I was not sundered from thee, but thou wert a part of me; whereas for the others, yea, even for our daughter, thine and mine, they were but images and shows of men, and I longed to depart from them, and to see thy body and to feel thine heart beating. And by then so evil was I grown that my very shame had fallen from me, and my will to die: nay, I longed to live, thou and I, and death seemed hateful to me, and the deeds before death vain and foolish.

"Where then was my glory and my happy life, and the hope of the days fresh born every day, though never dying? Where then was life, and Thiodolf that once had lived?

"But now all is changed once more; I loved thee never so well as now, and great is my grief that we must sunder, and the pain of farewell wrings my heart. Yet since I am once more Thiodolf the Mighty, in my heart there is room for joy also. Look at me, O Wood-Sun, look at me, O beloved! tell me, am I not fair with the fairness of the warrior and the helper of the folk? Is not my voice kind, do not my lips smile, and mine eyes shine? See how steady is mine hand, the friend of the folk! For mine eyes are cleared again, and I can see the kindreds as they are, and their desire of life and scorn of death, and this is what they have made me myself. Now therefore shall they and I together earn the merry days to come, the winter hunting and the spring sowing, the summer haysel, the ingathering of harvest, the happy rest of midwinter, and Yuletide with the memory of the Fathers, wedded to the hope of the days to be. Well may they bid me help them who have holpen me! Well may they bid me die who have made me live!

"For whereas thou sayest that I am not of their blood, nor of their adoption, once more I heed it not. For I have lived with them, and eaten and drunken with them, and toiled with them, and led them in battle and the place of wounds and slaughter; they are mine and I am theirs; and through them am I of the whole earth, and all the kindreds of it; yea, even of the foemen, whom this day the edges in mine hand shall smite.

"Therefore I will bear the Hauberk no more in battle; and belike my body but once more: so shall I have lived and death shall not have undone me.

"Lo thou, is not this the Thiodolf whom thou hast loved? no changeling of the Gods, but the man in whom men have trusted, the friend of Earth, the giver of life, the vanquisher of death?"

And he cast himself upon her, and strained her to his bosom and kissed her, and caressed her, and awoke the bitter-sweet joy within her, as he cried out: "O remember this, and this, when at last I am gone from thee!"

But when they sundered her face was bright, but the tears were on it, and she said: "O Thiodolf, thou wert fain hadst thou done a wrong to me so that I might forgive thee; now wilt thou forgive me the wrong I have done thee?"

"Yea," he said, "Even so would I do, were we both to live, and how much more if this be the dawn of our sundering day! What hast thou done?"

The Hauberk's History

She said: **"I lied to thee concerning the Hauberk when I said that no evil weird went with it: and this I did for the saving of thy life."**

He laid his hand fondly on her head, and spake smiling: "Such is the wont of the God-kin, because they know not the hearts of men. Tell me all the truth of it now at last."

She said:

HEAR THEN THE TALE OF THE HAUBERK AND THE TRUTH THERE IS TO TELL:
There was a maid of the God-kin, and she loved a man right well,
Who unto the battle was wending; and she of her wisdom knew
That thence to the folk-hall threshold should come back but a very few;
And she feared for her love, for she doubted that of these he should not be;
So she wended the wilds lamenting, as I have lamented for thee;
And many wise she pondered, how to bring her will to pass
(E'en as I for thee have pondered), as her feet led over the grass,
Till she lifted her eyes in the wild-wood, and lo! She stood before
The Hall of the Hollow-places; and the Dwarf-lord stood in the door

And held in his hand the Hauberk, whereon the hammer's blow
The last of all had been smitten, and the sword should be hammer now.
Then the Dwarf beheld her fairness, and the wild-wood many-leaved
Before his eyes was reeling at the hope his heart conceived;
So sorely he longed for her body; and he laughed before her and cried,
'O Lady of the Disir, thou farest wandering wide
Lamenting thy beloved and the folkmote of the spear,
But if amidst of the battle this child of the hammer he bear
He shall laugh at the foemen's edges and come back to thy lily breast
And of all the days of his life-time shall his coming years be best.'
Then she bowed adown her godhead and sore for the Hauberk she prayed;
But his greedy eyes devoured her as he stood in the door and said;
'Come lie in mine arms! Come hither, and we twain the night to wake!
And then as a gift of the morning the Hauberk shall ye take.'
So she humbled herself before him, and entered into the cave,
The dusky, the deep-gleaming, the gem-strewn golden grave.
But he saw not her girdle loosened, or her bosom gleam on his love,
For she set the sleep-thorn in him, that he saw, but might not move,
Though the bitter salt tears burned him for the anguish of his greed;
And she took the hammer's offspring, her unearned morning meed,
And went her ways from the rock-hall and was glad for her warrior's sake.
But behind her dull speech followed, and the voice of the hollow spake:
'Thou hast left me bound in anguish, and hast gained thine heart's desire;
Now I would that the dewy night-grass might be to thy feet as the fire,
And shrivel thy raiment about thee, and leave thee bare to the flame,
And no way but a fiery furnace for the road whereby ye came!
But since the folk of God-home we may not slay nor smite,
And that fool of the folk that thou lovest, thou hast saved in my despite,
Take with thee, thief of God-home, this other word I say:
Since the safeguard wrought in the ring-mail I may not do away
I lay this curse upon it, that whoso weareth the same,
Shall save his life in the battle, and have the battle's shame;
He shall live through wrack and ruin, and ever have the worse,
And drag adown his kindred, and bear the people's curse.'

Lo, THIS THE tale of the Hauberk, and I knew it for the truth:
And little I thought of the kindreds; of their day I had no ruth;
For I said, They are doomed to departure; in a little while must they wane,
And nought it helpeth or hindreth if I hold my hand or refrain.
Yea, thou wert become the kindred, both thine and mine; and thy birth
To me was the roofing of heaven, and the building up of earth.

I have loved, and I must sorrow; thou hast lived, and thou must die;
Ah, wherefore were there others in the world than thou and I?

He turned round to her and clasped her strongly in his arms again, and kissed her many times and said:

LO, HERE ART THOU FORGIVEN; AND HERE I SAY FAREWELL!
Here the token of my wonder which my words may never tell;
The wonder past all thinking, that my love and thine should blend;
That thus our lives should mingle, and sunder in the end!
Lo, this, for the last remembrance of the mighty man I was,
Of thy love and thy forbearing, and all that came to pass!
Night wanes, and heaven dights her for the kiss of sun and earth;
Look up, look last upon me on this morn of the kindreds' mirth!

Therewith he arose and lingered no minute longer, but departed, going as straight towards the Thing-stead and the Folk-mote of his kindred as the swallow goes to her nest in the hall-porch. He looked not once behind him, though a bitter wailing rang through the woods and filled his heart with the bitterness of her woe and the anguish of the hour of sundering.

27. THEY WEND TO THE MORNING BATTLE

Thiodolf returns to the camp and tells Arinbiorn that he is resuming his role as War-duke armed with the usual "war-gear and weapons." Together, he and Arinbiorn plan for the coming battle. Thiodolf tells of expecting to die near the end of this battle. Hall-Sun makes her own contribution to the battle plans. Thiodolf and Hall-Sun have one last conversation, and the Markmen leave for battle.

Now when Thiodolf came back to the camp the signs of dawn were plain in the sky, the moon was low and sinking behind the trees, and he saw at once that the men were stirring and getting ready for departure. He looked gladly and blithely at the men he fell in with, and they at him, and scarce could they refrain a shout when they beheld his face and the brightness of it. He went straight up to where the Hall-Sun was yet sitting under her namesake, with Arinbiorn standing before her amidst of a ring of leaders of hundreds and scores: but old Sorli sat by her side clad in all his war-gear.

When Thiodolf first came into that ring of men they looked doubtfully at him, as if they dreaded somewhat, but when they had well beheld him their faces cleared, and they became joyous.

He went straight up to Arinbiorn and kissed the old warrior, and said to him, "I give thee good morrow, O leader of the Bearings! Here now is come the War-duke! And meseems that we should get to work as speedily as may be, for lo the dawning!"

"Hail to thine hand, War-duke!" said Arinbiorn joyously; "there is no more to do but to take thy word concerning the order wherein we shall wend; for all men are armed and ready."

Said Thiodolf; "Lo ye, I lack war-gear and weapons! Is there a good sword here-by, a helm, a byrny [chain armor] and a shield? For hard will be the battle, and we must fence ourselves all we may."

"Hard by," said Arinbiorn, "is the war-gear of Ivar of our House, who is dead in the night of his hurts gotten in yesterday's battle: thou and he are alike in stature, and with a good will doth he give them to thee, and they are goodly things, for he comes of smithying blood. Yet is it a pity of Throng-plough that he lieth on the field of the slain."

But Thiodolf smiled and said: "Nay, Ivar's blade shall serve my turn to-day; and thereafter shall it be seen to, for then will be time for many things."

Planning for the Battle

So they went to fetch him the weapons; but he said to Arinbiorn, "Hast thou numbered the host? What are the gleanings of the Roman sword?"

Said Arinbiorn: "Here have we more than three thousand three hundred warriors of the host fit for battle: and besides this here are gathered eighteen hundred of the Wolfings and the Bearings, and of the other Houses, mostly from over the water, and of these nigh upon seven hundred may bear sword or shoot shaft; neither shall ye hinder them from so doing if the battle be joined."

Then said Thiodolf: "We shall order us into three battles; the Wolfings and the Bearings to lead the first, for this is our business; but others of the smaller Houses this side the water to be with us; and the Elkings and Galtings and the other Houses of the Mid-mark on the further side of the water to be in the second, and with them the more part of the Nether-mark; but the men of Up-mark to be in the third, and the stay-at-homes to follow on with them: and this third battle to let the wood cover them till they be needed, which may not be till the day of fight draws to an end, when all shall be needed: for no Roman man must be left alive or untaken by this even, or else must we all go to the Gods together.

"Hearken, Arinbiorn. I am not called fore-sighted, and yet meseems I see somewhat how this day shall go; and it is not to be hidden that I shall not see another battle until the last of all battles is at hand. But be of good cheer, for I shall not die till the end of the fight, and once more I shall be a man's help unto you.

"Now the first of the Romans we meet shall not be able to stand before us, for they shall be unready, and when their men are gotten ready and are fighting with us grimly, ye of the second battle shall hear the war-token, and shall fall on, and they shall be dismayed when they see so many fresh men come into the fight; yet shall they stand stoutly; for they are valiant men, and shall not all be taken unawares. Then, if they withstand us long enough, shall the third battle come forth from the wood, and fall on either flank of them, and the day shall be won. But I think not that they shall withstand us so long, but that the men of Up-mark and the stay-at-homes shall have the chasing of them. Now get me my war-gear, and let the first battle get them to the outgate of the garth."

So they brought him his arms; and meanwhile the Hall-Sun spake to one of the Captains, and he turned and went away a little space, and then came back, having with him three strong warriors of the Wolfings, and he brought them before the Hall-Sun, who said to them: "Ye three, Steinulf, Athalulf, and Grani the Grey, I have sent for you because ye are men both mighty in battle and deft wood-wrights and house-smiths; ye shall follow Thiodolf closely, when he winneth into the Roman garth, yet shall ye fight wisely, so that ye be not slain, or at least not all; ye shall enter the Hall with Thiodolf, and when ye are therein, if need be, ye shall run down the Hall at your swiftest, and mount up into the loft betwixt the Middle-hearth and the Women's-Chamber, and there shall ye find good store of water in vats and tubs, and this ye shall use for quenching the fire of the Hall if the foemen fire it, as is not unlike to be."

Then Grani spoke for the others and said he would pay all heed to her words, and they departed to join their company.

Now was Thiodolf armed; and Arinbiorn, turning about before he went to his place, beheld him and knit his brow, and said: "What is this, Thiodolf? Didst thou not swear to the Gods not to bear helm or shield in the battles of this strife? Yet hast thou Ivar's helm on thine head and his shield ready beside thee: wilt thou forswear thyself? So doing shalt thou bring woe upon the House."

"Arinbiorn," said Thiodolf, "where didst thou hear tell of me that I had made myself the thrall of the Gods? The oath that I sware was sworn when mine heart was not whole towards our people; and now will I break it that I may keep what of good intent there was in it, and cast away the rest. Long is the story; but if we journey together tonight I will tell it thee. Likewise I will tell it to the Gods if they look sourly upon me when I see them, and all shall be well."

A Farewell to Hall-Sun

He smiled as he spoke, and Arinbiorn smiled on him in turn and went his ways to array the host. But when he was gone Thiodolf was alone in that place with the Hall-Sun, and he turned to her, and kissed her, and caressed her fondly, and spake and said:

So fare we, O my daughter, to the sundering of the ways;
Short is my journey henceforth to the door that ends my days,
And long the road that lieth as yet before thy feet.
How fain were I that thy journey from day to day were sweet
With peace to thee and pleasure; that a noble warrior's hand
In its early days might lead thee adown the flowery land,
And thy children in its noon-tide cling round about thy gown,
And the wise that thy womb has carried when the sun is going down,
Be thy happy fellow-farers to tell the tale of Earth,
But I wot that for no such sweetness did we bring thee unto birth,
But to be the soul of the Wolfings till the other days should come,

And the fruit of the kindreds' harvest with thee is garnered home.
Yet if for no blithe faring thy life-day is ordained,
Yet peace that long endureth maybe thy soul hath gained;
And thy sorrow of this even thy latest grief shall be,
The grief wherewith thou singest the death-song over me.

She looked up at him and smiled, though the tears were on her face; then she said:

THOUGH TO-DAY THE GRIEF BEGINNETH YET THE BITTERNESS IS DONE.
Though my body wendeth barren 'neath the beams of the quickening sun,
Yet remembrance still abideth, and long after the days of my life
Shall I live in the tale of the morning, when they tell of the ending of strife;
And the deeds of this little hand, and the thought conceived in my heart,
And never again henceforward from the folk shall I fare apart.
And if of the Earth, my father, thou hast tidings in thy place
Thou shalt hear how they call me the Ransom and the Mother of happy days.

THEN SHE WEPT outright for a brief space, and thereafter she said:
Keep this in thine heart, O father, that I shall remember all
Since thou liftedst the she-wolf's nursling in the oak-tree's leafy hall.
Yea, every time I remember when hand in hand we went
Amidst the shafts of the beech-trees, and down to the youngling bent
The Folk-wolf in his glory when the eve of fight drew nigh;
And every time I remember when we wandered joyfully
Adown the sunny meadow and lived a while of life
'Midst the herbs and the beasts and the waters so free from fear and strife,
That thy years and thy might and thy wisdom, I had no part therein;
But thou wert as the twin-born brother of the maiden slim and thin,
The maiden shy in the feast-hall and blithe in wood and field.
Thus have we fared, my father; and e'en now when thou bearest shield,
On the last of thy days of mid-earth, twixt us 'tis even so
That the heart of my like-aged brother is the heart of thee that I know.

Then the bitterness of tears stayed her speech, and he spake no word more, but took her in his arms a while and soothed her and fondled her, and then they parted, and he went with great strides towards the outgoing of the Thing-stead.

There he found the warriors of his House and of the Bearings and the lesser Houses of Mid-mark, all duly ordered for wending through the wood. The dawn was coming on apace, but the wood was yet dark. But whereas the Wolfings led, and each man of them knew the wood like his own hand, there was no straying or disarray, and in less than a half-hour's space Thiodolf and the first battle were come to the wood behind the hazel-trees at the back of the hall, and before them was the dawning round about the Roof of the Kindred; the eastern heavens were brightening, and they could see all things clear without the wood.

28. OF THE STORM OF DAWNING

Fearing the Romans may attack those left behind at the Thing-stead, Thiodolf sends scouts to discover what his foes are doing. The battle is soon going well for the Markmen. The Roman general has his men withdraw to defenses they have prepared. Arinbiorn falls in battle. This part of the battle is called the Storm of Dawning.

Then Thiodolf bade Fox and two others steal forward, and see what of foemen was before them; so they fell to creeping on towards the open: but scarcely had they started, before all men could hear the tramp of men drawing nigh; then Thiodolf himself took with him a score of his House and went quietly toward the wood-edge till they were barely within the shadow of the beechwood; and he looked forth and saw men coming straight towards their lurking-place. And those he saw were a good many, and they were mostly of the dastards of the Goths; but with them was a Captain of an Hundred of the Romans, and some others of his kindred; and Thiodolf deemed that the Goths had been bidden to gather up some of the night-watchers and enter the wood and fall on the stay-at-homes.

So he bade his men get them aback, and he himself abode still at the very wood's edge listening intently with his sword bare in his hand. And he noted that those men of the foe stayed in the daylight outside the wood, but a few yards from it, and, by command as it seemed, fell silent and spake no word; and the morn was very still, and when the sound of their tramp over the grass had ceased, Thiodolf could hear the tramp of more men behind them. And then he had another thought, to wit that the Romans had sent scouts to see if the Goths yet abided on the vantage-ground by the ford, and that when they had found them gone, they were minded to fall on them unawares in the refuge of the Thing-stead and were about to do so by the counsel and leading of the dastard Goths; and that this was one body of the host led by those dastards, who knew somewhat of the woods.

So he drew aback speedily, and catching hold of Fox by the shoulder (for he had taken him alone with him) he bade him creep along through the wood toward the Thing-stead, and bring back speedy word whether there were any more foemen near the wood thereaway; and he himself came to his men, and ordered them for onset, drawing them up in a shallow half moon, with the bowmen at the horns thereof, with the word to loose at the Romans as soon as they heard the war-horn blow: and all this was done speedily and with little noise, for they were well nigh so arrayed already.

Thus then they waited, and there was more than a glimmer of light even under the beechen leaves, and the eastern sky was yellowing to sunrise. The other warriors were like hounds in the leash eager to be slipped; but Thiodolf stood calm and high-hearted turning over the memory of past days, and the time he thought of seemed long to him, but happy.

Scarce had a score of minutes passed, and the Romans before them, who were now gathered thick behind those dastards of the Goths, had not moved, when back comes Fox and tells how he has come upon a great company of the Romans led by their thralls of the Goths who were just entering the wood, away there towards the Thing-stead.

"But, War-duke," says he, "I came also across our own folk of the second battle duly ordered in the wood ready to meet them; and they shall be well dealt with, and the sun shall rise for us and not for them."

Then turns Thiodolf round to those nighest to him and says, but still softly:

Hear ye a word, O people, of the wisdom of the foe!
Before us thick they gather, and unto the death they go.
They fare as lads with their cur-dogs who have stopped a fox's earth,
And standing round the spinny [thorny thicket], now chuckle in their mirth,
Till one puts by the leafage and trembling stands astare
At the sight of the Wood-wolf's father arising in his lair—
They have come for our wives and our children, and our sword-edge shall they meet;
And which of them is happy save he of the swiftest feet?

The Storm of Dawning Begins

Speedily then went that word along the ranks of the Kindred, and men were merry with the restless joy of battle: but scarce had two minutes passed ere suddenly the stillness of the dawn was broken by clamour and uproar; by shouts and shrieks, and the clashing of weapons from the wood on their left hand; and over all arose the roar of the Markmen's horn, for the battle was joined with the second company of the Kindreds. But a rumour and murmur went from the foemen before Thiodolf's men; and then sprang forth the loud sharp word of the captains commanding and rebuking, as if the men were doubtful which way they should take. Amidst all which Thiodolf brandished his sword, and cried out in a great voice:

Now, now, ye War-sons!
Now the Wolf waketh!
Lo how the Wood-beast
Wendeth in onset.
E'en as his feet fare
Fall on and follow!

And he led forth joyously, and terrible rang the long refrained gathered shout of his battle as his folk rushed on together devouring the little space between their ambush and the hazel-beset green-sward.

In the twinkling of an eye the half-moon had lapped around the Roman-Goths and those that were with them; and the dastards made no stand but turned about at once, crying out that the Gods of the Kindreds were come to aid and none could withstand them. But these fleers thrust against the band of Romans who were next to them, and bore them aback, and great was the turmoil; and when Thiodolf's storm fell full upon them, as it failed not to do, so close were they driven together that scarce could any man raise his hand for a stroke.

For behind them stood a great company of those valiant spearmen of the Romans, who would not give way if anywise they might hold it out: and their ranks were closely serried, shield nigh touching shield, and their faces turned toward the foe; and so arrayed, though they might die, they scarce knew how to flee. As they might these thrust and hewed at the fleers, and gave fierce words but few to the Roman-Goths, driving them back against their foemen: but the fleers had lost the cunning of their right hands, and they had cast away their shields and could not defend their very bodies against the wrath of the kindreds; and when they strove to flee to the right hand or to the left, they were met by the horns of the half-moon, and the arrows began to rain in upon them, and from so close were they shot at that no shaft failed to smite home.

There then were the dastards slain; and their bodies served for a rampart against the onrush of the Markmen to those Romans who had stood fast. To them were gathering more and more every minute, and they faced the Goths steadily with their hard brown visages and gleaming eyes above their iron-plated shields; not casting their spears, but standing closely together, silent, but fierce. The light was spread now over all the earth; the eastern heavens were grown golden-red, flecked here and there with little crimson clouds: this battle was fallen near silent, but to the North was great uproar of shouts and cries, and the roaring of the war-horns, and the shrill blasts of the brazen trumpets.

Now Thiodolf, as his wont was when he saw that all was going well, had refrained himself of hand-strokes, but was here and there and everywhere giving heart to his folk, and keeping them in due order, and close array, lest the Romans should yet come among them. But he watched the ranks of the foe, and saw how presently they began to spread out beyond his, and might, if it were not looked to, take them in flank; and he was about to order his men anew to meet them, when he looked on his left hand and saw how Roman men were pouring thick from the wood out of all array, followed by a close throng of the kindreds: for on this side the Romans were outnumbered and had stumbled unawares into the ambush of the Markmen, who had fallen on them straightway and disarrayed them from the first. This flight of their folk the Romans saw also, and held their men together, refraining from the onset, as men who deem that they will have enough to do to stand fast.

But the second battle of the Markmen, (who were of the Nether-mark, mingled with the Mid-mark) fought wisely, for they swept those fleers from before them, slaying many and driving the rest scattering, yet held the chase for no long way, but wheeling about came sidelong on toward the battle of the Romans and Thiodolf. And when Thiodolf saw that, he set up the whoop of victory, he and his, and fell fiercely on the Romans, casting everything that would fly, as they rushed on to the handplay; so that

Tolkien Warriors—The House of the Wolfings

there was many a Roman slain with the Roman spears that those who had fallen had left among their foemen.

The Romans Withdraw

Now the Roman captains perceived that it availed not to tarry till the men of the Mid and Nether-marks fell upon their flank; so they gave command, and their ranks gave back little by little, facing their foes, and striving to draw themselves within the dike and garth, which, after their custom, they had already cast up about the Wolfing Roof, their stronghold.

Now as fierce as was the onset of the Markmen, the main body of the Romans could not be hindered from doing this much before the men of the second battle were upon them; but Thiodolf and Arinbiorn with some of the mightiest brake their array in two places and entered in amongst them.

And wrath so seized upon the soul of Arinbiorn for the slaying of Otter, and his own fault towards him, that he cast away his shield, and heeding no strokes, first brake his sword in the press, and then, getting hold of a great axe, smote at all before him as though none smote at him in turn; yea, as though he were smiting down tree-boles for a match against some other mighty man; and all the while amidst the hurry, strokes of swords and spears rained on him, some falling flatwise and some glancing sideways, but some true and square, so that his helm was smitten off and his hauberk rent adown, and point and edge reached his living flesh; and he had thrust himself so far amidst the foe that none could follow to shield him, so that at last he fell shattered and rent at the foot of the new clayey wall cast up by the Romans, even as Thiodolf and a band with him came cleaving the press, and the Romans closed the barriers against friend and foe, and cast great beams adown, and masses of iron and lead and copper taken from the smithying-booths of the Wolfings, to stay them if it were but a little.

Then Thiodolf bestrode the fallen warrior, and men of his House were close behind him, for wisely had he fought, cleaving the press like a wedge, helping his friends that they might help him, so that they all went forward together. But when he saw Arinbiorn fall he cried out: "Woe's me, Arinbiorn! that thou wouldest not wait for me; for the day is young yet, and over-young!"

There then they cleared the space outside the gate, and lifted up the Bearing Warrior, and bare him back from the rampart. For so fierce had been the fight and so eager the storm of those that had followed after him that they must needs order their battle afresh, since Thiodolf's wedge which he had driven into the Roman host was but of a few and the foe had been many and the rampart and the shot-weapons were close anigh. Wise therefore it seemed to abide them of the second battle and join with them to swarm over the new-built slippery wall in the teeth of the Roman shot.

In this, the first onset of the Morning Battle, some of the Markmen had fallen, but not many, since but a few had entered outright into the Roman ranks; and when they first rushed on from the wood but three of them were slain, and the slaughter was all of the dastards and the Romans; and afterwards not a few of the Romans were slain, what by Arinbiorn, what by the others; for they were fighting fleeing, and before their eyes was the image of the garth-gate which was behind them; and they stumbled against each other as they were driven sideways against the onrush of the Goths, nor were they now standing fair and square to them, and they were hurried and confused with the dread of the onset of them of the two Marks.

As yet Thiodolf had gotten no great hurt, so that when he heard that Arinbiorn's soul had passed away he smiled and said: "Yea, yea, Arinbiorn might have abided the end, for ere then shall the battle be hard."

So now the Wolfings and the Bearings met joyously the kindreds of the Nether Mark and the others of the second battle, and they sang the song of victory arrayed in good order hard by the Roman rampart, while bowstrings twanged and arrows whistled, and sling-stones hummed from this side and from that. And of their song of victory thus much the tale telleth:

Now hearken and hear
Of the day-dawn of fear,
And how up rose the sun
On the battle begun.
All night lay a-hiding,
Our anger abiding,
Dark down in the wood
The sharp seekers of blood;
But ere red grew the heaven we bore them all bare,
For against us undriven the foemen must fare;
They sought and they found us, and sorrowed to find,
For the tree-boles around us the story shall mind,
How fast from the glooming they fled to the light,
Yeasaying the dooming of Tyr of the fight.

Hearken yet and again
How the night gan to wane,
And the twilight stole on
Till the world was well won!
E'en in such wise was wending
A great host for our ending;
On our life-days e'en so
Stole the host of the foe;
Till the heavens grew lighter, and light grew the world,
And the storm of the fighter upon them was hurled,
Then some fled the stroke, and some died and some stood,
Till the worst of the storm broke right out from the wood,
And the war-shafts were singing the carol of fear,
The tale of the bringing the sharp swords anear.

Come gather we now,
For the day doth grow.
Come, gather, ye bold,
Lest the day wax old;
Lest not till to-morrow
We slake our sorrow,
And heap the ground
With many a mound.
Come, war-children, gather, and clear we the land!
In the tide of War-father the deed is to hand.
Clad in gear that we gilded they shrink from our sword;
In the House that we builded they sit at the board;
Come, war-children, gather, come swarm o'er the wall
For the feast of War-father to sweep out the Hall!

Now amidst of their singing the sun rose upon the earth, and gleamed in the arms of men, and lit the faces of the singing warriors as they stood turned toward the east.

In this first onset of battle but twenty and three Markmen were slain in all, besides Arinbiorn; for, as aforesaid, they had the foe at a disadvantage. And this onset is called in the tale the Storm of Dawning.

29. Of Thiodolf's Storm

The Battle of the Morning begins. The Markmen surround the Romans in their improvised fort. With each of the fort's four gates under attack, the Romans fear that the gods are against them but resolve to fight on. The Markmen bring in tree trunks to bridge the ditch and rampart. The Roman general decides to break though the Markmen's lines. That is a mistake, since it would have been better to inflict heavy losses on the Markmen by repelling attacks before fleeing. Hall-Sun foretells the Markmen's victory, even as the Romans fight on valiantly and desperately, in fear for how badly they have treated the Goths. Seeing the Markmen are winning, Thiodolf takes some men to save the Hall, which the Romans have set on fire. At the Hall, he meets the Roman captain. The two fight. The Roman is killed and Thiofolf is wounded with the Roman's short sword. The Markmen rush to put out the fire and release those held captive there. Thiodolf dies in the Hall, but the fire is put out.

The Goths tarried not over their victory; they shot with all the bowmen that they had against the Romans on the wall, and therewith arrayed themselves to fall on once more. And Thiodolf, now that the foe were covered by a wall, though it was but a little one, sent a message to the men of the third battle, them of Up-mark to wit, to come forward in good array and help to make a ring around the Wolfing Stead, wherein they should now take the Romans as a beast is taken in a trap. Meanwhile, until they came, he sent other men to the wood to bring tree-boles to batter the gate, and to make bridges whereby to swarm over the wall, which was but breast-high on the Roman side, though they had worked at it ceaselessly since yester-day morning.

In a long half-hour, therefore, the horns of the men of Up-mark sounded, and they came forth from the wood a very great company, for with them also were the men of the stay-at-homes and the homeless, such of them as were fit to bear arms. Amongst these went the Hall-Sun surrounded by a band of the warriors of Up-mark; and before her was borne her namesake the Lamp as a sign of assured victory. But these stay-at-homes with the Hall-Sun were stayed by the command of Thiodolf on the crown of the slope above the dwellings, and stood round about the Speech-Hill, on the topmost of which stood the Hall-Sun, and the wondrous Lamp, and the men who warded her and it.

When the Romans saw the new host come forth from the wood, they might well think that they would have work enough to do that day; but when they saw the Hall-Sun take her stand on the Speech-Hill with the men-at-arms about her, and the Lamp before her, then dread of the Gods fell upon them, and they knew that the doom had gone forth against them. Nevertheless they were not men to faint and die because the Gods were become their foes, but they were resolved rather to fight it out to the end against whatsoever might come against them, as was well seen afterwards.

Now they had made four gates to their garth [enclosure] according to their custom, and at each gate within was there a company of their mightiest men, and each was beset by the best of the Markmen. Thiodolf and his men beset the western gate where they had made that fierce onset. And the northern gate was beset by the Elkings and some of the kindreds of the Nether-mark; and the eastern gate by the rest of the men of Nether-mark; and the southern gate by the kindreds of Up-mark.

All this the Romans noted, and they saw how that the Markmen were now very many, and they knew that they were men no less valiant than themselves, and they perceived that Thiodolf was a wise Captain; and in less than two hours' space from the Storm of Dawning they saw those men coming from the wood with plenteous store of tree-trunks to bridge their ditch and rampart; and they considered how the day was yet very young, so that they might look for no shelter from the night-tide; and as for any aid from their own folk at the war-garth aforesaid, they hoped not for it, nor had they sent any messenger to the Captain of the garth; nor did they know as yet of his overthrow on the Ridge.

The Romans Flee their Garth

Now therefore there seemed to be but two choices before them; either to abide within the rampart they had cast up, or to break out like valiant men, and either die in the storm, or cleave a way through, whereby they might come to their kindred and their stronghold south-east of the Mark.

This last way then they chose; or, to say the truth, it was their chief captain who chose it for them, though they were nothing loth thereto: for this man was a mocker, yet hot-headed, unstable, and nought wise in war, and heretofore had his greed minished his courage; yet now, being driven into a corner, he had courage enough and to spare, but utterly lacked patience; for it had been better for the Romans to have abided one or two onsets from the Goths, whereby they who should make the onslaught would at the least have lost more men than they on whom they should fall, before they within stormed forth on them; but their pride took away from the Romans their last chance. But their captain, now that he perceived, as he thought, that the game was lost and his life come to its last hour wherein he would have to leave his treasure and pleasure behind him, grew desperate and therewith most fierce and cruel.

So all the captives whom they had taken (they were but two score and two, for the wounded men they had slain) he caused to be bound on the chairs of the high-seat clad in their war-gear with their swords or spears made fast to their right hands, and their shields to their left hands; and he said that the Goths should now hold a Thing wherein they should at last take counsel wisely, and abstain from folly. For he caused store of faggots and small wood smeared with grease and oil to be cast into the hall that it might be fired, so that it and the captives should burn up altogether; "So," said he, "shall we have a fair torch for our funeral fire;" for it was the custom of the Romans to burn their dead.

Thus, then, he did; and then he caused men to do away the barriers and open all the four gates of the new-made garth, after he had manned the wall with the slingers and bowmen, and slain the horses, so that the woodland folk should have no gain of them. Then he arrayed his men at the gates and about them duly and wisely, and bade those valiant footmen fall on the Goths who were getting ready to fall on them, and to do their best. But he himself armed at all points took his stand at the Man's-door of the Hall, and swore by all the Gods of his kindred that he would not move a foot's length from thence either for fire or for steel.

So fiercely on that fair morning burned the hatred of men about the dwellings of the children of the Wolf of the Goths, wherein the children of the Wolf of Rome were shut up as in a penfold of slaughter.

Hall-Sun Fortells Victory

Meanwhile the Hall-Sun standing on the Hill of Speech beheld it all, looking down into the garth of war; for the new wall was no hindrance to her sight, because the Speech-Hill was high and but a little way from the Great Roof; and indeed she was within shot of the Roman bowmen, though they were not very deft in shooting.

So now she lifted up her voice and sang so that many heard her; for at this moment of time there was a lull in the clamour of battle both within the garth and without; even as it happens when the thunder-storm is just about to break on the world, that the wind drops dead, and the voice of the leaves is hushed before the first great and near flash of lightening glares over the fields. So she sang:

NOW THE LATEST HOUR COMETH AND THE ENDING OF THE STRIFE;
And to-morrow and to-morrow shall we take the hand of life,

And wend adown the meadows, and skirt the darkling wood,
And reap the waving acres, and gather in the good.
I see a wall before me built up of steel and fire,
And hurts and heart-sick striving, and the war-wright's fierce desire;
But there-amidst a door is, and windows are therein;
And the fair sun-litten meadows and the Houses of the kin
Smile on me through the terror my trembling life to stay,
That at my mouth now flutters, as fain to flee away.
Lo e'en as the little hammer and the blow-pipe of the wright
About the flickering fire deals with the silver white,
And the cup and its beauty groweth that shall be for the people's feast,
And all men are glad to see it from the greatest to the least;
E'en so is the tale now fashioned, that many a time and oft
Shall be told on the acre's edges, when the summer eve is soft;
Shall be hearkened round the hall-blaze when the mid-winter night
The kindreds' mirth besetteth, and quickeneth man's delight,
And we that have lived in the story shall be born again and again
As men feast on the bread of our earning, and praise the grief-born grain.

As she made an end of singing, those about her understood her words, that she was foretelling victory, and the peace of the Mark, and for joy they raised a shrill cry; and the warriors who were nighest to her took it up, and it spread through the whole host round about the garth, and went up into the breath of the summer morning and went down the wind along the meadow of the Wolfings, so that they of the Wain-burg, who were now drawing somewhat near to Wolfstead heard it and were glad.

The Battle Grows Fiercer

But the Romans when they heard it knew that the heart of the battle was reached, and they cast back that shout wrathfully and fiercely, and made toward the foe. There-withal those mighty men fell on each other in the narrow passes of the garth; for fear was dead and buried in that Battle of the Morning.

On the North gate Hiarandi of the Elkings was the point of the Markmen's wedge, and first clave the Roman press. In the Eastern gate it was Valtyr, Otter's brother's son, a young man and most mighty. In the South gate it was Geirbald of the Shieldings, the Messenger.

In the west gate Thiodolf the War-duke gave one mighty cry like the roar of an angry lion, and cleared a space before him for the wielding of Ivar's blade; for at that moment he had looked up to the Roof of the Kindred and had beheld a little stream of smoke curling blue out of a window thereof, and he knew what had betided, and how short was the time before them. But his wrathful cry was taken up by some who had beheld that same sight, and by others who saw nought but the Roman press, and terribly it rang over the swaying struggling crowd.

Then fell the first rank of the Romans before those stark men and mighty warriors; and they fell even where they stood, for on neither side could any give back but for a little space, so close the press was, and the men so eager to smite. Neither did any crave peace if he were hurt or disarmed; for to the Goths it was but a little thing to fall in hot blood in that hour of love of the kindred, and longing for the days to be. And for the Romans, they had had no mercy, and now looked for none: and they remembered their dealings with the Goths, and saw before them, as it were, once more, yea, as in a picture, their slayings and quellings, and lashings, and cold mockings which they had dealt out to the conquered foemen without mercy, and now they longed sore for the quiet of the dark, when their hard lives should be over, and all these deeds forgotten, and they and their bitter foes should be at rest for ever.

Most valiantly they fought; but the fury of their despair could not deal with the fearless hope of the Goths, and as rank after rank of them took the place of those who were hewn down by Thiodolf and the Kindred, they fell in their turn, and slowly the Goths cleared a space within the gates, and then began to spread along the wall within, and grew thicker and thicker. Nor did they fight only at the gates; but made them bridges of those tree-trunks, and fell to swarming over the rampart, till they had cleared it of the bowmen and slingers, and then they leaped down and fell upon the flanks of the Romans; and the host of the dead grew, and the host of the living lessened.

Moreover the stay-at-homes round about the Speech-Hill, and that band of the warriors of Up-mark who were with them, beheld the Great Roof and saw the smoke come gushing out of the windows, and at last saw the red flames creep out amidst it and waver round the window jambs like little banners of scarlet cloth. Then they could no longer refrain themselves, but ran down from the Speech-Hill and the slope about it with great and fierce cries, and clomb the wall where it was unmanned, helping each other with hand and back, both stark warriors, and old men and lads and women: and thus they gat them into the garth and fell upon the lessening band of the Romans, who now began to give way hither and thither about the garth, as they best might.

Thus it befell at the West-gate, but at the other gates it was no worser, for there was no diversity of valour between the Houses; nay, whereas the more part and the best part of the Romans faced the onset of Thiodolf, which seemed to them the main onset, they were somewhat easier to deal with elsewhere than at the West gate; and at the East gate was the place first won, so that Valtyr and his folk were the first to clear a space within the gate, and to tell the tale shortly (for can this that and the other sword-stroke be told of in such a medley?) they drew the death-ring around the Romans that were before them, and slew them all to the last man, and then fell fiercely on the rear-ward of them of the North gate, who still stood before Hiarandi's onset.

There again was no long tale to tell of, for Hiarandi was just winning the gate, and the wall was cleared of the Roman shot-fighters, and the Markmen were standing on the top thereof, and casting down on the Romans spears and baulks of wood and what-soever would fly. There again were the Romans all slain or put out of the fight, and the two bands of the kindred joined together, and with what voices the battle-rage had left them cried out for joy and fared on together to help to bind the sheaves of war which Thiodolf's sickle had reaped. And now it was mere slaying, and the Romans, though they still fought in knots of less than a score, yet fought on and hewed and thrust without more thought or will than the stone has when it leaps adown the hill-side after it has first been set agoing.

But now the garth was fairly won and Thiodolf saw that there was no hope for the Romans drawing together again; so while the kindreds were busied in hewing down those knots of desperate men, he gathered to him some of the wisest of his warriors, amongst whom were Steinulf and Grani the Grey, the deft wood-wrights (but Athalulf had been grievously hurt by a spear and was out of the battle), and drave a way through the confused turmoil which still boiled in the garth there, and made straight for the Man's-door of the Hall.

Thiodolf Fights the Roman Captain

Soon he was close thereto, having hewn away all fleers that hindered him, and the doorway was before him. But on the threshold, the fire and flames of the kindled hall behind him, stood the Roman Captain clad in gold-adorned armour and surcoat of sea-born purple; the man was cool and calm and proud, and a mocking smile was on his face: and he bore his bright blade unbloodied in his hand.

Thiodolf stayed a moment of time, and their eyes met; it had gone hard with the War-duke, and those eyes glittered in his pale face, and his teeth were close set together; though he had fought wisely, and for life, as he who is most valiant ever will do, till he is driven to bay like the lone wood-wolf by the hounds, yet had he been sore mishandled. His helm and shield were gone, his hauberk rent; for it was no dwarf-wrought coat, but the work of Ivar's hand: the blood was running down from his left arm, and he was hurt in many places: he had broken Ivar's sword in the medley, and now bore in his hand a strong Roman short-sword, and his feet stood bloody on the worn earth anigh the Man's-door.

He looked into the scornful eyes of the Roman lord for a little minute and then laughed aloud, and therewithal, leaping on him with one spring, turned sideways, and dealt him a great buffet on his ear with his unarmed left hand, just as the Roman thrust at him with his sword, so that the Captain staggered forward on to the next man following, which was Wolfkettle the eager warrior, who thrust him through with his sword and shoved him aside as they all strode into the hall together. Howbeit no sword fell from the Roman Captain as he fell, for Thiodolf's side bore it into the Hall of the Wolfings.

Most wrathful were those men, and went hastily, for their Roof was full of smoke, and the flames flickered about the pillars and the wall here and there, and crept up to the windows aloft; yet was it not wholly or fiercely burning; for the Roman fire-raisers had been hurried and hasty in their work. Straightway then Steinulf and Grani led the others off at a run towards the loft and the water; but Thiodolf, who went slowly and painfully, looked and beheld on the dais those men bound for the burning, and he went quietly, and as a man who has been sick, and is weak, up on to the dais, and said: "Be of good cheer, O brothers, for the kindreds have vanquished the foemen, and the end of strife is come."

The Death of Thiodolf

His voice sounded strange and sweet to them amidst the turmoil of the fight without; he laid down his sword on the table, and drew a little sharp knife from his girdle and cut their bonds one by one and loosed them with his blood-stained hands; and each one as he loosed him he kissed and said to him, "Brother, go help those who are quenching the fire; this is the bidding of the War-duke."

But as he loosed one after other he was longer and longer about it, and his words were slower. At last he came to the man who was bound in his own high-seat close under the place of the wondrous Lamp, the Hall-Sun, and he was the only one left bound; that man was of the Wormings and was named Elfric; he loosed him and was long about it; and when he was done he smiled on him and kissed him, and said to him: "Arise, brother! go help the quenchers of the fire, and leave to me this my chair, for I am weary: and if thou wilt, thou mayst bring me of that water to drink, for this morning men have forgotten the mead of the reapers!"

Then Elfric arose, and Thiodolf sat in his chair, and leaned back his head; but Elfric looked at him for a moment as one scared, and then ran his ways down the hall, which now was growing noisy with the hurry and bustle of the quenchers of the fire, to whom had divers others joined themselves.

There then from a bucket which was still for a moment he filled a wooden bowl, which he caught up from the base of one of the hall-pillars, and hastened up the Hall again; and there was no man nigh the dais, and Thiodolf yet sat in his chair, and the hall was dim with the rolling smoke, and Elfric saw not well what the War-duke was doing. So he hastened on, and when he was close to Thiodolf he trod in something wet, and his heart sank for he knew that it was blood; his foot slipped therewith and as he put out his hand to save himself the more part of the water was spilled, and mingled with the blood. But he went up to Thiodolf and said to him, "Drink, War-duke! here hath come a mouthful of water."

But Thiodolf moved not for his word, and Elfric touched him, and he moved none the more. Then Elfric's heart failed him and he laid his hand on the War-duke's hand, and looked closely into his face; and the hand was cold and the face ashen-pale; and Elfric laid his hand on his side, and he felt the short-sword of the Roman leader thrust deep therein, besides his many other hurts.

So Elfric knew that he was dead, and he cast the bowl to the earth, and lifted up his hands and wailed out aloud, like a woman who hath come suddenly on her dead child, and cried out in a great voice: "Hither, hither, O men in this hall, for the War-duke of the Markmen is dead! O ye people, Hearken! Thiodolf the Mighty, the Wolfing is dead!" And he was a young man, and weak with the binding and the waiting for death, and he bowed himself adown and crouched on the ground and wept aloud.

Hall-Sun Enters the Hall

But even as he cried that cry, the sunlight outside the Man's-door was darkened, and the Hall-Sun came over the threshold in her ancient gold-embroidered raiment, holding in her hand her namesake the wondrous Lamp; and the spears and the war-gear of warriors gleamed behind her; but the men tarried on the threshold till she turned about and beckoned to them, and then they poured in through the Man's-door, their war-gear rent and they all befouled and disarrayed with the battle, but with proud and happy faces: as they entered she waved her hand to them to bid them go join the quenchers of the fire; so they went their ways.

But she went with unfaltering steps up to the dais, and the place where the chain of the Lamp hung down from amidst the smoke-cloud wavering a little in the gusts of the hall. Straightway she made the Lamp fast to its chain, and dealt with its pulleys with a deft hand often practised therein, and then let it run up toward the smoke-hidden Roof till it gleamed in its due place once more, a token of the salvation of the Wolfings and the welfare of all the kindreds.

Then she turned toward Thiodolf with a calm and solemn face, though it was very pale and looked as if she would not smile again. Elfric had risen up and was standing by the board speechless and the passion of sobs still struggling in his bosom. She put him aside gently, and went up to Thiodolf and stood above him, and looked down on his face a while: then she put forth her hand and closed his eyes, and stooped down and kissed his face.

Then she stood up again and faced the Hall and looked and saw that many were streaming in, and that though the smoke was still eddying overhead, the fire was well nigh quenched within; and without the sound of battle had sunk and died away. For indeed the Markmen had ended their day's work before noontide that day, and the more part of the Romans were slain, and to the rest they had given peace till the Folk-mote should give Doom concerning them; for pity of these valiant men was growing in the hearts of the valiant men who had vanquished them, now that they feared them no more. And this second part of the Morning Battle is called Thiodolf's Storm.

So now when the Hall-Sun looked and beheld that the battle was done and the fire quenched, and when she saw how every man that came into the Hall looked up and beheld the wondrous Lamp and his face quickened into joy at the sight of it; and how most looked up at the high-seat and Thiodolf lying leaned back therein, her heart nigh broke between the thought of her grief and of the grief of the Folk that their mighty friend was dead, and the thought of the joy of the days to be and all the glory that his latter days had won. But she gathered heart, and casting back the dark tresses of her hair, she lifted up her voice and cried out till its clear shrillness sounded throughout all the Roof:

"O men in this Hall the War-duke is dead! O people hearken! for Thiodolf the Mighty hath changed his life: Come hither, O men, Come hither, for this is true, that Thiodolf is dead!"

30. Thiodolf Is Borne Out of the Hall and Otter Is Laid Beside Him

Hearing that Thiodolf is dead, the Goths flock to the Hall. There Hall-Sun calls for some of those who had fought well in the battles of the last few days. She orders them to carry Thiodolf's body to a burial mound. Otter's body is also found and taken to be with Thiodolf's. Hall-Sun speaks of their deaths. Asmund of the Daylings arrives on horseback too late for the battle.

So when they heard her voice they came thither flockmeal [one-by-one], and a great throng mingled of many kindreds was in the Hall, but with one consent they made way for the Children of the Wolf to stand nearest to the dais. So there they stood, the warriors mingled with the women, the swains with the old men, the freemen with the thralls: for now the stay-at-homes of the House were all gotten into the garth, and the more part of them had flowed into the feast-hall when they knew that the fire was slackening.

Hall-Sun Calls for the Valiant in Battle

All these now had heard the clear voice of the Hall-Sun, or others had told them what had befallen; and the wave of grief had swept coldly over them amidst their joy of the recoverance of their dwelling-place; yet they would not wail nor cry aloud, even to ease their sorrow, till they had heard the words of the Hall-Sun, as she stood facing them beside their dead War-duke. Then she spake: "O Sorli the Old, come up hither! thou hast been my fellow in arms this long while."

So the old man came forth, and went slowly in his clashing war-gear up on to the dais. But his attire gleamed and glittered, since over-old was he to thrust deep into the press that day, howbeit he was wise in war. So he stood beside her on the dais holding his head high, and proud he looked, for all his thin white locks and sunken eyes.

But again said the Hall-Sun: "Canst thou hear me, Wolfkettle, when I bid thee stand beside me, or art thou, too, gone on the road to Valhall?"

Forth then strode that mighty warrior and went toward the dais: nought fair was his array to look on; for point and edge had rent it and stained it red, and the flaring of the hall-flames had blackened it; his face was streaked with black withal, and his hands were as the hands of a smith among the thralls who hath wrought unwashen in the haste and hurry when men look to see the war-arrow abroad. But he went up on to the dais and held up his head proudly, and looked forth on to the hall-crowd with eyes that gleamed fiercely from his stained and blackened face.

Again the Hall-Sun said: "Art thou also alive, O Egil the messenger? Swift are thy feet, but not to flee from the foe: Come up and stand with us!"

Therewith Egil clave the throng; he was not so roughly dealt with as was Wolfkettle, for he was a bowman, and had this while past shot down on the Romans from aloof; and he yet held his bended bow in his hand. He also came up on to the dais and stood beside Wolfkettle glancing down on the hall-crowd, looking eagerly from side to side.

Yet again the Hall-Sun spake: "No aliens now are dwelling in the Mark; come hither, ye men of the kindreds! Come thou, our brother Hiarandi of the Elkings, for thy sisters, our wives, are fain of thee. Come thou, Valtyr of the Laxings, brother's son of Otter; do thou for the War-duke what thy father's brother had done, had he not been faring afar. Come thou, Geirbald of the Shieldings the messenger! Now know we the deeds of others and thy deeds. Come, stand beside us for a little!"

Forth then they came in their rent and battered war-gear: and the tall Hiarandi bore but the broken truncheon of his sword; and Valtyr a woodman's axe notched and dull with work; and Geirbald a Roman cast-spear, for his own weapons had been broken in the medley; and he came the last of the three, going as a belated reaper from the acres. There they stood by the others and gazed adown the hall-throng.

But the Hall-Sun spake again: "Agni of the Daylings, I see thee now. How camest thou into the hard hand-play, old man? Come hither and stand with us, for we love thee. Angantyr of the Bearings, fair was thy riding on the day of the Battle on the Ridge! Come thou, be with us. Shall the Beamings whose daughters we marry fail the House of the Wolf to-day? Geirodd, thou hast no longer a weapon, but the fight is over, and this hour thou needest it not. Come to us, brother! Gunbald of the Vallings, the Falcon on thy shield is dim with the dint of point and edge, but it hath done its work to ward thy valiant heart: Come hither, friend! Come all ye and stand with us!"

As she named them so they came, and they went up on to the dais and stood altogether; and a terrible band of warriors they looked had the fight been to begin over again, and they to meet death once more. And again spake the Hall-Sun:

"Steinulf and Grani, deft are your hands! Take ye the stalks of the war blossoms, the spears of the kindreds, and knit them together to make a bier for our War-duke, for he is weary and may not go afoot. Thou Ali, son of Grey; thou hast gone errands for me before; go forth now from the garth, and wend thy ways toward the water, and tell me when thou comest back what thou hast seen of the coming of the Wain-burg. For by this time it should be drawing anigh."

So Ali went forth, and there was silence of words for a while in the Hall; but there arose the sound of the wood-wrights busy with the wimble and the hammer about the bier. No long space had gone by when Ali came back into the hall panting with his swift running; and he cried out: "O Hall-Sun, they are coming; the last wain hath crossed the ford, and the first is hard at hand: bright are their banners in the sun."

Thiodolf's Funeral Procession

Then said the Hall-Sun: "O warriors, it is fitting that we go to meet our banners returning from the field, and that we do the Gods to wit what deeds we have done; fitting is it also that Thiodolf our War-duke wend with us. Now get ye into your ordered bands, and go we forth from the fire-scorched hall, and out into the sunlight, that the very earth and the heavens may look upon the face of our War-duke, and bear witness that he hath played his part as a man.

Then without more words the folk began to stream out of the Hall, and within the garth which the Romans had made they arrayed their companies. But when they were all gone from the Hall save they who were on the dais, the Hall-Sun took the waxen torch which she had litten and quenched at the departure of the host to battle, and now she once more kindled it at the flame of the wondrous Lamp, the Hall-Sun. But the wood-wrights brought the bier which they had made of the spear-shafts of the kindred, and they laid thereon a purple cloak gold-embroidered of the treasure of the Wolfings, and thereon was Thiodolf laid.

Then those men took him up; to wit, Sorli the Old, and Wolfkettle and Egil, all these were of the Wolfing House; Hiarandi of the Elkings also, and Valtyr of the Laxings, Geirbald of the Shieldings, Agni of the Daylings, Angantyr of the Bearings, Geirodd of the Beamings, Gunbald of the Vallings: all these, with the two valiant wood-wrights, Steinulf and Grani, laid hand to the bier.

So they bore it down from the dais, and out at the Man's-door into the sunlight, and the Hall-Sun followed close after it, holding in her hand the Candle of Returning. It was an hour after high-noon of a bright midsummer day when she came out into the garth; and the smoke from the fire-scorched hall yet hung about the trees of the wood-edge. She looked neither down towards her feet nor on the right side or the left, but straight before her. The ordered companies of the kindreds hid the sight of many fearful things from her eyes; though indeed the thralls and women had mostly gleaned the dead from the living both of friend and foe, and were tending the hurt of either host. Through an opening in the ranks moreover could they by the bier behold the scanty band of Roman captives, some standing up, looking dully around them, some sitting or lying on the grass talking quietly together, and it seemed by their faces that for them the bitterness of death was passed.

Forth then fared the host by the West gate, where Thiodolf had done so valiantly that day, and out on to the green amidst the booths and lesser dwellings. Sore then was the heart of the Hall-Sun, as she looked forth over dwelling, and acre, and meadow, and the blue line of the woods beyond the water, and bethought her of all the familiar things that were within the compass of her eyesight, and remembered the many days of her father's loving-kindness, and the fair words wherewith he had solaced her life-days. But of the sorrow that wrung her heart nothing showed in her face, nor was she paler now than her wont was. For high was her courage, and she would in no wise mar that fair day and victory of the kindreds with grief for what was gone, whereas so much of what once was, yet abided and should abide for ever.

Then fared they down through the acres, where what was yet left of the wheat was yellowing toward harvest, and the rye hung grey and heavy; for bright and hot had the weather been all through these tidings. Howbeit much of the corn was spoiled by the trampling of the Roman bands.

So came they into the fair open meadow and saw before them the wains coming to meet them with their folk; to wit a throng of stout carles of the thrall-folk led by the war-wise and ripe men of the Steerings. Bright was the gleaming of the banner-wains, though for the lack of wind the banners hung down about their staves; the sound of the lowing of the bulls and the oxen, the neighing of horses and bleating of the flocks came up to the ears of the host as they wended over the meadow.

They made stay at last on the rising ground, all trampled and in parts bloody, where yesterday Thiodolf had come on the fight between the remnant of Otter's men and the Romans: there they opened their ranks, and made a ring round about a space, amidmost of which was a little mound whereon was set the bier of Thiodolf. The wains and their warders came up with them and drew a garth of the wains round about the ring of men with the banners of the kindreds in their due places.

There was the Wolf and the Elk, the Falcon, the Swan, the Boar, the Bear, and the Green-tree: the Willow-bush, the Gedd, the Water-bank and the Wood-Ousel, the Steer, the Mallard and the Roe-deer: all these were of the Mid-mark. But of the Upper-mark were the Horse and the Spear, and the Shield, and the Daybreak, and the Dale, and the Mountain, and the Brook, and the Weasel, and the Cloud, and the Hart. Of the Nether-mark were the Salmon, and the Lynx, and the Lingworm, the Seal, the Stone, and the Sea-mew; the Buck-goat, the Apple-tree, the Bull, the Adder, and the Crane.

There they stood in the hot sunshine three hours after noon; and a little wind came out of the west and raised the pictured cloths upon the banner-staves, so that the men could now see the images of the tokens of their Houses and the Fathers of old time.

Otter's Body Arrives

Now was there silence in the ring of men; but it opened presently and through it came all-armed warriors bearing another bier, and lo, Otter upon it, dead in his war-gear with many a grievous wound upon his body. For men had found him in an ingle [angle] of the wall of the Great Roof, where he had been laid yesterday by the Romans when his company and the Bearings with the Wormings made their onset: for the Romans had noted his exceeding valour, and when they had driven off the Goths some of them brought him dead inside their garth, for they would know the name and dignity of so valorous a man.

So now they bore him to the mound where Thiodolf lay and set the bier down beside Thiodolf's, and the two War-dukes of the Markmen lay there together: and when the warriors beheld that sight, they could not forbear, but some groaned aloud, and some wept great tears, and they clashed their swords on their shields and the sound of their sorrow and their praise went up to the summer heavens.

Now the Hall-Sun holding aloft the waxen torch lifted up her voice and said:

O WARRIORS OF THE WOLFINGS, BY THE TOKEN OF THE FLAME
That here in my right hand flickers, ye are back at the House of the Name,
And there yet burneth the Hall-Sun beneath the Wolfing Roof,

And the flame that the foemen quickened hath died out far aloof.
Ye gleanings of the battle, lift up your hearts on high,
For the House of the War-wise Wolfings and the Folk undoomed to die.
But ye kindreds of the Markmen, the Wolfing guests are ye,
And to-night we hold the high-tide, and great shall the feasting be,
For to-day by the road that we know not a many wend their ways
To the Gods and the ancient Fathers, and the hope of the latter days.
And how shall their feet be cumbered if we tangle them with woe,
And the heavy rain of sorrow drift o'er the road they go?
They have toiled, and their toil was troublous to make the days to come;
Use ye their gifts in gladness, lest they grieve for the Ancient Home!
Now are our maids arraying that fire-scorched Hall of ours
With the treasure of the Wolfings and the wealth of summer flowers,
And this eve the work before you will be the Hall to throng
And purge its walls of sorrow and quench its scathe and wrong.

She looked on the dead Thiodolf a moment, and then glanced from him to Otter
and spake again:

O KINDREDS, HERE BEFORE YOU TWO MIGHTY BODIES LIE;
Henceforth no man shall see them in house and field go by
As we were used to behold them, familiar to us then
As the wind beneath the heavens and the sun that shines on men;
Now soon shall there be nothing of their dwelling-place to tell,
Save the billow of the meadows, the flower-grown grassy swell!
Now therefore, O ye kindreds, if amidst you there be one
Who hath known the heart of the War-dukes, and the deeds their hands have
    done,
Will not the word be with him, while yet your hearts are hot,
Of our praise and long remembrance, and our love that dieth not?
Then let him come up hither and speak the latest word
O'er the limbs of the battle-weary and the hearts outworn with the sword.

She held her peace, and there was a stir in the ring of men: for they who were anigh
the Dayling banner saw an old warrior sitting on a great black horse and fully armed.
He got slowly off his horse and walked toward the ring of warriors, which opened before him; for all knew him for Asmund the old, the war-wise warrior of the Daylings,
even he who had lamented over the Hauberk of Thiodolf. He had taken horse the day
before, and had ridden toward the battle, but was belated, and had come up with them
of the Wain-burg just as they had crossed the water.

31. Old Asmund Speaketh Over the War-dukes: The Dead Are Laid in Mound

Asmund speaks over the bodies of Otter and Thiodorf. Hall-Sun speaks, and they celebrate the victory with a feast. The dead are buried in mounds, and the damage the Romans did is repaired. About this time the Romans, "began to stay the spreading of their dominion, or even to draw in its boundaries somewhat."

Now while all looked on, he went to the place where lay the bodies of the War-dukes, and looked down on the face of Otter and said:

O Otter, there thou liest! and thou that I knew of old,
When my beard began to whiten, as the best of the keen and the bold,
And thou wert as my youngest brother, and thou didst lead my sons
When we fared forth over the mountains to meet the arrowy Huns,
And I smiled to see thee teaching the lore that I learned thee erst.
O Otter, dost thou remember how the Goth-folk came by the worst,
And with thee in mine arms I waded the wide shaft-harrowed flood
That lapped the feet of the mountains with its water blent with blood;
And how in the hollow places of the mountains hidden away
We abode the kindreds' coming as the wet night bideth day?
Dost thou remember, Otter, how many a joy we had,
How many a grief remembered has made our high-tide glad?
O fellow of the hall-glee! O fellow of the field!
Why then hast thou departed and left me under shield?
I the ancient, I the childless, while yet in the Laxing hall
Are thy brother's sons abiding and their children on thee call.

O kindreds of the people! the soul that dwelt herein,
This goodly way-worn body, was keen for you to win
Good days and long endurance. Who knoweth of his deed
What things for you it hath fashioned from the flame of the fire of need?
But of this at least well wot we, that forth from your hearts it came
And back to your hearts returneth for the seed of thriving and fame.
In the ground wherein ye lay it, the body of this man,
No deed of his abideth, no glory that he wan,
But evermore the Markmen shall bear his deeds o'er earth,
With the joy of the deeds that are coming, the garland of his worth.

He was silent a little as he stood looking down on Otter's face with grievous sorrow, for all that his words were stout. For indeed, as he had said, Otter had been his battle-fellow and his hall-fellow, though he was much younger than Asmund; and they had been standing foot to foot in that battle wherein old Asmund's sons were slain by his side.

After a while he turned slowly from looking at Otter to gaze upon Thiodolf, and his body trembled as he looked, and he opened his mouth to speak; but no word came from it; and he sat down upon the edge of the bier, and the tears began to gush out of his old eyes, and he wept aloud. Then they that saw him wondered; for all knew the stoutness of his heart, and how he had borne more burdens than that of eld, and had not cowered down under them. But at last he arose again, and stood firmly on his feet, and faced the Folk-mote, and in a voice more like the voice of a man in his prime than of an old man, he sang:

WILD THE STORM IS ABROAD
Of the edge of the sword!
Far on runneth the path
Of the war-stride of wrath!
The Gods hearken and hear
The long rumour of fear
From the meadows beneath
Running fierce o'er the heath,
Till it beats round their dwelling-place builded aloof
And at last all up-swelling breaks wild o'er their roof,
And quencheth their laughter and crieth on all,
As it rolleth round rafter and beam of the Hall,
Like the speech of the thunder-cloud tangled on high,
When the mountain-halls sunder as dread goeth by.

So THEY THROW the door wide
Of the Hall where they bide,
And to murmuring song
Turns that voice of the wrong,
And the Gods wait a-gaze
For that Wearer of Ways:
For they know he hath gone
A long journey alone.
Now his feet are they hearkening, and now is he come,
With his battle-wounds darkening the door of his home,
Unbyrnied, unshielded, and lonely he stands,
And the sword that he wielded is gone from his hands—
Hands outstretched and bearing no spoil of the fight,
As speechless, unfearing, he stands in their sight.

WAR-FATHER GLEAMS
Where the white light streams

Round kings of old
All red with gold,
And the Gods of the name
With joy aflame.
All the ancient of men
Grown glorious again:
Till the Slains-father crieth aloud at the last:
'Here is one that belieth no hope of the past!
No weapon, no treasure of earth doth he bear,
No gift for the pleasure of Godhome to share;
But life his hand bringeth, well cherished, most sweet;
And hark! the Hall singeth the Folk-wolf to greet!'

As the rain of May
On earth's happiest day,
So the fair flowers fall
On the sun-bright Hall
As the Gods rise up
With the greeting-cup,
And the welcoming crowd
Falls to murmur aloud.
Then the God of Earth speaketh; sweet-worded he saith,
'Lo, the Sun ever seeketh Life fashioned of death;
And to-day as he turneth the wide world about
On Wolf-stead he yearneth; for there without doubt
Dwells the death-fashioned story, the flower of all fame.
Come hither new Glory, come Crown of the Name!'

All men's hearts rose high as he sang, and when he had ended arose the clang of sword and shield and went ringing down the meadow, and the mighty shout of the Markmen's joy rent the heavens: for in sooth at that moment they saw Thiodolf, their champion, sitting among the Gods on his golden chair, sweet savours around him, and sweet sound of singing, and he himself bright-faced and merry as no man on earth had seen him, for as joyous a man as he was. But when the sound of their exultation sank down, the Hall-Sun spake again:

Now wendeth the sun westward, and weary grows the Earth
Of all the long day's doings in sorrow and in mirth;
And as the great sun waneth, so doth my candle wane,
And its flickering flame desireth to rest and die again.
Therefore across the meadows wend we aback once more
To the holy Roof of the Wolfings, the shrine of peace and war.
And these that once have loved us, these warriors images,

Tolkien Warriors—The House of the Wolfings

Shall sit amidst our feasting, and see, as the Father sees
The works that menfolk fashion and the rest of toiling hands,
When his eyes look down from the mountains and the heavens above all lands,
And up from the flowery meadows and the rolling deeps of the sea.
There then at the feast with our champions familiar shall we be
As oft we are with the Godfolk, when in story-rhymes and lays
We laugh as we tell of their laughter, and their deeds of other days.

COME THEN, YE sons of the kindreds who hither bore these twain!
Take up their beds of glory, and fare we home again,
And feast as men delivered from toil unmeet to bear,
Who through the night are looking to the dawn-tide fresh and fair
And the morn and the noon to follow, and the eve and its morrow morn,
All the life of our deliv'rance and the fair days yet unborn.

So she spoke, and a murmur arose as those valiant men came forth again. But lo, now were they dight in fresh and fair raiment and gleaming war-array. For while all this was a-doing and a-saying, they had gotten them by the Hall-Sun's bidding unto the wains of their Houses, and had arrayed them from the store therein.

So now they took up the biers, and the Hall-Sun led them, and they went over the meadow before the throng of the kindreds, who followed them duly ordered, each House about its banner; and when they were come through the garth which the Romans had made to the Man's-door of the Hall, there were the women of the House freshly attired, who cast flowers on the living men of the host, and on the dead War-dukes, while they wept for pity of them. So went the freemen of the Houses into the Hall, following the Hall-Sun, and the bearers of the War-dukes; but the banners abode without in the garth made by the Romans; and the thralls arrayed a feast for themselves about the wains of the kindreds in the open place before their cots and the smithying booths and the byres.

And as the Hall-Sun went into the Hall, she thrust down the candle against the threshold of the Man's-door, and so quenched it. Long were the kindreds entering, and when they were under the Roof of the Wolfings, they looked and beheld Thiodolf set in his chair once more, and Otter set beside him; and the chiefs and leaders of the House took their places on the dais, those to whom it was due, and the Hall-Sun sat under the wondrous Lamp her namesake.

Now was the glooming falling upon the earth; but the Hall was bright within even as the Hall-Sun had promised. Therein was set forth the Treasure of the Wolfings; fair cloths were hung on the walls, goodly broidered garments on the pillars: goodly brazen cauldrons and fair-carven chests were set down in nooks where men could see them well, and vessels of gold and silver were set all up and down the tables of the feast. The pillars also were wreathed with flowers, and flowers hung garlanded from the walls over the precious hangings; sweet gums and spices were burning in fair-wrought censers of brass, and so many candles were alight under the Roof, that scarce had it looked more ablaze when the Romans had litten the faggots therein for its burning amidst the hurry of the Morning Battle.

There then they fell to feasting, hallowing in the high-tide of their return with victory in their hands: and the dead corpses of Thiodolf and Otter, clad in precious glistering raiment, looked down on them from the High-seat, and the kindreds worshipped them and were glad; and they drank the Cup to them before any others, were they Gods or men.

But before the feast was hallowed in, came Ali the son of Grey up to the High-seat, bearing something in his hand: and lo! It was Throng-plough, which he had sought all over the field where the Markmen had been overcome by the Romans, and had found it at last. All men saw him how he held it in his hand now as he went up to the Hall-Sun and spake to her.

But she kissed the lad on the forehead, and took Throng-plough, and wound the peace-strings round him [it] and laid him [it] on the board before Thiodolf; and then she spake softly as if to herself, yet so that some heard her: "O father, no more shalt thou draw Throng-plough from the sheath till the battle is pitched in the last field of fight, and the sons of the fruitful Earth and the sons of Day meet Swart and his children at last, when the change of the World is at hand. Maybe I shall be with thee then: but now and in meanwhile, farewell, O mighty hand of my father!"

Thus then the Houses of the Mark held their High-tide of Returning under the Wolfing Roof with none to blame them or make them afraid: and the moon rose and the summer night wore on towards dawn, and within the Roof and without was there feasting and singing and harping and the voice of abundant joyance: for without the Roof feasted the thralls and the strangers, and the Roman war-captives.

But on the morrow the kindreds laid their dead men in mound betwixt the Great Roof and the Wild-wood. In one mound they laid them with the War-dukes in their midst, and Arinbiorn by Otter's right side; and Thiodolf bore Throng-plough to mound with him.

But a little way from the mound of their own dead, toward the south they laid the Romans, a great company, with their Captain in the midst: and they heaped a long mound over them not right high; so that as years wore, and the feet of men and beasts trod it down, it seemed a mere swelling of the earth not made by men's hands; and belike men knew not how many bones of valiant men lay beneath; yet it had a name which endured for long, to wit, the Battle-toft.

Thiodolf's Howe

But the mound whereunder the Markmen were laid was called Thiodolf's Howe [here 'Howe' refers to a mound] for many generations of men, and many are the tales told of him; for men were loth to lose him and forget him: and in the latter days men deemed of him that he sits in that Howe not dead but sleeping, with Throng-plough laid before him on the board; and that when the sons of the Goths are at their sorest need and the falcons cease to sit on the ridge of the Great Roof of the Wolfings, he will wake and come forth from the Howe for their helping. But none have dared to break open that Howe and behold what is therein.

But that swelling of the meadow where the Goths had their overthrow at the hands of the Romans, and Thiodolf fell to earth unwounded, got a name also, and was called the Swooning Knowe; and it kept that name long after men had forgotten wherefore it was so called.

Now when all this was done, and the warriors of the kindreds were departed each to his own stead, the Wolfings gathered in wheat-harvest, and set themselves to make good all that the Romans had undone; and they cleansed and mended their Great Roof and made it fairer than before, and took from it all signs of the burning, save that they left the charring and marks of the flames on one tie-beam, the second from the dais, for a token of the past tidings. Also when Harvest was over the Wolfings, the Beamings, the Galtings, and the Elkings, set to work with the Bearings to rebuild their Great Roof and the other dwellings and booths which the Romans had burned; and right fair was that house.

But the Wolfings throve in field and fold, and they begat children who grew up to be mighty men and deft of hand, and the House grew more glorious year by year.

The tale tells not that the Romans ever fell on the Mark again; for about this time they began to stay the spreading of their dominion, or even to draw in its boundaries somewhat. And this is all that the tale has to tell concerning the House of the Wolfings and the Kindreds of the Mark.

—The End—

INTRODUCING THE STORY OF DESIDERIUS

Trilogies are popular with both authors and readers. Much like the three volumes of *The Lord of the Rings*, William Morris planned to create a trilogy of historical novels with related themes. We've read the first in that series, *The House of the Wolfings*. The second in the series, *The Roots of the Mountains*, is available also.

Unfortunately, Morris never completed the third, writing only a little over 5300 words of the first chapter. His daughter called it *The Story of Desiderius* (after the main character). She published it in *The Collected Works of William Morris* (1914), and that's the version we have here. Since much remained unresolved in the fragment, she inserted the names of characters inside square brackets much as I have done with obscure words in this book. Keep in mind that this is a rough draft that was never intended for publication.

The contrasts between the worlds of the two previous volumes and that of *Desiderius* resembles that we find in Tolkien between the warrior-farmers of Rohan and the civilized but increasingly decadent city dwellers of Minas Tirith. We can even think of the Wolfings and Rohan as resembling the Anglo-Saxons of old England, while the world in which Desiderius lives and that of Minas Tirith resemble the ancient Roman empire.

Beyond the presence of a handsome young man and hints of a possible romance with a lovely slave girl, the world this fragment describes bears little resemblance to the other two tales in the Morris trilogy. Rather than a vibrant agricultural community where even slaves are respected, we find ourselves in a large city, perhaps west of the Alps near the coast of what is today northern Italy or southern France.

The city is linked to a powerful "master city of the world," probably a reference to Rome at the height of its power. The rich live in idle ease, slaves are typically abused, and the poor suffer in misery and dependence. This decaying, cosmopolitan world also roughly resembles the Minas Tirith-based sequel to *The Lord of the Rings* that Tolkien began but abandoned as too depressing.

From this fragment, we can guess at the plot. In his other two tales, Morris placed his romantically besotted hero in a conflict between love for a beautiful woman and loyalty to his group, so it's easy to suspect Desiderius' interest in the mysteriously un-slavish slave girl will lead him to clash with his own family or with the city's elite, perhaps in defense of either the unknown group the girl calls her own or the city's many poor. It also seems likely that his scheming mother, Julia, will play a major role, perhaps in opposition to Desiderius.

This novel might have also been intended to be more political than the others. That's suggested by the biblical passage at the end of the third paragraph, which alludes to Psalm 94:3, "Lord, how long shall the wicked, how long shall the wicked triumph?" (Bible, KJV) That Psalmist goes on to say: "And he shall bring upon them their own iniquity, and shall cut them off in their own wickedness; yea, the LORD our God shall cut them off." Morris may have intended to create a tale that was about justice rather than war and class conflict rather than tribal warfare. With that, I leave you to you develop your own theory about how this fragment might have developed.

The Story of Desiderius (A Fragment)

Once upon a time in years long ago there dwelt a young man, Desiderius, in a certain city. The said city was huge and built gloriously as for the dwellings of its rich men. A great market there was and on one side thereof a noble mote-house [perhaps a castle-like building surrounded by a moat] where were held the councils of the city, howbeit the Elders that sat in the said councils, though they were oft of many words, might as well have been packs of wool or sacks of wheat with scarlet cloaks thrown over them for all the wielding of their words over the fortunes of the said city.

For he who in men's eyes was its ruler and master was a rich man sent from the master city of the world that he might gather the taxes and tributes to send back again to that fountain of all might, so that rich men might dwell therein, doing nought and wasting the lives of their slaves till richer men than they should arise to take their possessions and slay them. And of the said taxes might the ruler or the head man of the city we have told of take what he durst for his own behoof, though whiles forsooth it turned out that he had but been gathering for another, some captain or chieftain of the aliens, or even a thrall grown rich through many villainies who should buy his guards and wheedle his women, and so enter into his chamber of dais and thrust him through his purple waled gown [one whose cloth has a woven texture like corduroy] and reign in his stead, to fall in like manner when the time was ripe thereto.

But in that city were many other glorious houses, as temples of the Gods with their shrines and their altars, and mote-houses of the Gilds of Crafts, and palaces of the Elders, and of the rich men who were many, for the thralls and the poor folk were without number, and houses of the captains of war who lay far otherwise than the warriors who were underneath them, and courts of law builded somewhat like minsters and great churches of our day wherein the judge was the Bishop, [the canons] the lawyers and the canticles that were sung therein were lawyers' lies and judges' cruelty, and the amens were the chuckling of the rich over the poor, and the Mass sung therein they offered to a sack stuffed with of gold, and the Host and the daily victim was the life of the poor, and the Bread and Wine of Communion was the thankless labour of the poor and the blood of the thrall and the tears of his day that gaineth nought and his night that knoweth no rest—How long, O Lord, how long?

Such were the noble buildings of this city, and well had it been if there had been no others. But well ye may wot that since there were rich men therein there were many and worser than these: lairs and dens for the poor folk to lay their heads, foul and close and of evil odours, burnt by the sun, made bitter by the frost and the wind. Ah, if the dwellers therein had only bethought them for once how many they were and how few their masters and yeomen! But out on it they knew nought of the joys of battle and the hope and toil of the freeman; though of these were most free in name and were fed from time to time with dog's food and dog's bidding that they might lie quiet in the sun and huddle into warm corners when colder weather was to hand; nor even rise up and take the food from those who hoarded it and needed it not, and the houses from those who must leave them empty or fill them with poor clad in fair raiment—their slaves born in the house or bought with a price.

Now this city was builded on the two sides of a great river joined by a bridge of boats, the midmost whereof opened to give passage to great ships which could come all the way up from the sea to the quays thereof, bearing in their hollow bellies the wealth of the shores of that country and of far off lands. A great wall of hewn stone went all about the city except where it was cleft by the river; where indeed were builded great towers to guard a chain that barred the ingate to all foemen, and on that wall were many towers for defence and for shelter of the soldiers that warded it, men paid with a price for the risking of their lives and the shedding of their blood. For you must know that the citizens would have nought to do with such work, nor would gird themselves of with steel except for hunting and whiles it maybe to murder men in some private quarrel for pelf or lust or vengeance.

But in the south-east ingle [angle] of the aforesaid wall on a mound raised by men's hands was a great castle wherein dwelt the soldiers and their captain, and whoso was master of these and had the captain for his henchman was master of the whole city and might do what he would so long as they suffered it. The said city stood amidst a wide plain which stretched away far to the westward and was covered with green fields and acres and orchards and gardens sprinkled over with little woods of oak and poplar and sweet chestnut, with fair country steads betowered and walled of the rich men and hamlets of hovels for their slaves—for there were few free peasants or none therein: no yeomen, no franklins [freeholders who are not nobles but own extensive land], nought but rich men and their bailiffs and stewards over the slaves. All this was on the west side of the river.

On the east it was much the same for a little way, except that instead of the little woods was one great forest well tree-grown that came down from low-rising grounds ten miles away, and so to say flooded a great part of the eastern plain and thrust down a tongue close to the walls of the city itself: plentiful were the deer of this great wild-wood, hart and hind and elk and bears and lynxes and wild-cats and wolves and boars and roe deer: and the lords of that city loved to hunt there when they might do so without hardship.

Beyond the wood and the low hills rose high bare downs of the shepherd folk and beyond those again rocky fells dark blue in the distance, and when the sky was clear above and beyond it all could you see the snowy tops of the Wall of the World [perhaps the Alps] like white clouds far away. Through all that flat country where the wood was not were many roads wide and narrow, but all hard and good even in the winter and the rainy season, but through the wood was but one great wheel-road that went straight up towards the mountains; though indeed there were paths through the thicket a many which a man might follow on foot or on horseback if he had enough of patience in him.

Desiderius and His Family

In this city then dwelt Desiderius the son of a rich merchant; he was but of twenty-four winters, a man very goodly of fashion, not very tall but clean limbed and well knit. So that he had a carle's might in him though he was sleek-skinned and soft-handed; for no work had his body done save feeding itself, save it were at whiles hunting and riding, and such play of swordsmanship and wrestling and stone-casting as they taught in the school of arms of that city. His hair was black, short and curly, his face berry-brown with grey eyes and red lips; a fresh and fair swain much to be desired by all women kind.

His father hight [named] [Aurelian] was a well-looking carle of forty-five winters, a courteous man of many words, greedy of gain but open-handed when the gain lay in his coffers; not tyrannous himself but winking at the deeds of tyrants if it were for his gain; so that they who were over his thralls and other poor men wotted [knew] that they might do as they would so that no tales reached his [ear].

Wherefore did they the more abound in tyranny and with torments and the threat of torments locked the lips and tied up the tongues of the poor folk whom they oppressed. But if by any chance they let a true tale slip through it did them but little harm, for the master would indeed being rich and soft of mood give money to the poor man, and if he were thrall would set him free, or at least promise so to do with many fair words. And foul words also would he rain down without stint on the head of the hireling oppressor: but there was an end of all, and next week or next day would the same thing be done and merrily would go the mill that ground the gold.

As for the mother of Desiderius the lawful wife of Aurelian (who indeed had as many wives as seemed good to him) she had seen forty summers but was a stately woman and still very fair; for her face was like the marble image of a good imager, so right and true were all the lines therein and so shapely was the compass of it. Dark smooth and fine was her hair, her lips full and red, her skin smooth and clear of of hue, her limbs and all her body excellently fashioned, her eyes great and grey like her son's and seeming as if they were the very windows of a true and simple soul.

This was her seeming, which was but a painted show: for inwardly she was a fool, false and cruel, of many moods indeed but none of them good, a liar so that no one could say whether any word of hers were false or true; a fawner and a flatterer to make the time pass pleasantly: a friend in the morning, a stranger at mid-day, a foe in the evening: a woman cruel in deeds of set purpose if the mood took her, and always cruel without set purpose, whereas she cared for no soul of man or beast what grief might happen to them either with her or without her. Lovers had she had in her time and yet had: their love lasted but a little while; for presently they found that there was nought to be loved in her save her fair body; whereas she was not one of those evil women with whom soul and body are interwoven for good and ill and they are at once both beautiful and evil: creatures whom some taint and venom hath seized on and driven them past the natural perversity of women, and yet left them women still. Such was the mother of Desiderius and he wotted well to his great grief what she was.

Withal his father's brother dwelt in the house, Tatian by name, a man like to his brother both in body and in speech, but different from him in many ways. For whereas Aurelian had thriven ever in his dealings Tatian had never thriven except when he was on other men's business. Forsooth he was a man who cared not and could not draw bridle on any desire he had be it great or small, and since he was a goodly and full-blooded man he had many desires both great and small. He would fain have been the King of the World; but if he had come to his kingship he would have complained of the sun that burned him on the morning of his triumph. Yet was he rather restless than idle, and was wishful to have some business ever on his hands, which he did well till he wearied of it, as soon happened.

Like his brother he was easy of temper, yet not being rich like him and having few to run his errands, his kindness was soon swept away by the incoming flood of his desire for some goodly thing. For it is to be said of him that he loved all goodly things which a true man ought to love, but yet not as a true man should love them; nor had he any love for doing well to other men at his own expense though he deemed all men good—that is good enough for his service. Truly he had many companions but never a friend saving his brother, who loved him as well as he could love anything and better than he loved aught else, and being a rich man gave him spending-money at will so long as he abode in his house, and set him awork doing what he could not easily spoil, and suffered him to make himself great in the house, and was fain to see him happy.

Such were the near kin of Desiderius who dwelt in the house with him, and he had neither brother nor sister.

The Story Begins

Now on the afternoon of a day of early summer he sat in the court of his father's house, and that court was a fair and dainty place after the fashion of those days: a pillared square from the outside of which opened the doors of the chambers great and small, and in the midst of it a pool of clear water with a fountain which had been open to the air save for a gay-stained linen cloth hung over it with poles and cords. The floor was of marble wrought with a fair pattern of little squares of many colours, the pillars were of marble white and green with gilded chapiters [the upper part of a column], and on the wall of the court were painted pictures from the tales of the poets.

There then sat Desiderius, who had but that forenoon come back from an errand of his father's down the water, which had kept him three days from home: he had bathed and clad himself in fresh raiment since his return, and was now as fair-looking a rich young man as might be as he sat with the rumour of the city in his ears mingled with the cooing of the doves on the roof without. Yet his brows were knitted and his face overcast with the weary discontent of a young man of the rich who hath no toil to weary him and no hope to lighten toil, and who yet is not a fool to eat and drink and be merry without deeds.

As he sat pondering with no mirth in his heart of what the coming days should bring him, he of heard footsteps coming from the outer court where dwelt the servants and thralls, and presently a man came under the pillars and made slowly towards him: he was a big man fat and white with no hair on his face, with large eyes like a calf's that told no tale of him, and soft rolling lips that told him to be a greedy man of money and a belly-god. He was clad in a scarlet coat laced with silver and broidered about his neck with the similitude of a thrall's chain: in his hand was an ebony staff ringed with silver and jewelled with blue mountain-stones: it was clear to be seen of him that he was a man who had lost his manhood, a eunuch. He was the chief thrall of Aurelian and the master of the thralls; a glutton as aforesaid. He was cruel when he was bidden to it, and his cruelty lay light on him for he put it all on his masters and had no will of his own in the matter, and when he squeezed others for his own gain he squeezed them not beyond measure, and was otherwise not an ill man, lying not more than behoves a thrall and a half-man. His name was [Felix] and Aurelian had great trust in him.

He came up to Desiderius and bent a knee before him and said, "Hail to our young master: the house is glad to have thee again." And he stood before him smiling as one who is not afraid. But Desiderius just nodded his head and looked at him without speaking. Then said the thrall," May I speak or shall I go?"

Said Desiderius, "Speak on unless thou hast something new to say in which case hold thy peace."

The thrall's smile spread wider over his face and he said: "My lord thy father hath lent more money to the Prefectus of the city."

"No news is that," said Desiderius.

Said Felix, "We had tidings first that our soldiers have overcome a host of the barbarians, and next that these tidings are false and that they have been overcome."

"*That* is no news," said the young man: "go on with my full leave." And his scorn wrinkled his face into a smile.

Again said the thrall: "The dole of corn to the poor was double last week, so rich hath the city grown."

"Thou art rich in thy no news," said Desiderius. "Go on."

Said Felix, "My lady thy mother hath sent her damsel Pulcheria away to the fieldhouse being weary of her."

Desiderius said nought but sat up in his chair as one who throws off listlessness.

Again quoth the thrall: "She hath bought her a new damsel, and hath bidden me hide from all the price she hath given for her, and I will do her bidding and thine also to tell thee no news."

He held his peace and Desiderius said nought but abode him awhile and he said: "Yet when my lady thy mother cometh from her chamber thou mightest cast a glance at her handmaids, and forget not that though thy father hath bought me and thy mother sendeth me on her errands, if I might give myself to any it would be to thee, my lord."

Desiderius looked on him thoughtfully for some while and then his face cleared and he said to him smiling: "Well what is thy last no news?"

Said the thrall folding his hands across his breast, "That I need a gold piece or two, sweet lord."

Desiderius laughed and said, "That is the crown of thy no news: put forth thine hand and search my sleeve and as robbers are wont take what thou findest." And he held forth his left arm. Felix was not long in his search and drew forth a purse from its due lurking place and then cast himself down before the young man and fell to kissing his feet and the hem of his garment.

"Nay nay," said Desiderius, "go thy ways and count it: thou wilt be rich when I set thee free, for—"

He broke off short and Felix rising up said with a chuckling laugh, "Say out thy thought, my lord; thou meanest that I have nought to cast away money on the great waster of money, to wit the fair woman. Yea, yea, I shall be rich."

The smiles went out of Desiderius' face and he looked kindly on the thrall whose face darkened as he said in a low voice almost a whisper yet fervently withal: "My lord, thou art young and hitherto thou hast heeded this half-man but as a pander and a pimp: thou hast needed no trustiness, nor belike would all thy riches have bought it if thou hadst. But as I said even now in jest, thou desiredst what I can give to thee that I will give: and may happen the time may come when thou wilt ask for trustiness and good service, and of all the people in this town thou wilt find it in this half-man, this woman-herd." And he bowed himself down lowly and so departed whence he had come.

Desiderius left alone sat in his chair listlessly a while and then rose and walked up and down betwixt the pillars for a longer while, and then once more cast himself discontentedly in the chair again and gave a sigh as one ill-pleased both with himself and the world.

A Pretty Slave-girl

But he had not sat there long before one of the doors which gave into the hall opened and there came out a young and fair woman bare-armed and bare-footed, clad in a gown of light blue all spangled and broidered with gold which reached scantily to her ankles: she bore a chair in her arms silver-plated and gilded in places which she set down near the edge of the water.

Desiderius scarce turned to note her; and then lay back again in his chair looking up at the sun-smitten awning, while there came out from the said chamber two more young women bearing great fans in their hands and then two others, one with divers toys in her hands, the other bearing a little white sharp-nosed dog with a gold collar round its neck; all these were clad as to fashion of their gowns like the first, but of divers colours, mostly pink and yellow flowered very fairly.

The Mother of Desiderius

After them came a grey-headed carline, thin and tall, clad in a long gown of Indian gold. All these stood in order about the silver chair, the old woman close to it. And then came forth a very comely and stately dame clad in a long sweeping gown of fine white linen with purple welt a hands-breadth wide going down each side from the shoulders to the hem. The dame was dark-eyed, black-haired, smooth-cheeked as a young woman; her lips like scarlet threads, her arms very full and fair: she was much like to Desiderius in the face, as was like to be, for indeed this was his mother of whom we have told.

She went proudly amidst the maidens, who were her thralls, and sat down on the silver chair and reached out her hand to one of the damsels who gave her a golden pomace-box with some sponge of essence in it. The dame took it, but as she did so chanced to look at the hand that gave it, and therewith sat up on her chair and took the damsel's hand by the wrist and held it out and looked at it and knit her brows and muttered: "This is no thrall's hand: I wish—"

She stayed and dropped it and looked up at the woman who reddened not nor changed countenance in any wise, but stood like an image of stone so that the Dame's eyes fell before hers, and she smiled but somewhat sickly, and turning her face saw her son who had risen up to greet her. He bent his knee and took her hand and kissed it and she drew him to her and kissed his smooth cheek and patted it, and then one of the

Tolkien Warriors—The House of the Wolfings

women brought his chair and set it beside hers and he sat down by her: and the weariness of thought faded from his face and he sat as one in all ease looking straight before him, and she smiled on him since for a while she loved him as she had when he was but a youngling: and also there was none to take her thoughts from him. Then she turned to him a little and said: "Well, dear son, when didst thou come within doors again?"

"Two hours ago, Mother," he said.

She said: "I wonder why thy father must be ever sending thee on business that Tatian could do as well as thou; and he knows thy love of the city and my loneliness, how none come near me save him and his brother, now all is changed at the Castle."

Desiderius smiled yet scarce happily and he said: "Nay, Mother, I am well content to get out of these walls, if it were but for a while; and I am fain of having an errand of some one else since I have none of mine own."

"Poor boy," she said," thou weariest of life already like I did when I was of thine age. I have borne enough of it since." And she sighed.

But Desiderius said: "But I am no wise weary, Mother: or dost thou see wrinkles on my face?"

She looked at him somewhat fondly as if she saw her own face in a mirror, and said," Nay Desiderius, so it is with me and my kindred that sorrow doth not trouble our faces or roughen our skins: we are of the race of kings though I have wedded a mere rich man."

And she took his hand and fondled it, but he drew a little away from her and his face clouded. Then she said: "Did ye get the Indian onyxes down the water, and the Persian opals?"

"Yea," he said, "and of the best they are."

"And the book of plays," she said, "the African book?"

"Yea," said he, "as well writ as maybe."

"Are they anigh?" said she.

"In my chamber," he said and rose up to go thither. But even therewith came a man into the hall goodly of presence with a fair face and black hair and short beard: somewhat big-nosed he was, his eyes long but not wide opened,his lips full and loosely fashioned: he was clad in a watchet [pale or light blue] coat embroidered with gold and exceeding dainty: he had a staff in his hand with a golden apple to it—and this was Tatian his father's brother. He drew near to greet them and [Julia] looked on him smiling though as now she loved him little, and Desiderius nodded his head and reached his hand to him and hailed him and then made a step towards his chamber, but as he did so turned and saw Tatian look at [Julia] and her women as it he would be thought to let his eyes stray aimlessly amongst them, but yet fixing themselves at last.

So Desiderius' were drawn whereas his kinsman looked, and even therewith he remembered the word of the eunuch about the new thrall, and his eyes met the eyes of the woman whose hand his mother had taken up; and therewith his heart sank and rose again and a pain which yet was sweet filled his whole soul, and he felt that his face burned as the blood rushed to his head, and he scarce knew where he was.

And as for her, at first she looked at him as she had looked at his mother and as if she would turn away in a moment of time; but suddenly her face grew troubled and she flushed red, and then paled, and put her hand to her bosom as if in pain, and still she looked at Desiderius.

Then he heard someone speaking and like the breaking of a dream saw his mother looking on him, a cold smile on her lips, her eyes scanning him curiously as she said, "Now son, thou mayest go fetch the jewels and the book; thine uncle will spare thee a while, though thou hast not seen him this long while." She spoke this with an evil smile: for she wotted well that no love was spilt between Desiderius and his uncle.

But Desiderius started when she had spoken and turning swiftly on his heel went to his chamber and sought the jewels and the book like one in a dream and came back again at once; and when he came again amongst the pillars of the hall he saw that the young women-slaves were gone and his uncle also and his mother sat there alone with the nurse beside her. Desiderius turned pale and frowned and his mother smiled as if in answer to some thought within her: and he came up to her as one whose thoughts are elsewhere, and said listlessly,"Here are thy toys, Mother, so please you," and so stood before her.

She took the gems which were very goodly of their kind and laid the book beside her and made great joy of those matters, or seemed to, but yet looked up at Desiderius from time to time [as] if she would read something in his face, while he for his part stood there saying nothing and scarce seeing her. At last she took up the playbook, and turning over its leaves and looking down thereon said to him: "Thou hast done well for me; when art thou going down the water again?"

He enforced himself to answer and said, "I know not: my father will bid me."

She said, "Thou saidst e'en now that thou wouldst be glad to go: art thou still of the same mind?"

"Why not," he said, "it was but within the hour that I said it," and he smiled faintly thinking in himself that much had happened in an hour.

She spake in awhile and said: "Young folk are fitful, son. But tell me are there women where thou goest or why art thou fain of leaving the city?"

He looked at her with wide open eyes and said: "Women, Mother? Yea surely how should it be otherwise?"

"O wise youth," she said, laughing in his face, "why wilt thou make thyself simple? Thou knowest what my word means."

"Nay, Mother," he said, "there are none for me."

"Well well," she said, "I would not pry into thy secrets, but one thing I would counsel thee, buy thee a fair young thrall or two such as the chapmen keep lovely with much pains, rather than hang about paying court to some great woman, for whom thou mayst be slain or grievously beaten some day or who at the least will waste all thy good and send thee away empty at last."

"Mother," he said frowning, "thou art wrong, the deer is not in that bush."

"Well well," she said, "a wilful man, a wilful man; it is well that thou art rich at least." She laughed aloud and her laugh sounded like the voice of the skilful player rippling up and down about the holes of the flute.

And he laughed in turn and somewhat merrily, for he was pleased to think that she had not noted his eyes upon her new-bought thrall; and he said: "Less than love makes it pleasant for me down yonder, for near the river mouth I meet Julianus the son of Ammianus and his house is fair, but to us the sand-plain and the downs fairer: for there about we fly our falcons at the geese and mallard, and course the bustard over the long ridges of the down."

"Yea," said his mother, "that we believe: but fair is the huntress among the gods when she kilts [gathers up] her skirts and takes her bow in hand and such there maybe with you. I grudge thee not dear lad so thou art happy. But lo! Here cometh thy father."

And therewith indeed came a man out of the inner chamber into the hall, a dark and goodly man much like to his brother, but brisker and more alert in his gait though he was shorter and burlier; the lines of his face better knit; his mouth firmer and more cleanly cut, his brow beetling more, his eyes keener: in short the master of the two brethren. He went up to Desiderius and embraced him and kissed his forehead and bade him welcome home; and Desiderius was fain of him for he loved him and there was much kindness between them.

—*The End*—

CPSIA information can be obtained
at www.ICGtesting.com
Printed in the USA
LVHW100757220722
724097LV00004B/390